American Indians
as Depicted on Song Sheet Covers
Since 1833

This book is the first in the series:

Illustrated Song Sheets: Reflections of Popular Culture

Including

American Indians
The American West
African Americans
Kids Will Be Kids
Marilyn & Sultry Film Goddesses
Christmas: Popular Singers
Doo-Wop to Rock Groups
The Folk Music Revival of the 1960s

American Indians as Depicted on Song Sheet Covers Since 1833

*Includes a Comprehensive Annotated Bibliography
of Sheet Music Books and a Listing of Illustrators of American Indian Song Sheets*

Frank D. Tinari

Sunstone Press
Santa Fe

© 2024 by Frank D. Tinari
All Rights Reserved
No part of this book may be reproduced in any form or by any electronic or mechanical means including information storage and retrieval systems without permission in writing from the publisher, except by a reviewer who may quote brief passages in a review.

Sunstone books may be purchased for educational, business, or sales promotional use. For information please write: Special Markets Department, Sunstone Press, P.O. Box 2321, Santa Fe, New Mexico 87504-2321.

Printed on acid-free paper
∞

Library of Congress Cataloging-in-Publication Data

Names: Tinari, Frank D., 1943- author.
Title: American Indians as depicted on song sheet covers since 1833 : includes a comprehensive annotated bibliography of sheet music books and a listing of illustrators of American Indian song sheets / Frank D. Tinari.
Other titles: Illustrated song sheets, reflections of popular culture.
Description: Santa Fe : Sunstone Press, [2024] | Series: Illustrated song sheets, reflections of popular culture | Includes bibliographical references and index. | Summary: "A comprehensive guide to American Indian images featured on over 700 colorful song sheet covers"-- Provided by publisher.
Identifiers: LCCN 2024021553 | ISBN 9781632933850 (paperback)
Subjects: LCSH: Tinari, Frank D., 1943---Catalogs and collections. | Indians of North America--Portraits. | Indians of North America--Collectibles. | Music title pages--Private collections. | LCGFT: Bibliographies.
Classification: LCC ML112.5 .T55 2024 | DDC 741.6/6--dc23/eng/20240612
LC record available at https://lccn.loc.gov/2024021553

WWW.SUNSTONEPRESS.COM
SUNSTONE PRESS / POST OFFICE BOX 2321 / SANTA FE, NM 87504-2321 /USA
(505) 988-4418

DEDICATION

To Barbara, my wife of fifty-four years, my inspiration, partner, lover, counselor, editor, mother of our daughters, and the love of my life. Looking forward to some day joining you, my love, in eternity.

CONTENTS

Acknowledgments ~ 8
Preface to the Series ~ 9
Bibliography of Illustrated Song Sheet Reference Books ~ 17
Introduction ~ 24

1. Beginnings ~ 32
2. American Indians Romanticized ~ 61
3. Notable Names ~ 179
4. Humorous and Whimsical Treatments ~ 197
5. Song Sheets from Other Countries ~ 207
6. Post-1930 Song Sheets: Nostalgia Meets Stereotype ~ 229

American Indian Song Sheet Illustrators ~ 259
Song Title Index ~ 265
About the Author ~ 277

ACKNOWLEDGMENTS

To provide high quality images for this book, I used a flatbed scanner of song sheets from my collection. Some images were scanned from books. I also had the benefit of researching and, in some instances, acquiring high quality images from public sources such as the libraries of Johns Hopkins University, Baylor University, Mississippi State University, Duke University, Indiana University, Wayne State University, and University of Arizona. For his more than helpful assistance, special thanks go to Sam Bessen, Assistant Curator of the Lester S. Levy Sheet Music Collection at the Sheridan Libraries of Johns Hopkins University. In addition, the staff of the Walsh Library, Seton Hall University, efficiently obtained books for my use via interlibrary requests.

I am greatly indebted to the many song sheet collectors who have chosen to author books about the hobby. Throughout the book, specific citation credit is given to their work and contributions whenever they are used.

In addition to the many books, libraries, and institutions that the author has relied upon, this undertaking has received the benefit of individuals who have contributed their knowledge and resources. Collectors and sellers of song sheets have been gracious in providing requested images. One such helpful resource has been Alex Hassan, musician and song sheet expert, who provided me a number of song sheet cover images. Especially noteworthy has been the extensive assistance of Sandy Marrone, longtime collector, seller and appraiser of sheet music. Sandy lent numerous song sheets to the author for scanning, and many images contained in the volumes of this series were taken from her large, wide-ranging collection. I thank her very much for her assistance. Each such image is noted as from her collection. C. Mark Clardy, sheet music collector and docent at the Sid Richardson Museum, Ft. Worth, Texas, also was kind enough to provide song sheet images that are cited in this book. In the same vein, any reproduction of a song sheet cover taken from another source is given proper citation.

My nephew Frank A. Nastro is to be commended for his selfless assistance in digitally cleaning some of the song sheet cover images exhibited in this series of books.

Special thanks are extended to our daughter Alexandra Tinari who served as my writing editor and compassionate critic of previous manuscript drafts. Alex lived and worked on the Rosebud Reservation in South Dakota for several years with the Sicangu Lakota; she was given honorary membership in the tribe and the name of Ho Na'umpi win (One Whose Voice is Heard) at a Pow Wow that our family attended.

Any errors or omissions that remain are fully your author's responsibility.

—Frank D. Tinari
2024

PREFACE TO THE SERIES

Though I am an economist by profession, one could say my avocation has always been a deep interest and love for art and music. When I was toddler, I think my innate love for music was reinforced by mom who loved to hum and sing along with tunes of the 1940s heard on the radio. I started collecting 45 rpm records and LPs in my high school days during which time I headed my school's "Poster Club" with designs that promoted various school events. Growing up in an ethnic Italian New York neighborhood in the 1950s, I spent many nights harmonizing doo-wop music with my buddies under a streetlight on the corner of the block. In the 1980s and 1990s, I was the guitar-strumming cantor at our parish Sunday "folk" mass. That experience inspired me to compose worship songs that were later recorded by vocalists and choirs on a CD entitled *If I Ask*. I was able to combine my love for music with my economics interests in a path-breaking journal article, "From Rhythm and Blues to Broadway: Using Music to Teach Economics" (*The Journal of Economic Education*, Vol. 31, June 2000), cited numerous times in subsequent literature. And during our continuing long marriage, my wife and I traveled extensively and always brought back artwork, sculpture, and hand-crafted items from Europe, China, Peru, Turkey, and Africa.

For my 45rpm record collection, in addition to the music itself, I liked to collect the colorful picture sleeves that were issued. I always had an eye out for them as I perused estate and garage sales. Many years ago, I had the occasion to visit John Ritchie in Oregon to see his record collection. But it was his collection of sheet music of the early rock and roll era that caught my fancy.[1] Then, about twenty years ago, my search for music on eBay led to an encounter with illustrated sheet music covers. I stopped collecting records and began accumulating what I viewed as attractive artwork that happened to be on song sheets.[2]

Collecting is one thing. But writing books about those collections is another. A review of the Bibliography of Illustrated Song Sheet Reference Books presented in this book will reveal that there are over 90 books that focus on the illustration of sheet music covers. Thus, one might reasonably ask: Isn't another book, let alone a series of books, redundant? It would seem so—except when one considers the nearly unlimited genres and subjects that are of interest to collectors, and which have not had in-depth examination. Just how many topical subjects are found among all produced popular sheet music may never be tallied. In her brief museum exhibition survey of nineteenth century sheet music, Nancy R. Davison touches on the following genres: minstrel shows, dancing, portraits, yacht racing, fashionable resorts, Negroes, war, presidents, misfortunes, children, temperance, ethnic groups, feminine fashion, bicycle, fires, railroads, baseball, variety shows, marching songs, telephone, and political campaigns.[3] A colleague and fellow collector, Sandy Marrone, once counted the categories of her substantial song sheet collection. When the number of music sheets dealing with U.S. states started to build, she subdivided them into individual states. The same process occurred with so many of her other themes such that the total number of categories and sub-categories in her collection nears one thousand. John Edward Hasse, former curator at the Smithsonian's National Museum of Natural History, told me that the Sam DeVincent Collection of Illustrated American Sheet Music that he helped acquire for the Museum had been gathered by Sam into a collection of more than 1,200 categories.

The reader will surmise, as I have, that it would be a herculean task to list all possible collecting genres, topics, or themes. Although there have been published several comprehensive books on certain song sheet themes (such as Danny Crew's excellent catalogs on suffragist music, and U.S. Presidents)[4], only a sprinkling of illustrated song sheet covers of any given genre has been covered thoroughly in available reference books.[5] Given the substantial gaps, what is needed is a series of comprehensive books on specific subjects of song sheet cover artwork not addressed by other authors.

The present series, Illustrated Song Sheets: Reflections of Popular Culture, attempts to fill the appreciable void that exists for a wide variety of song sheet genres. Whether it is songs about Native Americans, pretty women, movie stars, doo wop groups, or folk singers, to name just a few, these reference books aim to present a comprehensive overview of the most notable, most artistic, and most interesting song sheet images within each chosen genre. As such, these volumes will serve as an invaluable aid to not only sheet music collectors but also historians of the eras on which each volume touches. As Gene Utz writes: "Sheet music traces history, whether of a country or an age, of sentiment or satire." (*Collecting Paper: An Identification and Value Guide*, 1993, p. 55.) In the Foreward to Davison's exhibition guide, Howard H. Peckham, Museum Director, puts it this way:

> We look upon this sheet music as source material for social history. ... The sentiments expressed, the events celebrated, the places commemorated, the persons admired, the attitudes revealed, the increasing popularity of sheet music—these are the stuff that help us reconstruct the feelings of past times. (p. 3)

This book and, indeed, the entire series of books for collectors, then, is a natural evolution in the publication of song sheet books in that each volume presents comprehensive, in-depth coverage of a particular subject that has not been presented in thorough fashion heretofore. Each book builds upon, incorporates, and expands the coverage of selected illustrated song sheets found in prior books, and cites the contributions of prior authors whenever they are used.

Yet one may question the legitimacy of song sheet illustration as art. Are illustrators really artists? Marian Klamkin, author of *Old Sheet Music: A Pictorial History*, argues that song sheet covers "are the contemporary artists' interpretation of the popular songs that they were hired to illustrate ...." (p. 1) She goes on to explain as follows:

From an artistic point of view sheet music is unique in that almost from its inception, the published piece of popular music brought three forms of art together in a manner where they are interdependent for the final success of the product. ... [For example] the early lithographs are as important an expression of American popular art as are the words and the notes to be found within the covers of a published song. (pp. 1-2)

One particularly insightful discussion is found in the program that accompanied a sheet music display at the Elvehjem Museum of Art of the University of Wisconsin. Its author Jean M. Bonin explains in *The Art of Sheet Music: American Life in Our Piano Benches* that song sheet design and illustration have never been considered a high art form:

> The very popularity of the music itself, as well as its primary appeal to musicians, rather than "art collectors," has too frequently excluded sheet music from consideration as a visual art form. Yet, the illustrated and highly decorative covers encasing the majority of these musical scores are very much a visual art form. Produced for commercial distribution in the United States and abroad, they, in fact, effectively reflect the stylistic tastes and historical attitudes of their time. The covers of these musical scores were from the very beginning designed by some of the leading artists of their respective periods and utilized some of the most sophisticated and advanced printing techniques then being developed. (Foreword, p. 2)

Thus, to song sheet collectors, historians and social commentators, the visual art exhibited on the covers is very much admired and appreciated. Bonin puts it this way:

> ...pictorial art was clearly a valued and coveted part of American popular sheet music. Its pieces merit our attention because of their widespread historical presence in our parlors and dance halls and for the imagination and craftsmanship which they exhibit. (p. 4)

That word "craftsmanship" seems a good way of describing the efforts of the many illustrators who were engaged to illustrate and, thus, help promote the sale of song sheets. In the process, the cover illustrations and photographs also unintentionally give us a glimpse of the culture and history of their time. Davison explains:

> Sheet music illustration in the United States began in earnest about 1825 and flourished throughout the remainder of the century. During the fifty years of its most fruitful era American sheet music illustration recorded the passing scene in city views, cartoons, political events and personages, and portraits of heroes and performers. Ever changing tastes and fashions in music, theatre, and popular culture in general appear in lithographs, engravings, and wood engravings on sheet music. (p. 5)

Yes, at its heart, the purpose of song sheet illustration was and continues to be commercial—to help sell vocal and instrumental musical compositions. That has been true of other illustrative crafts, particularly with respect to the sale of magazines, prints, dime paperbacks, comic books and contemporary novels whose dust jackets over the decades have featured artistic expression. While numerous such illustrations are pedestrian, some stand out and can be appreciated for their artistry, as you will see in many of the song sheet cover images presented in this book and the others in this series.

Individual song sheets are the focus of the series which, thereby, leaves out illustrated folios, song collections and songsters that have been popular for over one hundred years. In *Doo-dah! Stephen Foster and the Rise of American Popular Culture* (1997), Emerson explains that popular songs "were disseminated not only by sheet music but by songsters—collections of lyrics, for the most part without music, that were often published in pocket-sized volumes." (p. 44) Folios continue to be published today, often with a focus on either a particular performer ('greatest hits") or a theme ("Academy Award winners", Christmas songs, etc).

So, we look to past decades to find song sheet covers that were meant to attract the eye and help promote the song within. In *Tunes of the Twenties and All That Jazz*, Robert Rawlins explains:

> Prior to the 20s, sheet music sales were the primary indicator of a song's popularity Typically, the covers were illustrated by an artist hired by the publishing firm to depict a scene expressing what the song meant. We have no way of knowing if the songwriters or publishers told artists what to draw, or if the artists were given carte blanche to let their imaginations soar. What we do know is that covers played some part in telling the public what the song was about. (p. xvii)

But how was the decision made in selecting song sheets for inclusion in this book and the others in the series? Two criteria were used: the visual appeal of a cover's artwork or photography, and/or the historical significance of an illustrated cover. Not included are the many musical pieces that were published without illustrated covers or those with covers that appear, to this collector, uninteresting or unattractive.[6] The selection process is solely that of the author and necessarily involves subjective judgment. *However, it is hoped that the song sheets listed, as well as those pictured in each book, represent a relatively comprehensive overview of collectible, interesting and attractive song sheets in their respective genre.*

Mention was made a moment ago of both artwork and photography. Although photography was created and introduced in the mid-nineteenth century, it was not heavily used in the early design of song sheet covers. In that century, illustrator-artists began using lithography methods to design and illustrate sheet music covers, though few signed their artwork. America was just a few years behind England where lithography first began to be used around 1820 in producing sheet music cover illustrations. Bonin explains: "... the history of sheet music illustration is largely faceless. Many imprints from the nineteenth century carry only the name of the lithography firm, which is at least a thread of evidence. ... Only rarely in those days is there an artist's signature." (p. 4) Davison discusses the introduction of lithography to sheet music production:

> Lithography, invented in Austria in 1798, was imported to the United States in the early 1820s and after a few early experiments and false starts it became a popular, inexpensive, and comparatively rapid means of reproducing pictures. One of the first commercially

successful firms to produce lithographs in the United States was "Pendleton's Lithography" of Boston. The two Pendleton brothers, William and John, went into business in 1825 and published the first dated, lithographically illustrated sheet music cover in March, 1826. (p. 7)

Writing in England at the start of the twentieth century, Imeson exclaims that "a history of music-illustration would, to a great extent, be a history of lithography in this country." (p. 6)

Toward the end of the nineteenth century, color lithographs (chromolithography) became increasingly used in the world of academic and commercial publication (think Audubon or Currier & Ives), followed closely by song sheet cover illustration. Major music publishers began employing full-time illustrators, driven by the rising demand for song sheets for use primarily in homes across America.

By far the major form of entertainment for numerous households in the nineteenth and early twentieth centuries was playing the piano and singing the tunes. Piano purchases by families in the U.S. began in earnest in the latter part of the nineteenth century and continued until the new entertainment forms of radio and cinema became their competition. In the early adoption of pianos for the home, here, again, England took the lead:

> Another reason for the increasing popularity of music sheets in the mid-19th-century was the introduction of the upright piano about 1827. It was small enough to be accommodated in the parlours of modest homes, and its early acquisition denoted a certain status to envious friends and neighbours. ... the upright painoforte was soon a feature of many homes. Jullien's quadrilles, polkas, mazurkas and waltzes were purchased for home performance during the 1840s .... (Victoria & Albert Museum, *Victorian Illustrated Sheet Music*, p. 5.)

According to Arthur Loesser: "In 1860, for example, seventy Americans bought a new piano every working day." (*Men, Women and Pianos: A Social History*, p. 512.) And, as reported in Rawlins (p. 262), in 1909 alone (the peak year for piano sales) over 364,000 pianos were sold in the U.S.[7] Sales of sheet music followed. Songs were often first heard in music halls that became increasingly affordable for the middle class in the latter part of the nineteenth century. Department stores set up counters for the sale of popular song sheets, including performers who would play and promote the tunes. Sunday newspaper supplements printed songs and some companies used songs as advertisements. In *American Sheet Music with Prices: A Guide to Collecting Sheet Music from 1775 to 1975*, Daniel B. Priest reports that:

> From 1902 to 1907, about 100 different songs had reached a sales level of more than 100,000 while 40 had gone over 200,000. Four had been jumbo sellers with Williams and Van Alstyne's "In the Shade of the Old Apple Tree" topping out at 700,000. ... "After the Ball" was the first to go over one million. (p. 26)

Purchased song sheets got heavy use—witness the many extant copies that show wear and tear, markings, splitting spines, yellowing due to exposure to sun, water stains and other indicators of use. Some families had their song sheets bound in hard covers, thereby helping to preserve them. Although the American Civil War effectively stopped distribution of goods including sheet music between North and South, Davison observes: "Sheet music and its accompanying activities were such a part of American life that even civil war did not seriously disrupt the writing, illustrating, publishing, and sale of music for home performance." (p. 24) After the war, the technological innovations of train travel and telegraphy helped spur the distribution of song sheets far from their sources. Music publishers in New York and Boston could now communicate promotion of their songs and have them distributed throughout the midwest and beyond by traveling salesmen. In *Doo-dah!*, Emerson explains that innovations in transportation and communications as well as printing expedited the home delivery of sheet music:

> The canal, the steamboat, the railroad, the telegraph, the high-speed rotary steam press, the paper-cutting machine, color lithography, new ways to convert rags into paper—all these forces converged in Stephen Foster's childhood to revolutionize Jacksonian America

and make popular culture in general, and pop music in particular, possible. (p. 43)

But song sheets were also widely used in venues outside the home. The explosion of sheet music sales began with the extended use of new technologies during what Max Morath terms the Exposition Era, from 1893's Columbian Exposition (Chicago) to 1904's Louisiana Purchase Exposition (St. Louis). In his Introduction to Robert A. Fremont's *Favorite Songs of the Nineties* (1973) Morath puts it well: "recorded, mass-printed and promoted, illustrated with colored slides, punched into piano rolls, endlessly performed in tandem with silent movies at the nickelodeons. No wonder music became an industry." (p. viii)

Rawlins states that the decade of the 1920s was the most prolific decade for American popular music, increasing the demand for sheet music via a variety of entertainment establishments:

The number of songs written and live bands performing them was simply staggering. An average of more than 225 Broadway shows opened every year, each with more than a dozen original songs, not to mention all of the stand-alone songs, made popular by vaudeville performers or dance bands. And all of these songs—tens of thousands of them, were performed in theaters, cabarets, hotels, dance halls, movie houses, and speakeasies throughout the country. (pp. 259-60)

As to the use of photography to decorate song sheet covers, it became increasingly found on song sheets that featured a particular vocalist or actor who may have been well received in a vaudeville or playhouse production. Davison (pp. 22-23) notes that:

...successful photo-mechanical printing process was not developed until the late 1890s. ... The half-tone process, perfected about the turn of the century, solved the problems of representing the wide range of grays found in photographs and of printing photographs on the same equipment and in the same press run as type.

Thus, the golden era of illustrated popular song sheet production extends only through the first quarter of the twentieth century. Swift-moving technological changes contributed to the shift from pure illustration to full use of photographs. In his colorful way, Max Wilk, author of *Memory Lane: The Golden Age of American Popular Music*, summarizes the causes of the subsequent decline of the song sheet:

Mr. Thomas A. Edison's invention of the talking-machine, with its cylinders that brought performers' voices into the parlour, began to chip away at the popularity of the published song. By the early 1920's, there appeared the radio; every home became equipped with its own crystal set. On a clear night, one could listen to other voices crooning—from as far away as Bridgeport! Soon, every consumer owned his own Atwater Kent super-heterodyne, and dust began to gather on the closed lid of the family Steinway. By the time 1928 was upon us, with the introduction of the talking-picture, the days of sheet-music had passed. Why should anyone try to compete with Al Jolson singing on a phonograph record, or from the silver screen? The professional performers had taken over. (p. 9)

Commentators have noted likewise that it was the period roughly from 1920 to 1935 that witnessed a seismic shift in the way our country entertained itself. We shifted from being *active players or producers* of musical entertainment for each other to becoming *passive consumers* of professional performances, a change that was reflected in the declining sales of song sheets. By the early 1930s, two-thirds of American homes had one or more radios. John Edward Hasse summed the shift succinctly: "As people flocked to buy radios, sales of other music machines—pianos, player pianos, and phonographs—plummeted." (Remembering the Radio Revolution 100 Years On, *Wall Street Journal*, Nov. 9, 2020)

However, song sheets did not disappear. From the 1930s onward, Broadway shows, movies, radio programs and jukeboxes became the foundation for song sheet designs, featuring the photographs (and, sometimes, caricatures) of popular actors, movie stars and vocalists. Now, performing artists were helping to sell song sheets. In the present digital era, hard-copy music sheets have lost most of their reason for being, though to some extent they are still being produced with covers featuring performers of hit tunes.

The various books that comprise our series, Illustrated Song Sheets: Reflections of Popular Culture, may be divided into those that focus on artistic illustration of song sheet covers and those that make full or heavy use of photography. The artistry type includes song sheets dealing with genres such as American Indians, pretty women, the far west, African Americans, cartoons and animation, automobiles, dance, and so much more. Despite their commercial purpose, many song illustrators transcended that purpose. Their work may be enjoyed on their own terms, as art. Over 100 years ago, Imeson observed that the artistry exhibited on song sheet covers made them valuable and collectible in themselves because "most of the blocks, plates or stones from which these obsolete titles were printed have long since been defaced or destroyed." (p. 9)

The photography type includes songs from the cinema, Broadway shows, country and western, pop singers, rock and roll stars, folk music, and other categories.

I hope that you, dear reader, will find these books enlightening, informative, interesting and, most of all, artistically appealing—much as the song sheets did for me in acquiring and collecting them.

A Note on Song Sheet Sizes

Before around 1920, most song sheets were published in large-size. These sheets vary slightly in size but are approximately 10.5 to 10.75 inches (wide) by 13.5 to 14.0 inches (high). Along with the sale of pianos during the nineteenth century came the sale of piano stools and music cabinets to hold sheet music. Colleague Sandy Marrone related to me that with the later production of piano benches, large sheets music had to be trimmed to fit. In addition, due to efforts to preserve paper during WWI, the U. S. government asked music publishers to shrink the size of their paper to 9 x12 inches and to reduce the number of pages. In the books in this series, 9 x 12 song sheets are referred to as standard size, and are identified by the abbreviation ST. Some publishers went farther and produced much smaller sheets of approximately 5" in width and 9" in height. These are referred to as war size and abbreviated WS. Since the late 1950s, song sheets have been slightly reduced from standard size to 8.5 x 11 inches.

SOURCES CITED

From Bibliography of Illustrated Song Sheet Reference Books

Imeson, W. E. *Illustrated Music Titles and their Delineators.* London, self-published, 1912.

Bonin, Jean M. *American Life in Our Piano Benches: The Art of Sheet Music.* University of Wisconsin, 1985.

Crew, Danny O. *Presidential Sheet Music: An Illustrated Catalogue of Published Music Associated with the American Presidency and Those Who Sought the Office.* Jefferson, NC: McFarland & Company, Inc., 2001.

Crew, Danny O. *Suffragist Sheet Music: An Illustrated Catalogue of Published Music Associated with the Women's Rights and Suffrage Movement in America, 1795–1921, with Complete Lyrics.* Jefferson, NC: McFarland & Company, Inc., 2002.

Davison, Nancy R. *American Sheet Music Illustration: Reflections of the Nineteenth Century* (A Guide to an Exhibition in the Museum of Art, October 12 – November 18, William L. Clements Library, University of Michigan), 1973.

Emerson, Ken. *Doo-dah!: Stephen Foster and the Rise of American Popular Culture.* NY: Simon & Schuster, 1997

Fremont, Robert A., ed. *Favorite Songs of the Nineties: Complete Original Sheet Music for 89 Songs.* NY: Dover Publications, Inc., 1973.

Hasse, John Edward, Ed. *Ragtime: Its History, Composers, and Music.* NY: Schirmer Books, 1985.

Jackson, Richard, ed. *Stephen Foster Song Book: Original Sheet Music of 40 Songs by Stephen Collins Foster.* Selected, with Introduction and Notes, by Richard Jackson. Mineola, NY: Dover Publications, Inc., 1974.

Klamkin, Marian. *Old Sheet Music: A Pictorial History.* NY: Hawthorn Books, Inc., 1975.

Priest, Daniel B. *American Sheet Music with Prices: A Guide to Collecting Sheet Music from 1775 to 1975.* Des Moines: Wallace Homestead Book Co., 1978.

Rawlins, Robert. *Tunes of the Twenties and All That Jazz: The Stories Behind the Songs.* Clayton, NJ: Rookwood House Publishing, 2015.

Ritchie, John W. and John W. Teel. *Rock 'n Roll Sheet Music: A Reference and Price Guide to the Golden Age of Rock & Roll – the '50s and Early '60s.* Portland, OR: John Ritchie, 2000.

Victoria & Albert Museum. *Victorian Illustrated Music Sheets.* London: Her Majesty's Stationery Office, 1981.

Wilk, Max. *Memory Lane: The Golden Age of American Popular Music.* NY: Ballantine Books, 1976.

Additional References

Ehrlich, Cyril. *The Piano: A History.* London: J. M. Dent, 1976.

Fabricant, Solomon. *The Output of Manufacturing Industries, 1899–1937.* NY: National Bureau of Economic Research, 1940.

Hasse, John Edward. Remembering the Radio Revolution 100 Years On, *Wall Street Journal*, Nov. 9, 2020.

Loesser, Arthur. *Men, Women and Pianos: A Social History.* NY: Simon & Schuster, 1954.

NOTES

1. Ritchie is co-author with John W. Teel of *Rock 'n Roll Sheet Music: A Reference and Price Guide to the Golden Age of Rock & Roll – the '50s and Early '60s*.

2. The term "song sheet" is used throughout to refer to popular songs issued as sheet music. The broader term, less preferred for our purposes, "sheet music," encompasses popular and classical compositions, with and without cover illustration.

3. Davison, Nancy R. *American Sheet Music Illustration: Reflections of the Nineteenth Century*, 1973.

4. Crew, Danny O. *Presidential Sheet Music*, 2001, and *Suffragist Sheet Music*, 2002.

5. Books containing song sheet cover images have been published on individual composers including Irving Berlin, E.T. Paull, James Reese Europe, Stephen Foster, Joseph F. Lamb, Cole and the Johnson Brothers, Scott Joplin, and James Scott. Also, there are published books covering specific topics including Abraham Lincoln, Confederate Songs, Ku Klux Klan, Ragtime, Early African American Songs, Classic Blues, Broadway & Hollywood Songs, Songs of New York City, Cowboy Songs, Tin Pan Alley Western Songs, Hawaiian Music, Baseball, and others. For specific titles, see the Bibliography of Illustrated Song Sheet Reference Books listed in this book.

6. For a notable example, most of the song sheet covers of tunes composed and issued by Stephen Foster in the mid-nineteenth century featured highly ornamental words only, but no illustration. See Richard Jackson, ed., *Stephen Foster Song Book: Original Sheet Music of 40 Songs by Stephen Collins Foster*, 1974.

7. Sales data were compiled by Solomon Fabricant in *The Output of Manufacturing Industries, 1899–1937* (pp. 597-99) and Cyril Ehrlich, *The Piano: A History* (p. 221). The author is grateful to John Edward Hasse for including these references on piano sales information in his book, *Ragtime: Its History, Composers, and Music*.

BIBLIOGRAPHY OF ILLUSTRATED SONG SHEET REFERENCE BOOKS

(With notations regarding inclusion of cover illustrations)

It is safe to predict that, in the near future, many books—on widely diverse subjects—will be illustrated with facsimiles of old song and music-titles.
—W. E. Imeson, 1912 (p. 18)

Eighteenth and Nineteenth Centuries

This section includes comprehensive reference books that focus on sheet music produced in the eighteenth through the early twentieth centuries. Many of these books provide in-depth discussion of the development of the sheet music industry, while others provide comprehensive listings of popular song sheets.

1912: *Illustrated Music Titles and their Delineators.* W. E. Imeson. London, self-published. (nine b&w illustrations) This is the first book believed to have been written about song sheet illustration. The 'delineators' in the title refer to biographies of British song sheet illustrators.

1941: *Early American Sheet Music: Its Lure and Its Lore, 1768–1889.* Harry Dichter and Elliott Shapiro. NY: R. R. Bowker Co. (includes some b&w illustrations)

1948: *Morning, Noon and Night in London.* Sacheverell Sitwell. London: Macmillan & Co. (selective color illustrations of British song sheets)

1967: *Grace Notes in American History: Popular Sheet Music from 1820 to 1900.* Lester. S. Levy. Norman: University of Oklahoma Press. (b&w illustrations)

1969: *Victorian Music Covers.* Doreen and Sidney Spellman. (2nd Ed: 1972) Park Ridge, NJ: Noyes Press. (b&w and some color illustrations)

1970: *Prints in and of America to 1850.* John D. Morse, Ed. Published for The Henry Francis du Pont Winterthur Museum. Charlottesville: The University Press of Virginia. (b&w illustrations)

1971: *Flashes of Merriment: A Century of Humorous Songs in American, 1805–1905.* Lester S. Levy. Norman: University of Oklahoma Press. (b&w illustrations)

1972: *Victorian Sheet Music Covers.* Ronald Pearsall. South Devon: David & Charles Ltd. (extensive b&w illustrations)

1973: *The Lure of the Striped Pig: The Illustration of Popular Music in America, 1820–1870.* David Tatham. Barre, Mass.: Imprint Society. (color and b&w illustrations)

1973: *American Sheet Music Illustration: Reflections of the Nineteenth Century* (A Guide to an Exhibition in the Museum of Art, October 12– November 18, William L. Clements Library, University of Michigan). Nancy R. Davison (includes four b&w song sheet images)

1973: *Favorite Songs of the Nineties: Complete Original Sheet Music for 89 Songs.* Robert A. Fremont, Ed. NY: Dover Publications, Inc. (b&w illustrations)

1975: *Give Me Yesterday: American History in Song, 1890–1920.* Lester S. Levy. Norman: University of Oklahoma Press. (b&w illustrations)

1975: *Music for Patriots, Politicians, and Presidents: Harmonies and Discords of the First Hundred Years.* Vera Brodsky. Lawrence. NY: Macmillan Publishing Co., Inc. (b&w and some color illustrations)

1976: *Picture the Songs: Lithographs from the Sheet Music of Nineteenth Century America.* Lester S. Levy. Baltimore: Johns Hopkins University Press. (color and b&w illustrations)

1981: *Victorian Illustrated Music Sheets.* Victoria & Albert Museum. London: Her Majesty's Stationery Office. (25 color illustrations)

Reference Books Without Song Sheet Cover Images

Though without cover images, these books by Stubblebine, Crew and others are valued by collectors, and especially sellers, to identify titles and publication dates of song sheets, particularly those from cinema and stage productions.

1991: *Cinema Sheet Music: A Comprehensive Listing of Published Film Music from* Squaw Man *(1914) to* Batman *(1989).* Donald J. Stubblebine. Jefferson, NC: McFarland &Company, Inc.

1996: *Broadway Sheet Music: A Comprehensive Listing of Published Music from Broadway and Other Stage Shows, 1918–1993.* Donald J. Stubblebine. Jefferson, NC: McFarland & Company, Inc.

1997: *British Cinema Sheet Music: A Comprehensive Listing of Film Music Published in the United Kingdom, Canada and Australia, 1916 Through 1994.* Donald J. Stubblebine. Jefferson, NC: McFarland & Company, Inc.

1998: *Early Blues: Volume Three.* Richard L. Riley. Roseville, CA: PianoMania Music Publishing. (Spiral-bound with no illustrations except for color illustrations on the exterior & interior of the front and back covers)

2002: *Early Broadway Sheet Music 1843–1918.* Donald J. Stubblebine. Jefferson, NC: McFarland & Company, Inc.

2006: *American Political Music; Vol. 1: Introduction, Alabama-New York; Vol. 2: New York-General, Indexes.* Danny O. Crew. Jefferson, NC: McFarland & Company, Inc.

Song Sheet Price Guides

In books identified as "price guides," the authors have attempted to assign values to song sheets. But the explosion of second-hand selling sites on the internet has unearthed hundreds of thousands of song sheets garnered from estate sales, house attics, and piano benches, thereby impacting monetary values. Most of the books listed in this section were published before the internet became widely used. Thus, their valuations are not especially helpful. They are included here for the sake of thoroughness.

1976: *Introducing the Song Sheet: A Collector's Guide with Current Price List.* Helen Westin. NY: Thomas Nelson, Inc. (color illustrations)

1978: *American Sheet Music with Prices: A Guide to Collecting Sheet Music from 1775 to1975.* Daniel B. Priest. Des Moines: Wallace Homestead Book Co. (b&w with some color illustrations)

1991: *Sheet Music: A Price Guide.* Debbie Dillon. Gas City, IN: L-W Book Sales. (b&w illustrations)

1995: *Sheet Music: A Price Guide (with Revised Prices).* Debbie Dillon. Gas City, IN: L-W Book Sales. (b&w illustrations)

1995: *The Sheet Music Reference & Price Guide.* Marie-Reine A. Pafik and Anna Marie Guiheen. Paducah, KY: Collector Books. (some small color illustrations)

2000: *The Sheet Music Reference & Price Guide.* Second Ed. Marie-Reine A. Pafik and Anna Marie Guiheen. Paducah, KY: Collector Books. (some small color illustrations)

2000: *Rock 'n' Roll Sheet Music: A Reference and Price Guide to the Golden Age of Rock &Roll– the '50s and Early '60s.* John W. Ritchie and John W. Teel. Portland, OR: John Ritchie. (b&w illustrations)

2006: *Collecting Rock 'n' Roll Sheet Music of the 1960s.* Valerie Carallo. Atglen, PA: Schiffer Publishing, Ltd. (profusely color illustrated)

2007: *Words by Ira Gershwin Sheet Music: A Pictorial Price Guide*. Thomas Inglis and Janice Grower. Vena Books.

2010: *1001 Rags: 1897–1920 Rags & Ragtime Sheet Music – A Pictorial Price Guide*. Thomas Inglis. Vena Books. (b&w illustrations)

Multiple-Topic Song Sheet Books

This section includes books that feature song sheets in several topical areas or genres. As such, their coverage of each included genre is selective.

1973: *Memory Lane: 1890 to 1925 / Ragtime, Jazz, Foxtrot and other popular music and music covers selected by Max Wilk*. Max Wilk. London: Studio International Publications, Ltd. (numerous color illustrations)

1975: *Old Sheet Music: A Pictorial History*. Marian Klamkin. NY: Hawthorn Books, Inc. (many b&w and some color illustrations)

1976: *Memory Lane: The Golden Age of American Popular Music*. Max Wilk. NY: Ballantine Books. (This is a reissue of his 1973 book; numerous color illustrations)

1985: *American Life in Our Piano Benches: The Art of Sheet Music*. Jean M. Bonin. University of Wisconsin. (b&w and a few color illustrations)

1989: *I Hear America Singing: A Nostalgic Tour of Popular Sheet Music*. Lynn Wenzel and Carol J. Binkowski. NY: Crown Publishers, Inc. (numerous color images)

1997: *The Gold in Your Piano Bench: Collectible Sheet Music, Tearjerkers, Black Songs, Rags & Blues*. Marion Short. Atglen, PA: Schiffer Publishing Ltd. (profusely color illustrated)

1997: *More Gold in Your Piano Bench: Collectible Sheet Music, Inventions, Wars, and Disasters*. Marion Short. Atglen, PA: Schiffer Publishing Ltd. (profusely color illustrated)

1998: *From Saginaw Valley to Tin Pan Alley: Saginaw's Contribution to American Popular Music, 1890–1955* (Great Lakes Books Series). R. Grant Smith. Detroit, MI: Wayne State University Press, 1998. (numerous b&w and some color illustrations)

1998: *Covers of Gold: Collectible Sheet Music, Sports, Fashion, Illustration and the Dance*. Marion Short. Atglen, PA: Schiffer Publishing Ltd. (profusely color illustrated)

2013: *North Dakota Composers: An Album of Sheet Music Covers 1887-2008*. Yvonne McDonald and Rudolf Polt. Morrisville, NC: Lulu Publishing (self-publisher). (b&w and color illustrations)

2014: *Visions of Music: Sheet Music in the Twentieth Century*. Tony Walas. Milwaukee: Hal Leonard Books. (profuse color illustrations)

Single Topic Song Sheet Sources

This section includes specialized collectors' references focusing on singular song sheet subjects, themes or composers.

1957: *A Pictorial Bibliography of the First Editions of Stephen C. Foster*. James J. Fuld. Philadelphia: Musical Americana. (dozens of mostly b&w illustrations)

1989: *E. T. Paull's Compositions*. Wayland Bunnell. The Sheet Music Exchange, Vol. VII, No. 2, April. [stapled set of pages] (b&w illustrations)

1991: *For a Cowboy Has to Sing*. Jim Bob Tinsley. Orlando, FL: University of Central Florida Press. (color illustrations of 60 songs)

1992: *From Cakewalks to Concert Halls: An Illustrated History of African American Popular Music from 1895 to 1930*. Thomas L. Morgan and William Barlow. Washington, DC: Elliott & Clark Publishing. (color illustrations)

1998: *From Footlights to "The Flickers": Collectible Sheet Music, Broadway*

Shows and Silent Movies. Marion Short. Atglen, PA: Schiffer Publishing Ltd. (profusely color illustrated)

1999: *Collectible Sheet Music: Hollywood Movie Songs*. Marion Short. Atglen, PA: Schiffer Publishing Ltd. (profusely color illustrated)

2001: *Presidential Sheet Music: An Illustrated Catalogue of Published Music Associated with the American Presidency and Those Who Sought the Office*. Danny O. Crew. Jefferson, NC: McFarland & Company, Inc. (b&w illustrations)

2002: *Suffragist Sheet Music: An Illustrated Catalogue of Published Music Associated with the Women's Rights and Suffrage Movement in America, 1795–1921, with Complete Lyrics*. Danny O. Crew. Jefferson, NC: McFarland & Company, Inc. (numerous b&w illustrations)

2003: *Ku Klux Klan Sheet Music: An Illustrated Catalogue of Published Music, 1867–2002*. Danny O. Crew. Jefferson, NC: McFarland & Company, Inc. (b&w illustrations)

2003: *Sheet Music Art of Irving Berlin*. Thomas Inglis. Atglen, PA: Schiffer Publishing Ltd. (profusely color illustrated)

2007: *The Baseball Songbook: Songs and Images from the Early Years of America's Favorite Pastime*. Jerry Silverman. Van Nuys, CA: Alfred Publishing Co., Inc. (dozens of b&w illustrations)

2007: *A Gilbert & Sullivan Guide: Illustrated Sheet Music*. Jonathan Smith. London: Arcadee Publishing, 2007. (profusely color illustrated)

2011: *Confederate Sheet Music*. E. Lawrence Abel. Jefferson, NC: McFarland & Co. (some b&w illustrations)

2012: *Rausmit der Kaiser (and Other Villains): An Album of Sheet Music Covers & Artwork*. (Title translated: Out with the Kaiser). Yvonne McDonald. Morrisville, NC: Lulu (self-publisher) (extensive color illustrations)

2016: Memori estoriche d'Italiane I cantidella Patria. 120 anni di spartitiillustrati dal Risorgimento alla Grande Guerra (1799–1922) [Translation: Historical memories of Italy in the songs of the Fatherland. 120 years of illustrated scores from the Risorgimento to the Great War (1799–1922).] Carlo Pagliucci. Rome, Italy: Palombi. (numerous color illustrations)

2017: *Talking Machine West: A History and Catalogue of Tin Pan Alley's Western Recordings, 1902–1918*. Michael A. Amundson. Norman: University of Oklahoma Press. (many color illustrations)

2020: *Abraham Lincoln Sheet Music: An Illustrated Catalogue of Sheet Music, Song Books and other Published Songs Associated with Our 16th President*. Danny O. Crew. Fort Mill: Lincoln Scholar Publishing LLC. (many b&w and color illustrations)

2021: *George Washington Sheet Music: An Illustrated Catalogue of Music Related to Our First President*. Danny O. Crew. Fort Mill: Lincoln Scholar Publishing LLC. (numerous color and b&w illustrations)

2022: *An Illustrated Bibliography of Sheet Music Covers Associated with James Weldon Johnson and John Rosamond Johnson*. Danny O. Crew. Fort Mill, SC: Lincoln Scholar Publishing LLC. [numerous color images]

2023: *An Illustrated Checklist of Sheet Music Associated with the Suwannee River*. Danny O. Crew. Fort Mill, SC: Lincoln Scholar Publishing LLC. [numerous color images]

2023: *An Illustrated Checklist of Sheet Music Covers Associated with the State of Florida*. Danny O. Crew. Fort Mill, SC: Lincoln Scholar Publishing LLC. [numerous color images]

Books Containing Images But Without Discussion

The books in this section present colorful song sheet images but do not provide any discussion or historical context for the depicted song sheet covers.

2011: *An International Album of Sheet Music Rarities, Vols. 1-17.* Rudolf Polt. Morrisville, NC: Lulu (self-publisher) (all seventeen volumes have extensive color illustrations, but with little discussion)

2012: *An International Album of Sheet Music Rarities, Vols. 18-23.* Rudolf Polt. Morrisville, NC: Lula (self-publisher) (extensive color illustrations, but with little discussion)

2012: *A Greta Garbo Sheet Music Album.* Rudolf Polt. Morrisville, NC: Lulu (self-publisher) (extensive color illustrations, but with little discussion)

2012: *A Marlene Dietrich Sheet Music Album.* Rudolf Polt. Morrisville, NC: Lulu (self-publisher) (extensive color illustrations, but with little discussion)

2012: *A Zarah Leander Sheet Music Album.* Rudolf Polt. Morrisville, NC: Lulu (self-publisher) (extensive color illustrations, but with little discussion)

2012: *100 Music Sheet Cover Girls.* Joe Tooley. Self-published. (color illustrations, one per page; not full cover images but trimmed; little discussion)

2013: *An International Album of Sheet Music Rarities, Vols. 24-25.* Rudolf Polt. Morrisville, NC: Lulu (self-publisher) (extensive color illustrations, but with little discussion)

2017: *Sheet Music Covers Vol. 1: The Jazz Era.* R. S. Rodella. Self-published. (50 color illustrations lacking description or commentary)

2017: *Sheet Music Covers Vol. 2: Romance.* R. S. Rodella. Self-published. (50 color illustrations lacking description or commentary)

2017: *Sheet Music Covers Vol. 3: Black Americana.* R. S. Rodella. Self-published. (50 color illustrations lacking description or commentary)

2017: *Sheet Music Covers Vol. 4: Polka, Tango, Two-Step.* R. S. Rodella. Self-published. (50 color illustrations lacking description or commentary)

2017: *Sheet Music Covers Vol. 5: Opera, Waltz, Ballet.* R. S. Rodella. Self-published. (50 color illustrations lacking description or commentary)

Books Not Focused on Song Sheet Cover Images

Although the books in this section include images of song sheet covers, their focus is not on song sheet illustration but on the musical compositions or their historical and cultural context. As such they provide useful background information for collectors of popular sheet music. The listing in this section is far from definitive since many other books would satisfy the criteria.

1939: *From Ragtime to Swingtime: The Story of the House of Witmark.* Isidore Witmark and Isaac Goldbert. NY: Lee Furman, Inc. (b&w illustrations)

1970: *Deac Martin's Book of Musical Americana.* Claude Trimble Martin. Englewood Cliffs, NJ: Prentice-Hall, Inc. (32 full-page color illustrations)

1971: *Ring Bells! Sing Songs! Broadway Musicals of the 1930s.* Stanley Green. New Rochelle, NY: Arlington House. (more than 50 b&w illustrations)

1973: *Classic Piano Rags: Complete Original Music for 81 Piano Rags.* Rudi Blesh. NY: Dover Publications, Inc. (81 b&w illustrations)

1974: *Stephen Foster Song Book: Original Sheet Music of 40 Songs by Stephen Collins Foster.* Selected, with Introduction and Notes, by Richard Jackson. Mineola, NY: Dover Publications, Inc. (four illustrated b&w covers)

1974: *Show Songs: From 'The Black Crook' to 'The Red Mill.'* Stanley Applebaum, Ed. NY, NY; Dover Publications. (numerous b&w illustrations)

1975: *Song Hits from the Turn of the Century: Complete Original Sheet Music for 25 Songs*. Paul Charosh and Robert A. Fremont, Eds. Mineola, NY, NY: Dover Publications, Inc. (25 b&w illustrations)

1975: *Ragtime Rarities: Complete Original Music for 63 Piano Rags*. Trebor Jay Tichenor. NY, NY: Dover Publications, Inc. (63 b&w illustrations)

1979: *Yesterdays: Popular Song in America*. Charles Hamm. NY: W. W. Norton & Co. (about two dozen b&w illustrations)

1981: *Scott Joplin: Complete Piano Works*. Vera Brodsky Lawrence, Ed. NY: The New York Public Library. (numerous b&w illustrations)

1982: *Scandalize My Name: Black Imagery in American Popular Music*. Sam Dennison. NY: Garland Publishing, Inc. (52 b&w illustrated covers)

1984: *The Illustrated Victorian Songbook*. Aline Waites and Robin Hunter. London: Sheldrake Press Ltd. (about 12 color illustrations)

1984: *Take Me Out to the Ball Game and Other Favorite Song Hits, 1906–1908*. Lester S. Levy (ed.) Mineola, NY: Dover Publications, Inc. (18 b&w illustrations)

1985: *Woman Composers of Ragtime*. Carolynn A. Lindeman. Theodore Presser Company. (5 b&w images)

1985: *Ragtime: Its History, Composers, and Music*. John Edward Hasse, Ed. NY: Schirmer Books. (eleven illustrated b&w covers)

1986: *Ragtime Gems: Original Sheet Music for 25 Ragtime Classics*. David A. Jasen. Mineola, NY: Dover Publications, Inc. (25 b&w illustrations)

1987: *Strains of Change: The Impact of Tourism on Hawaiian Music*. Elizabeth Tatar. Honolulu: Bishop Museum Press. (b&w and mostly color illustrations)

1988: *Scott Joplin: Complete Piano Rags*. David A. Jasen. Mineola, NY: Dover Publications, Inc. (38 b&w illustrations)

1988: *Tin Pan Alley: The Composers, The Songs, The Performers and Their Times*. David A. Jasen. NY: Donald I. Fine, Inc. (some b&w illustrations)

1989: *Peg O' My Heart and Other Favorite Song Hits, 1912 & 1913*. Stanley Applebaum, Ed. NY, NY: Dover Publications. (36 b&w illustrations)

1989: *American Solo Songs Through 1865*. Nicholas Tawa, ed. Vol. 1 of *Three Centuries of American Music: A Collection of American Sacred and Secular Music*. G. K. Hall & Co. (approximately 40 b&w illustrations)

1990: *American Solo Songs: 1866 Through 1910*. Nicholas Tawa, ed. Vol. 2 of *Three Centuries of American Music: A Collection of American Sacred and Secular Music*. G. K. Hall & Co. (approximately 50 b&w illustrations)

1990: *American Keyboard Music Through 1865*. J. Bunker Clark, ed. Vol. 3 of *Three Centuries of American Music: A Collection of American Sacred and Secular Music*. G. K. Hall & Co. (4 b&w illustrations)

1990: *American Keyboard Music: 1866 Through 1910*. Sylvia Glickman, ed. Vol. 4 of *Three Centuries of American Music: A Collection of American Sacred and Secular Music*. G. K. Hall & Co. (approximately 20 b&w illustrations)

1990: *The Complete Works of Harrison Fisher Illustrator*. Naomi Welch. Le Selva Beach, CA: Images of the Past. (9 color illustrations)

1991: *The Illustrated History of Wisconsin Music: 1840–1990*. Compiled and edited by Michael G. Corenthal. Milwaukee, WI: MGC Publications. (b&w illustrations)

1991: *Broadway: 125 Years of Musical Theatre*. Hollis Alpert. NY: Arcade Publishing. (about 20 small color illustrations)

1992: *The Music of James Scott*. Scott DeVeaux and, William Howland Kenney, eds. Washington, DC: Smithsonian Institution Press. (many b&w illustrations)

1993: *The Ziegfeld Touch: The Life and Times of Florenz Ziegfeld, Jr.* Richard and Paulette Ziegfeld. NY: Harry N. Abrams, Inc. (over 30 color illustrations)

1994: *The Voices That Are Gone: Themes in 19th-Century American Popular Song*. Jon W. Finson. NY: Oxford University Press. (16 b&w illustrations)

1997: *Cakewalks, Two-Steps and Trots*. David A. Jasen. Mineola, NY: Dover Publications. (b&w illustrations of 34 compositions)

1997: *Doo-dah! Stephen Foster and the Rise of American Popular Culture*. Ken Emerson. NY: Simon & Schuster. (several small b&w illustrations)

1998: *Beale Street and Other Classic Blues: 38 Works, 1901–1921*. David A. Jasen. Mineola, NY: Dover Publications, Inc. (b&w illustrations)

1999: *New York: Songs of the City*. Nancy Groce. NY: Watson-Guptill Publications. (numerous color illustrations)

2000: *That American Rag: The Story of Ragtime from Coast to Coast*. David A. Jasen and Gene Jones. NY: Schirmer Books. (b&w illustrations)

2007: *Ragtime: An Encyclopedia, Discography, and Sheetography*. David A. Jasen. NY: Routledge, 2014 (paperback) (19 b&w illustrations)

2007: *Doo Wop: The Music, The Times, The Era*. Cousin Bruce Morrow. NY: Sterling Publishing Co. (about 10 color illustrations)

2008: *The American Songbook: The Singers, The Songwriters, and The Songs*. Ken Bloom. NY: Black Dog & Leventhal, 2008. (numerous color illustrations)

2012: *The Music of James Reese Europe: Complete Published Works*. No author cited. NY: Edward B. Marks Music Company. (b&w illustrations)

2012: *Joseph F. Lamb: A Passion for Ragtime – Illustrated*. Carol J. Binkowski. NC: McFarland & Company, Inc. (some b&w illustrations)

2014: *150+ Stephen Foster Songs Songbook* (American Folk Songs Books) (Volume 1). Ironpower Publishing. .https://ironpowerpublishing.com. (b&w illustrations)

2015: *Tunes of the Twenties and All That Jazz: The Stories Behind the Songs*. Robert Rawlins. Clayton, NJ: Rookwood House Publishing. (small b&w and color illustrations)

2015: *The Songs of Cole and Johnson Brothers as Selected by J. Rosamond Johnson, with a Foreword by Thomas Riis*. No author specified. NY: Edward B. Marks Music Company. (about 25 b&w full-page illustrations)

2016: *The American Song Book: The Tin Pan Alley Era*. Philip Furia and Laurie Patterson. NY: Oxford University Press. (full-page b&w illustrations, 1 or 2 per chapter)

2018: *Ragtime Fingerstyle Ukulele: 15 Classic Rags Arranged For Solo Ukulele*. Fred Sokolow. Milwaukee: Hal Leonard, 2018. (small b&w illustrations)

INTRODUCTION

You are in for a visual treat as you peruse over 700 images of song sheet covers featuring American Indians. Whether you are an art aficionado, a sheet music collector, a student of American culture, an historian of American Indians, or someone interested in how song sheet illustrations reflected the public's view of American Indians, you will find much to appreciate in the images presented herein. This book is the first to compile a comprehensive catalog of illustrated song sheets depicting American Indians, featuring cover images and the names of their illustrators, when known. Although it is the result of new and independent research, it builds upon and is indebted to the pioneering efforts of the many authors who have discussed American Indian song sheets. Their comments about and descriptions of song sheets are cited in the book, as are commentaries by experts on American Indians.

In earlier centuries, the sights and sounds of American Indians captured the curiosity and imagination of white explorers of North America and the settlers that followed. Over time, they looked upon indigenous people in various ways—as exotic, noble, docile, fearless, savage, inferior, heathen, friend, foe, wise, backward and, finally, as a doomed race. Although sporadic painted and printed images of American Indians by European immigrant artists were produced in the Colonial period, including formal portraits of American Indian chiefs in 1710[1], most depictions of American Indians began in mid-nineteenth century narrative literature, prints, poetry, painting, and sculpture. Then came dime novels, song sheets, traveling shows, and photography, most often presenting American Indians in simplified, stereotypical fashion. Even the U.S. Treasury got in the act in 1899 by issuing a $5.00 bill featuring a head portrait of Running Antelope, the only American Indian ever depicted on U.S. paper currency.

The first decades of the twentieth century gave birth to radio, records, and silent cinema. Then, talking movies and, later, broadcast television brought to life the stereotypes of American Indians that had been developing over previous decades. As you will see, prevailing attitudes toward American Indians would find their reflection in musical compositions and the illustrated covers of song sheets that promoted them.

A Note on Nomenclature

During the initial preparation of this book, I grappled with the question of what the wording of its title should be. I had thought that use of "Native American" would be most accurate and respectful. But further research changed that view. The first was a mailing from the Smithsonian Institution's National Museum of the American Indian. When I visited its website, I discovered that, although its periodical magazine's name had been changed in the Fall of 2004 from '(National Museum of the) AMERICAN INDIAN' to '(National Museum of the American) INDIAN,' the term American Indian was and continues to be used. Of course, within the detailed descriptions of the Museum's purposes and its collections are found various other terms such as Native Americans, indigenous people, native peoples, and Indians.

In addition, Russell Means in his declaration "I am an American Indian, Not a Native American!" at an international conference of Indians from the Americas held in Geneva at the United Nations in 1977 stated that "we unanimously decided we would go under the term American Indian."[2]

In his book *Imagining Native America in Music* Michael Pisani tells how he grappled with terminology, finding "it difficult to account for every inconsistency of nomenclature."

While, for example, the label "Indian" has since Columbus's time traditionally signified a particular group of people (first the misconstrued "Indians" and then all native peoples of the Americas) as perceived by another group (Europeans), "Indian" has been reclaimed today as a term of unity among many First Peoples. (p. 5)

More recently, I received a mailing from a member of the Sicangu

Lakota tribe and President of the American Indian College Fund seeking support for "American Indian students."

Finally, "A Proclamation on Indigenous Peoples' Day issued by the U.S. President on October 8, 2021, includes the term: "Since time immemorial, American Indians, Alaska Natives, and Native Hawaiians have built vibrant and diverse cultures...."[3]

Although the terminology issue has not been resolved[4], in consideration of the sources cited here, and because the term "Indian" has been used for centuries and which, not coincidentally, has been used extensively in both scholarly and popular written works, and because there are 574 federally recognized tribes and over "1,000 distinct tribal entities or nations" in North America (Muckle, p. 1), I concluded that an appropriate term in the title for this book would be *American Indians*. This term is used throughout the book.

It is important to mention that few if any popular American Indian songs were composed by Indians who, instead, relied on oral and performance traditions to maintain a rich vein of ceremonial and celebratory songs. For the most part, American Indians did not have access to Western musical notation nor to a tradition of putting pen to paper.

> Earliest settlers in Plymouth and Massachusetts Bay remarked on native American music as being lullabies warbled to quiet the children…. In reality, native American music is American in a geographical sense only. Beautiful and haunting as it may be, it cannot be thought of as a precursor to American popular music….[5]

From about 1890 to 1920, inspired by the work of Czech composer Antonín Dvořák, who was director of the National Conservatory of Music in New York City (1892-95), American classical composers began to incorporate indigenous American Indian melodies and styles in classical pieces. "Compositions by Charles Wakefield Cadman, Arthur Farwell, Charles Sanford Skilton, Arthur Nevin, and many others appealed to classical music audiences during this time."[6] As part of this "Indianist Movement," they also "translated" American Indian tunes into Western style music with added enhancements and elaborations using Western instruments. Readers of this book will discover the images of several pieces composed by Cadman, one of the few composers of that era who attempted to straddle the gap between classical and popular music.

As explained in more detail in the Preface, sheet music production in nineteenth century America became increasingly widespread with the development of a middle class that was seeking leisure and entertainment activities. The production and sale of pianos for home use began a meteoric rise starting about mid-century, reaching an all-time peak in 1909.[7] With pianos came the demand for inexpensive and playable song sheets. Sheet music publishers began competing in this new market and, with the development of low-cost lithography methods, put illustrations on song sheet covers to help promote the sale of their songs. All kinds of songs were marketed including songs about American Indians as imagined by song writers and song sheet illustrators.

This by no means implies that American Indian people were treated with proper respect in the songs written about them. For the most part, American popular culture until the latter part of the twentieth century was not particularly sympathetic or sensitive to American Indians, who were characterized and referred to in condescending ways. Sheet music titles reflected this attitude, often incorporating terms such as redskin, squaw and injun. In *For a Cowboy Has to Sing,* Tinsley says that the 1903 song Hiawatha "set the pace for pseudo-Indian songs, followed a year later by 'Navajo,' the top Indian hit of 1904. Two youthful Tin Pan Alley composers, Egbert Van Alstyne and Harry Williams, based the latter song on a humourous theme of a black man proposing to a Navajo girl and promising to supply feathers for her hair if chickens were near."[8] Thus, song sheet cover images, objectionable as some of them may seem to the modern reader, present a fascinating insight into historical attitudes toward American Indians, careful analysis of which is still illuminating today.

Readers will find that, while a few song sheet covers incorporate photographs, the vast majority displayed in this book were issued with drawn or painted illustrations. In fact, illustrators were hired in droves by music publishers to enhance and promote the sale of new musical pieces by creating attractive cover images. Marion Short explains: "Artists Starmer, Carter, De Takacs, Etherington, Pfeiffer, and Frew have all contributed interesting, colorful, action-packed covers for sheet music of this [Indian intermezzo] genre. The large size Native American song covers are generally exquisitely rendered...."[9]

Illustrators worked for music publishers and often did not sign their work. Fortunately, a fair number of cover illustrations were signed, which allowed us to develop a listing of song sheets by artist names. This book's American Indian Song Sheet Illustrators lists the names of more than one hundred illustrators who signed their song sheet artwork.

Of the books listed in the accompanying Bibliography of Illustrated Song Sheet Reference Books, some contain images, commentary and information about song sheets depicting American Indians. A few have devoted an entire chapter or section to American Indian sheet music. Noteworthy is Amundson's very informative book that catalogs Tin Pan Alley's western recordings from 1902 to 1918. Though the focus of his book is on recordings made about the west, illustrations of a good number of song sheets dealing with American Indians are included. He comments on the reaction he had upon seeing song sheets in library collections and those that he purchased: "the music contained beautiful cover pages, highlighting scenes from the songs. Drawn by eastern artists who worked for the sheet music companies, these images proved to be a seemingly unknown collection of early twentieth-century western art." (p. 6)

Amundson's well-researched book catalogs fifty-four western recordings, including their lyrics and history, and includes thirty-six song sheets that have illustrations of American Indians on their cover. All of them are displayed in this volume. Also included herein are the thirty plus song sheet covers displaying American Indian themes presented in Marion Short's *Covers of Gold*.

Readers of this book will discover that song sheet illustrations portrayed American Indians, to a great extent, as romantic and even exotic, but rarely savage. This is of note because during this time the savage Indian stereotype frequently prevailed in many traveling shows, dime novels, theatrical performances and, later, motion pictures. This was also true in the art world. According to Ellwood Parry, two of the most persistent American Indian stereotypes in the popular mind were "the fiendish savage, ever thirsty for the blood of White men ... and the drunken half-breed, left to beg in city streets...."[10] But song sheet illustrations more often romanticized than demonized. Music composers and lyricists focused mostly on classic themes of love—found, lost, and unrequited—and nature as an unspoiled, romantic setting, including American Indian inhabitants. The American public didn't want to play music on their home piano about blood-thirsty massacres, drunken beggars, or shoot-outs; they wanted songs to reinforce their family values and feelings.[11] Illustrators were engaged to help sell the song sheets. This commercial motivation led to a de-emphasis of the savage and depraved Indian stereotypes, and a reliance on romanticized images.

Among the song sheets depicting American Indians presented in this volume, their cover illustrations may be characterized as falling broadly into three major types: historic events, Indian maidens, and Indian chieftains. Historic events reflect the historical reality of, as well as a sense of respect for, American Indians and are found primarily among the more than seventy-five lithographs produced in the nineteenth century that initiated song sheet depictions of American Indians.[12] Yet in the second half of the nineteenth century, illustrated songs depicting American Indians were produced at a rate of less than one per year. America was going through significant changes such as the Civil War and its aftermath, the opening of the railways to the western states, industrialization, the beginnings of public schools, and the forced settlement of Indians on reservations. It is notable that Currier & Ives' prints, displayed widely in American living rooms, featured scenes of family life, nature, modes of transport, and notable events, but few depicted American Indians.[13] In short, Indians were disappearing from the American conscience, especially in the Eastern half of the United States.

Then, around 1900 and continuing for several decades, depictions of American Indian women, often referred to as Indian maidens, started an explosion of songs about Indians. In part, this development appears to have been a fad incubated by musicians and lyricists of Tin Pan Alley that was in its heyday during this same period. Song writers seemed to be trying to outdo one another with tunes about young love, lost love,

love betrayed, and ill-fated love (such as between a "paleface" suitor and a young "Indian maiden" or "squaw"). Levy explains:

> Shortly after the start of the 1900s, all of a sudden the song writers were unleashing a superabundance of numbers about Indian girls … 'Iola,' 'Red Wing,' and other captivating maidens were presented musically to the public, who snapped up the songs by the hundreds of thousands."[14]

A viewing of the song sheet covers presented in this volume will reveal that pretty maidens comprise the largest type of American Indian song sheet illustration. The image of the Indian chief or warrior, also depicted in a romanticized way, mirrored the artistic treatment given Indian maiden songs. This promotion of the "noble Indian" image similarly sprung from the fads capturing the imagination of Tin Pan Alley.

In the first decades of the twentieth century, completion of the coast-to-coast land holdings of settlers, the ending of the vast westward migration, settlement of Indian tribes to reservations, and the realization that the centuries-old cultures of American Indians had been forcibly altered, all contributed to a sense of sorrow, historical reflection and idealization of American Indian life that came to be exhibited on some song sheet covers. In fact, songs such as The Passing of the Dakotahs, The Passing of the Red Man, Little White Rose (featured in Zane Grey's film *The Vanishing American*), and The Lost Phase, directly recognized the passing of a way of life American Indians had known for centuries.

Organization of the Book

This book is organized into six chapters. The first is titled Beginnings and includes illustrated song sheets from the nineteenth century that depict American Indians on their covers, mostly in an historical, respectful manner. Nearly all of these were produced using black and white lithography methods. Due to the historical importance of these song sheet images, it is only in this first chapter that they are listed in chronological order, beginning with We Have Met to Remember the Day published in 1833. The second chapter, American Indians Romanticized, contains the bulk of the song sheets presented in this volume. It is here where we find the many beautifully illustrated sheets from the first two decades of the twentieth century depicting American Indian women and "Indian braves." Chapter three, Notable Names, includes song sheets that depict famous chiefs and women such as Hiawatha, Geronimo, Pocahontas, Uncas, and other leaders. The fourth chapter, titled Humorous and Whimsical Treatments, includes what might be termed a second but smaller wave of song sheets produced in the 1920s. These songs told fanciful, humorous and, in some cases, mocking tales. The fifth chapter includes song sheets about American Indians that were published in other countries, primarily England and France. The sixth and final chapter lists song sheets depicting Indians that were published after 1930. A good number of these pieces were written for the purpose of teaching piano rather than to promote and sell tunes as was the case in prior decades.[15]

Starting around 1925, depictions of American Indians on song sheets began to diminish as other types of music and modern interests began capturing the attention of song writers. Contributing to the decline of songs written about the American Indian was, of course, an intellectual and cultural reappraisal of the treatment of American Indians at the hands of past explorers, settlers, and the U.S. government. In that atmosphere, tunesmiths could no longer write simple yet potentially offensive tunes about "Indian squaws" or "chieftains." Today, we are left with illustrated song sheets that represent a snapshot of American mainstream culture's dominant views of American Indians at a time in our history that is now more than a century old. In that light, the artistic beauty represented by numerous and attractive cover illustrations can still be appreciated. We hope, dear reader, that you will concur.

Format of the Song Listings

As noted earlier, the first chapter of the book lists song sheets chronologically and, within each year, lists the titles alphabetically. In each of the other five chapters, song sheets are listed alphabetically. In those parts, the articles "a", "an" and "the" that begin the titles of some songs are moved to the end of the listed title and are not considered when alphabetizing the listings. Immediately after each song title, the last name of the illustrator (if known) is given in parentheses, always with the abbreviated word (illust) for illustrator, followed by any other information about the cover's visual image. For pieces that are known to have been self-published, the term self-pub is utilized. Listed next are the names of the composers and lyricists, followed by the year of publication. Those few exceptions for which the publication date is unknown are characterized by n.d., meaning "no date." After the date, the source of the image is given in brackets. Finally, if there is any explanatory comment about a song's illustration or its theme by your author, and/or by other authors, these are given in an indented section. To demonstrate, the two examples that follow incorporate nearly all of elements described:

Golden Arrow (song) (illust Starmer) – Harry Williams & Egbert Van Alstyne 1909 [Courtesy Sandy Marrone]

> In this song's lyrics, a "virile Sioux brave whispers his love to Golden Arrow. 'You've pierced my heart it's true. Pretty Sioux, take me to be your fallen sparrow.'" (Short, *Covers of Gold*, p. 132)

Indian Love Moon (illust Manning) – Wm. J. McKenna, Christian Sinding & Frederic Watson 1924 ST [Tinari collection]

> The cover image is unusually simple compared to most of Manning's color-filled illustrations.

As you peruse the listings in the following chapters, you will notice that some listed song titles are not accompanied by a cover image. The reason is that, while being aware of a cover's illustration, your author was unable to acquire a good image for inclusion in this book. These are noted with an asterisk.

In those instances where the title of the piece printed on the cover is different from the title of the song on the inside music page, the song sheet is listed by the cover title, and the music title is included within the listing description.

A final note: over ninety percent of the song sheet cover images presented in this book have been scanned without alteration. The remainder were digitally "cleaned" slightly to eliminate distracting elements such as large signatures or tears on the covers. For that service I want to thank Frank A. Nastro who quickly and effectively responded to my requests.

Readers are encouraged to send to the author images of song sheet covers featuring American Indians that are not displayed in this book. I am compiling an image listing for public use and would appreciate receiving additional song sheet cover illustrations. Send your image and the date of the song sheet publication to tinarifr@shu.edu. High resolution jpg and jpeg formats are preferred. Unless otherwise instructed, I will give proper attribution to the source of each scan.

SOURCES

From Bibliography of Illustrated Song Sheet Reference Books

Amundson, Michael A. *Talking Machine West: A History and Catalogue of Tin Pan Alley's Western Recordings, 1902–1918.* Norman: University of Oklahoma Press, 2017.

Anonymous. *The Songs of Cole and Johnson Brothers as Selected by J. Rosamond Johnson, with a Foreword by Thomas Riis.* NY: Edward B. Marks Music Company, 2015.

Crew, Danny O. *Suffragist Sheet Music: An Illustrated Catalogue of Published Music Associated with the Women's Rights and Suffrage Movement in America, 1795–1921, with Complete Lyrics.* Jefferson, NC: McFarland & Company, Inc., 2002.

Dichter, Harry and Elliott Shapiro. *Early American Sheet Music: Its Lure and Its Lore, 1768–1889.* NY: R. R. Bowker Co., 1941.

Finson, Jon W. *The Voices That Are Gone: Themes in 19th-Century American Popular Song.* NY: Oxford University Press, 1994.

Lawrence, Vera Brodsky. *Music for Patriots, Politicians, and Presidents: Harmonies and Discords of the First Hundred Years.* NY: Macmillan Publishing Co., Inc., 1975.

Levy, Lester. S. *Give Me Yesterday: American History in Song, 1890–1920.* Norman: University of Oklahoma Press, 1975.

Levy, Lester. S. *Grace Notes in American History: Popular Sheet Music from 1820 to 1900.* Norman: University of Oklahoma Press, 1967.

Levy, Lester. S. *Picture the Songs: Lithographs from the Sheet Music of Nineteenth-Century America.* Baltimore: Johns Hopkins University Press, 1976.

Short, Marion. *Collectible Sheet Music: Hollywood Movie Songs.* Atglen, PA: Schiffer Publishing Ltd., 1999.

Short, Marion. *Covers of Gold: Collectible Sheet Music, Sports, Fashion, Illustration and the Dance.* Atglen, PA: Schiffer Publishing Ltd., 1998.

Short, Marion. *From Footlights to "The Flickers": Collectible Sheet Music, Broadway Shows and Silent Movies.* Atglen, PA: Schiffer Publishing Ltd, 1998.

Short, Marion. *The Gold in Your Piano Bench: Collectible Sheet Music, Tearjerkers, Black Songs, Rags & Blues.* Atglen, PA: Schiffer Publishing Ltd., 1997.

Short, Marion. *More Gold in Your Piano Bench: Collectible Sheet Music, Inventions, Wars, and Disasters.* Atglen, PA: Schiffer Publishing Ltd., 1997.

Tatham, David. *The Lure of the Striped Pig: The Illustration of Popular Music in America, 1820–1870.* Barre, Mass.: Imprint Society, 1973.

Tichenor, Trebor Jay, ed. *Ragtime Rarities: Complete Original Music for 63 Piano Rags.* Mineola, NY: Dover Publications, Inc., 1975.

Tinsley, Jim Bob. *For a Cowboy Has to Sing.* Orlando, FL: University of Central Florida Press. 1991.

Wenzel, Lynn and Carol J. Binkowski. *I Hear America Singing: A Nostalgic Tour of Popular Sheet Music.* NY: Crown Publishers, Inc., 1989.

Westin, Helen. *Introducing the Song Sheet: A Collector's Guide with Current Price List.* NY: Thomas Nelson, Inc., 1976.

Ziegfeld, Richard & Paulette. *The Ziegfeld Touch: The Life and Times of Florenz Ziegfeld, Jr.* NY: Harry N. Abrams, Inc., 1993.

Additional References

Berkhofer, Robert F., Jr. *The White Man's Indian: Images of the American Indian from Columbus to the Present.* NY: Alfred A. Knopf, 1978.

Coen, Rena Neumann. *The Indian as the Noble Savage in Nineteenth Century American Art.* PhD dissertation, University of Minnesota, 1969.

Coen, Rena Neumann. *The Red Man in Art.* Minneapolis: Lerner Publications Company, 1972.

Deloria, Philip J. *Indians in Unexpected Places.* Lawrence, KS: University Press of Kansas, 2004.

Edgerton, Samuel Y., Jr. "The Murder of Jane McCrea: The Tragedy of an American 'Tableau d'Histoire,'" *The Art Bulletin*, V. 47 (December 1965): 481-2.

Edwards, Bill, RagPiano.com, http://www.perfessorbill.com/pbmusic_paull.shtml

Fisher, William Arms. *One Hundred and Fifty Years of Music Publishing in the United States: An Historical Sketch with special reference to the pioneer publisher, Oliver Ditson Company, Inc.* Boston: Oliver Ditson Company, Inc., 1933.

Gale Research Company. *Currier & Ives: A Catalogue Raisonne, Vols. 1 & 2.* Detroit, MI: Gale Research Company, 1984.

Goldberg, Isaac. *Tin Pan Alley: A Chronicle of American Popular Music.* NY: Frederick Ungar Publishing Co., Inc., 1961 (paperback). First published in 1930.

Hall, Douglas E. *Edgewater: Images of America: New Jersey.* Charleston, SC: Arcadia Publishing, 2005.

Hasse, John Edward. *Ragtime: Its History, Composers, and Music.* NY: Schirmer Reference, 1985.

Hoxie, Frederick E., Ed. *Encyclopedia of North American Indians.* Boston: Houghton Mifflin Company, 1996.

Muckle, Robert J. *Indigenous Peoples of North America.* North York, Ontario: University of Toronto Press, Inc., 2012.

National Museum of the American Indian, www.AmericanIndian.si.edu

Parry, Ellwood. *The Image of the Indian and the Black Man in American Art, 1590–1900.* NY: George Braziller, 1974.

Pisani, Michael V. *Imagining Native America in Music.* New Haven: Yale University Press, 2005.

Pisani, Michael V. A Chronological Listing of Musical Works on American Indian Subjects. http://indianmusiclist.vassar.edu/

Smithsonian Institution Press. *American Printmaking: The First 150 Years.* Washington, DC: Chanticleer Press, Inc., 1969.

Wikipedia entries on Wenonah, Winona, and lacrosse.

Notes

1. Smithsonian Institution Press.
2. https://web.archive.org/web/20090503130744/http://www.peaknet.net/~aardvark/means.html
3. https://www.whitehouse.gov/briefing-room/presidential-actions/2021/10/08/a-proclamation-indigenous-peoples-day-2021/
4. https://en.wikipedia.org/wiki/Native_American_name_controversy
5. Wenzel & Binkowski, p. 1.
6. https://www.flutopedia.com
7. See the "Ragtime: From the Top" chapter in Hasse.
8. Tinsley, p. 1.
9. Short, *Covers of Gold*, p. 133.
10. Parry, p. 126.
11. There are exceptions of course. For example, Indian Snake Dance, published in 1925 by the Art Publication Society, St. Louis, was intended for piano instruction of beginners. The cover illustration depicts two Caucasian children dressed as Indians dancing around a girl tied to a tree trunk, a well-worn stereotype apparently quite acceptable to the editorial staff of the Society at the time. The cover image is not included in this book because it does not depict American Indians.
12. We note that many of the earliest song sheets dealing with American Indians were published without illustrated covers and are, thus, not included in this volume. Readers wanting to learn more about songs of the late 18th and early 19th centuries that focus on American Indians are referred to Pisani's webpage, A Chronological Listing of Musical Works on American Indian Subjects, and Dichter and Shapiro, *Early American Sheet Music: Its Lure and Its Lore*.
13. In the comprehensive volumes by Gale Research Company, *Currier & Ives: A Catalogue Raisonne*, I found less than 50 prints listed that deal with American Indians, which represents well under one percent of the 7,500 prints issued by the firm.
14. Lester Levy, *Give Me Yesterday*, p. 171.
15. More recent musical compositions such as Hank Williams' Kaw-Liga (1953), the Cowsills' 1968 song, Indian Lake, Paul Revere and Raiders' 1971 hit, Indian Reservation, and Billy Larkin's Indian Giver (1975) are not included in this book because their song sheet covers lack artistic expression of any aspect of American Indians.

1
BEGINNINGS

(All black and white lithographs unless otherwise noted)

In this section we list nearly all the known American Indian song sheets published in the nineteenth century that have cover illustrations of American Indian themes or depictions. Readers will find that many of the covers reproduced here were provided by the Lester S. Levy Collection of Sheet Music at the Sheridan Libraries of Johns Hopkins University. Levy was the author of several important books on early sheet music and his donated collection is still being catalogued. Nearly all the song sheet illustrations were produced using lithography methods. Given the historical importance of these song sheets, they are listed here in chronological order.

1833: We Have Met to Remember the Day, Rev. James Flint [Courtesy the Lester S. Levy Collection of Sheet Music, Sheridan Libraries, Johns Hopkins University]

The cover states: "Sung before the New England Society of the City and State of New York 22nd Dec. 1832 at their Anniversary in commemoration of the landing of the Pilgrims" The lithographic image displays a group of Pilgrims at the shoreline meeting an American Indian, with other Pilgrims from the Mayflower disembarking smaller boats at the water's edge.

1830s: Recollections of Buffalo, Francis Johnson [Courtesy the Lester S. Levy Collection of Sheet Music, Sheridan Libraries, Johns Hopkins University]

"Johnson (1792–1844), a talented composer of band and piano music, was leader of what was probably the finest American wind band of its period. He was an important musical figure in Philadelphia for many years and appeared with his band in command performance before Queen Victoria. He is the first American Negro composer for whom we have a significant body of published compositions." (Tatham, p. 54)

1835: Buffalo City Guards, Francis Johnson [Tatham, p. 55]

1837: The Indian Hunter, Eliza Cook & Henry Russell [Courtesy Sandy Marrone]

1837: The Roarers, John Holloway [Tatham, p. 59]

The depiction used on Recollections of Buffalo was used for the title page of this Johnson piece published in Philadelphia (Osbourn, n.d.). "The subject of this illustration, a buffalo hunt by Indians during a range fire, was unusual for its time (though in a few years it would be a stock subject for almanacs, magazines, and calendars) and particularly unusual for use as a decoration on a private militia company's publication. The primitive qualities of the illustration have been mentioned earlier in this book. Neither printer nor artist is known.... In any event, its unknown origins do not detract from its rank as one of the most memorable music title illustrations of its generation." (Tatham, p. 54) But some professional artists had been working the buffalo hunt theme. Alvan Fisher's *The Buffalo Hunt* was published in Boston's "The Token and Atlantic Souvenir," in 1835. (Parry, p. 84) The cover illustration of this song sheet is a near copy of that engraving.

The lithograph was produced by Thayer & Co. "Poetry by the young English poet Eliza Cook. [Also, editions of 1842, 1856, and 1866.] Arranged in 1865 for piano solo by J. B. Duvernoy." (Pisani, A Chronological Listing of Musical Works on American Indian Subjects) "Indian with tomahawk in right hand, bow and arrows in quiver slung over shoulder. Standing high above lake, with right knee resting on rock." (Dichter & Shapiro, p. 75) Russell (1812-1900) was an English ballad-singer and lyricist who visited Boston around 1840. His "descriptive ballads, *The Maniac*, *The Ship on Fire*, and *The Gambler's Wife* were being sung with melodramatic fervor in fashionable drawing-rooms." (Fisher, pp. 54 and 101)

The subtitle is given as: A Quick Step, Composed Expressly for the Rifle Rangers. A fierce lion appears to be roaring at an encampment of American Indians in their tepees. "The lion insignia of the Rifle Rangers.... The purpose of the [lion's] agitation is simply to express those qualities of courage, strength, and forcefulness that the Rangers identified in themselves." (Tatham, p. 58)

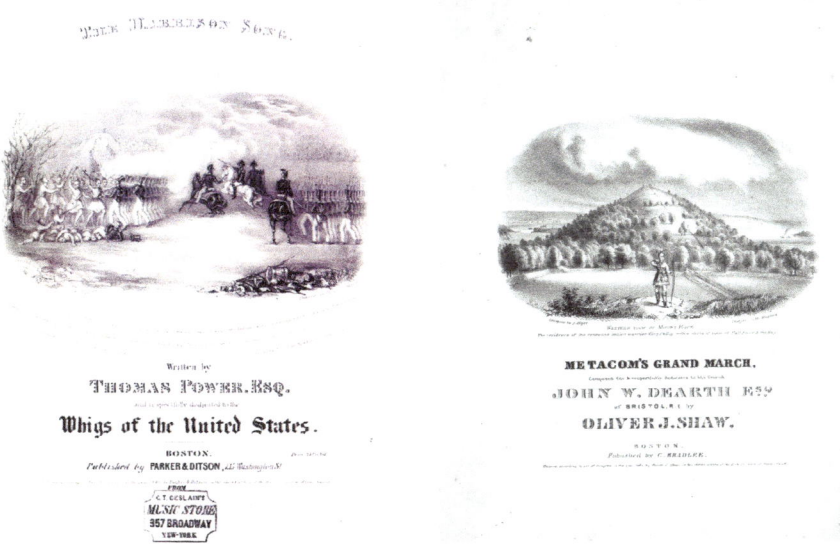

1839: Where Hudsons Wave, George P. Morris and Joseph Philip Knight [Courtesy the Lester S. Levy Collection of Sheet Music, Sheridan Libraries, Johns Hopkins University]

The lithographer is Luther Endicott who depicts a lone American Indian rowing in his canoe in a calm, bucolic Hudson River setting.

1840: The Harrison Song, Thomas Power [Courtesy the Lester S. Levy Collection of Sheet Music, Sheridan Libraries, Johns Hopkins University]

"Respectfully dedicated to the Whigs of the United States." The lithograph shows General Harrison leading troops against American Indian braves. The cover illustration "recalled the famous battle, even down to the tall black hats that Harrison's officers had worn to battle in 1811." (Lawrence, *Music for Patriots...*, p. 193)

1840: Metacom's Grand March, Oliver J. Shaw [Courtesy the Lester S. Levy Collection of Sheet Music, Sheridan Libraries, Johns Hopkins University]

Under the illustration is written: "Western view of Mount Hope. The residence of the renowned Indian warrior King Philip with a distant view of Fall River and the Bay." Historically, King Philip's War was, in proportion to the population and those in battle, one of the bloodiest and costliest wars in North America's history. For generations, English settlers and their descendants remembered this horrific experience.

*1840: National Lancers Grand Parade, John Holloway

Thayer's Lithographers of Boston was the source of the design. The cover states: A Quick Step Performed by the Boston Brass Band. Its illustration, identical to that of The Prize Banner Quick Step, listed later, is titled Indian Muster at Malden, Oct. 11, 1839, which could be connected to the Second Seminole Wars in Florida. Cavalry units and foot soldiers meet in a field, accompanying either a tribe representative or a captive American Indian on horseback, with military ceremony and encampment in the background.

1840: Old Tippecanoe [Courtesy the Lester S. Levy Collection of Sheet Music, Sheridan Libraries, Johns Hopkins University]

The name of the composer is not given anywhere in the song sheet. The cover inscription reads: "A Patriotic Song. Written, to be sung at Baltimore during the Young Men's Whig Convention, and most respectfully inscribed to The Young Ladies of the Monumental City by a Pennsylvanian." The illustration depicts events in the life of President William Harrison, including scenes of successful battles against Indians.

1840: A Song for New England, H. W. Elsworth [Courtesy the Lester S. Levy Collection of Sheet Music, Sheridan Libraries, Johns Hopkins University]

Each regional state is featured in a small cameo illustration. An American Indian is depicted only for Massachusetts.

1840: The Tippecanoe Quick Step, A. Walker [Courtesy the Lester S. Levy Collection of Sheet Music, Sheridan Libraries, Johns Hopkins University]

The scene depicts a military attack, presumably led by "Tippecanoe" Harrison, upon a band of American Indians. While the internal music to this piece is printed in traditional 'portrait' layout, the cover image is printed horizontally.

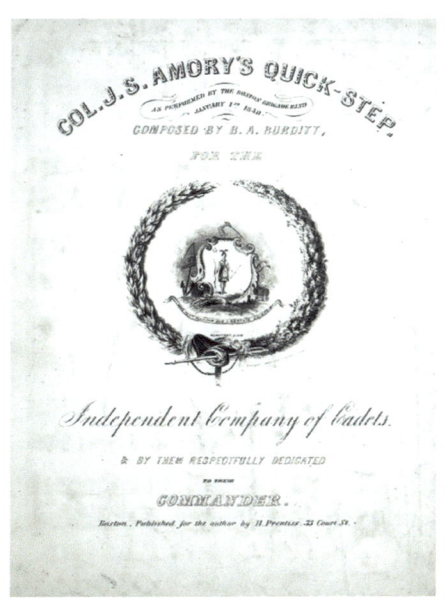

1840s: The Forester's Bride, H. Carl Schiller and Edward James Loder [Tinari collection]

1840: Col. J. S. Amory's Quick Step, B. A. Burditt [Courtesy the Lester S. Levy Collection of Sheet Music, Sheridan Libraries, Johns Hopkins University]

As performed by the Boston Brigade Band, January 1st, 1840. The small center image of the lithographed cover depicts a standing American Indian.

1840s: Shawmut Quick Step, Thomas Bricher [Courtesy the Lester S. Levy Collection of Sheet Music, Sheridan Libraries, Johns Hopkins University]

The lithographer-illustrator is given as R. Cooke, produced by B. W. Thayer Lithographers, Boston. The image depicts American Indians in canoes against a backdrop of tepees and forest.

1841: The Soldier and His Bride, George P. Morris and Henry Russell [Courtesy the Lester S. Levy Collection of Sheet Music, Sheridan Libraries, Johns Hopkins University]

"Founded on an event in the history of the American Revolutionary War." An inscription under the illustration states: "Accurate view of the scene where the murder of Miss McHugh (sp.) took place." The year was 1777. The lithograph depicts two American Indian men in the act of stabbing and killing a white woman. The inside music page includes a lengthy paragraph reciting detail of the event. The cover illustration harks back to a well-known painting by American artist John Vanderlyn titled The Death of Jane McCrae, picturing "an event that became, as a matter of fact, a *cause célèbre...*" (Coen, p. 57) The painting was exhibited in the Paris Salon of 1804. **According to Edgerton:** "Although Vanderlyn's painting began as an illustration for the Columbiad... it was the insipid engraving by Robert Smirke which finally accompanied the published text that was to inspire most subsequent representations... pandering to the egregious nineteenth century penchant for sentiment."

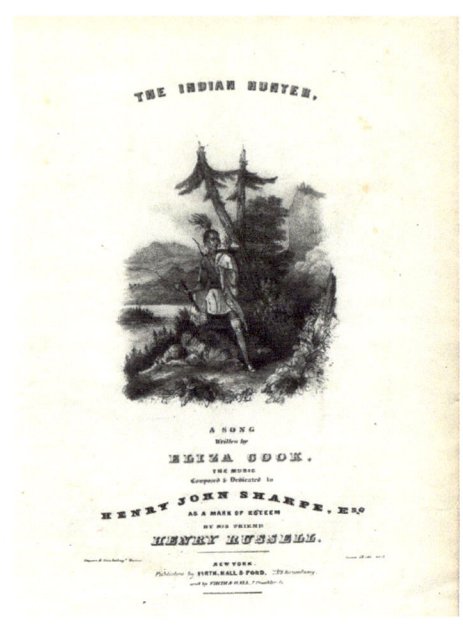

1841: The Chieftain's Daughter, George P. Morris and Henry Russell [Courtesy the Lester S. Levy Collection of Sheet Music, Sheridan Libraries, Johns Hopkins University]

The cover states: "Respectfully dedicated to General Winfield Scott by George Morris." This is a "sentimental song based on the Pocahontas story, with an introductory sketch of the romantic—and probably legendary—episode of the Indian maiden's successful life-saving appeal." (Levy, *Grace Notes*, p. 280) "Ye olde Indian executioner is holding a long sharp axe-like instrument, while Powhattan motions with left hand to wait." (Dichter & Shapiro, p. 74)

1841: Tippecanoe Slow Grand March, James M. Deems [Courtesy the Lester S. Levy Collection of Sheet Music, Sheridan Libraries, Johns Hopkins University]

"Most respectfully dedicated to William H. Harrison, President of the United States" The lithograph depicts two American Indian men hiding behind a tree, observing a cabin of, presumably, some white settlers.

1842: The Indian Hunter, Eliza Cook and Henry Russell [Tinari collection]

Published by Firth, Hall, & Pond. The poem is a lament in which the hunter questions what the white man wants with him and his home. See the original issue of 1837, shown previously.

1842: The Prize Banner Quick Step, H. Prentiss [Tinari collection]

The lithograph illustration is from Thayer's Lithographers, Boston. The header on the cover reads Prentiss Collection of Marches & Quick Steps. Eight tunes are listed, one of which is this selection. The illustration is titled Indian Muster at Malden, Oct. 11, 1839, the same as on the cover of 1840 National Lancers Grand Parade (listed previously), but which is not one of the eight tunes listed on this sheet. A song sheet bearing the same title was published in 1860, composed by D. H. Haskell. Its cover illustration is completely different and does not include any American Indians.

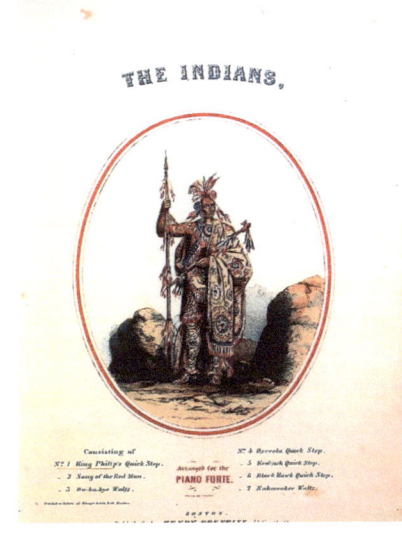

1843: King Philip's Quick Step [Courtesy the Lester S. Levy Collection of Sheet Music, Sheridan Libraries, Johns Hopkins University]

This piece is No. 1 of seven songs under the title "The Indians." The song was arranged by Nolcini for piano. The publisher was Henry Prentiss. There are seven pieces in this series, each published separately, using the same color lithographic cover illustration. "During the 1840's a Boston publisher named Henry Prentiss issued several instrumental pieces with such names as "The Osceola Quick Step," "The Keokuck Quick Step," and "The Nahmeokee Waltz" and found an artist to produce a cover design for these pieces portraying an Indian chief in full regalia." (Levy, *Grace Notes*, p. 285) The cover page is identical for the other six songs and is not shown for them.

§

*1843: The Song of the Red Man, A. F. Knight and Henry Prentiss.

This is Song No. 2 from "The Indians," arranged by Nolcini for piano, Henry Prentiss publisher. "For the only vocal number of the series, A. F. Knight composed the music for "The Song of the Red Man," whose plaintiff lament… [tells] the essential tragedy of the American Indians as revealed by a quick glance at the story of their migrations during the nineteenth century." (Levy, *Grace Notes*, p. 285)

§

*1843: On-ka-hye Waltz.

This is Song No. 3 from "The Indians," arranged by Nolcini for piano, Henry Prentiss, Publisher.

§

*1843: Osceola Quick Step.

From "The Indians" Song No. 4, arranged by Nolcini for piano, Henry Prentiss publisher. George Catlin (1796–1872) was among the best known and prolific painters of the Indian in the nineteenth century. In 1838 he painted a portrait of Osceola, a Seminole war leader whom Catlin visited. Osceola was the hero of an ill-fated uprising that had captured the public imagination. (Coen, *The Indian as the Noble Savage…*, pp. 82-91) A play in Philadelphia by the same name was written in 1841 by John H. Sherburne.

§

*1843: Keokuck Quick Step.

This is Song No. 5 from "The Indians," arranged by Nolcini for piano, Henry Prentiss publisher.

§

*1843: Black Hawk Quick Step, A. F. Knight, arranger.

This is Song No. 6 from "The Indians." Thayer & Co. was responsible for the color lithograph. This song sheet was published ten years after the publication of Black Hawk's autobiography, a best-seller having numerous subsequent editions. Born Ma-ka-tai-me-she-kia-kiak (1767–1838), Black Hawk of the Sauk American Indian tribe acted as a war chief with his band of warriors during the Black Hawk War of 1832 in the Illinois area. He continually resisted settler encroachment, fought several successful battles, but was eventually captured. During his captivity in 1833 he authored the first American Indian autobiography with the following extended title: The Autobiography of Ma-Ka-Tai-Me-She-Kia-Kiak, or Black Hawk, Embracing the Traditions of his Nation, Various Wars In Which He Has Been Engaged, and His Account of the Cause and General History of the Black Hawk War of 1832, His Surrender, and Travels Through the United States. Also Life, Death and Burial of the Old Chief, Together with a History of the Black Hawk War.

§

*1843: Nahmeokee Waltz.

This is Song No. 7 from "The Indians," arranged by Nolcini for piano, Henry Prentiss publisher.

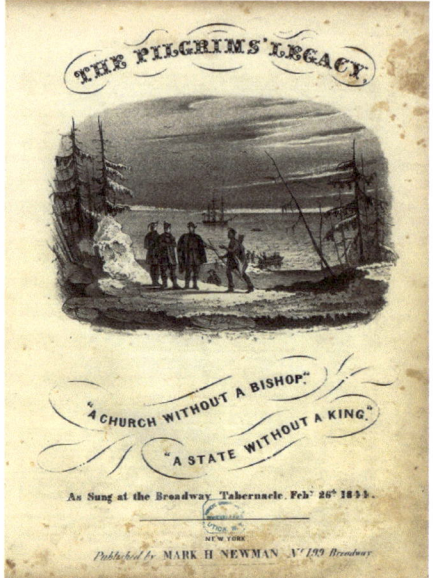

1844: The Pilgrim's Legacy [Courtesy the Lester S. Levy Collection of Sheet Music, Sheridan Libraries, Johns Hopkins University]

The composer is listed as follows: "An original Air and Chorus by An Amateur." The illustration depicts an American Indian meeting with a group of Pilgrims, with the Mayflower in the bay in the background, with the date of 1620 inscribed at the bottom. This is the same illustration found on the cover of We Have Met to Remember the Day, published in 1833 (see previously). The cover states: As Sung at the Broadway Tabernacle, Feb. 26th, 1844. The song praises the brave explorers who seek a home without domination by Church or King.

1844: The Puritans' Mistake, Oliver Ditson, publisher [Tinari collection]

The cover includes the following phrase, "A Church adorned with bishops, a State without a King" that is repeated in the verses of the song. It duplicates the cover illustration of We Have Met to Remember the Day but adds busts of a preacher and George Washington. The lyrics praise Washington for overthrowing the shackles of Britain and her king.

1844: Indian Hunter Quick Step, Henry Russell, arranged by Allen Dodworth [Courtesy Sandy Marrone]

Thayer & Co. was responsible for the lithograph. Arranged from Russell's popular song The Indian Hunter of 1837. The "Indian Hunter" theme was picked up in prints by Currier & Ives in 1845. (Gale Research, *Currier & Ives: A Catalogue Raisonne*, p. 344.)

1844: The Blue Juniata, Marion Dix Sullivan [Tinari collection]

This was a Bufford lithograph. "Indian girl at foot of lake holding beaded belt or ornament above head. Canoe at bank." (Dichter & Shapiro, p. 74) The Lester Levy Collection lists this as 1841, but Finson gives the date as 1844. (Finson, The *Voices That are Gone*, Illustration 7. 2)

1844: The Indian and His Bride, Francis H. Brown and George P. Morris [Courtesy the Lester S. Levy Collection of Sheet Music, Sheridan Libraries, Johns Hopkins University]

"Indian with sort of African head-dress (maybe we're wrong) sitting under foot of tree with coy looking bride at his side. Both dressed in what looks to us liked striped 'trade cloth.' Simple ornamental frame, rounded at top. Title in semi-circular design above illustration." (Dichter & Shapiro, p. 74)

   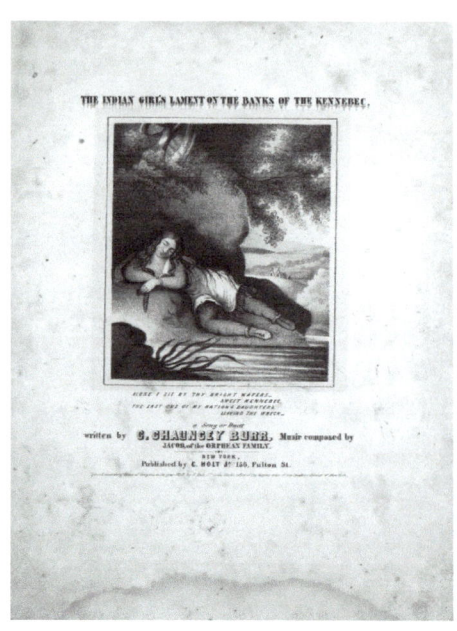

1845: The Spotted Fawn, W. D. Gallagher Esq. [Courtesy the Lester S. Levy Collection of Sheet Music, Sheridan Libraries, Johns Hopkins University]

The black-and-white illustration has stood the test of time, but the printed words on the front and back covers have faded to a pale yellow. The American Indian woman featured in the lithograph is standing by the water's edge, looking away at something that has caught her eye.

1845: The Spotted Fawn, W. D. Gallagher Esq. [Courtesy the Lester S. Levy Collection of Sheet Music, Sheridan Libraries, Johns Hopkins University]

The lithograph depicts a semi-nude American Indian woman doing her hair, presumably after bathing in the river.

1845: Cora (The Indian Maiden's Song) (illust Brandard) [London] – Shirley Brooks Esq. and Alexander Lee [sheetmusicwarehouse.co.uk]

The cover has the phrase "The Wild Free Wind" printed across the top. "Sung by Miss Mary Keeley in the New Burletta 'The Wigwam' performed with the greatest success at the Theatre Royal Lyceum."

1847: The Indian Girl's Lament on the Banks of the Kennebec, C. Chauncey Burr and Jacob of the Orphean Family [Courtesy the Lester S. Levy Collection of Sheet Music, Sheridan Libraries, Johns Hopkins University]

"Alone I sit by thy bright waters, Sweet Kennebec, The last one of my nation's daughters, leaving the wreck."

1847: La Belle Indienne, Albert W. Berg [Tinari collection]

The subtitle is given as Valse Brillante. Although the words on the cover are in French, the publisher is listed as Firth, Hall & Pond, New York. The lithograph is by Sarony & Major.

1848: The St. Lawrence Quadrilles, R. J. Fowler [Courtesy the Lester S. Levy Collection of Sheet Music, Sheridan Libraries, Johns Hopkins University]

Five sectional movements are contained within its six pages including "The Montreal," "Montmorence," "Les Voyageurs," and "Quebec, and the Thousand Islands."

1848: Fort Harrison March, C. H. Weber [Courtesy the Lester S. Levy Collection of Sheet Music, Sheridan Libraries, Johns Hopkins University]

The cover illustration depicts what appears to be a successful Indian attack on the fort. "Composed and Respectfully Dedicated to General Zachary Taylor."

1840s: Seek the Lodge Where the Red Men Live, T. Larkin Turner and Anne P. W. Pindell [Tinari collection]

The music page gives the song's title simply as Seek the Lodge. The lyrics tell of an American Indian woman urging her man to "shun the haunts of the pale faced one" and "seek the lodge where the red men live."

1850: Sachem's Daughter, J. E. A. Smith and Edward L. White [Courtesy the Lester S. Levy Collection of Sheet Music, Sheridan Libraries, Johns Hopkins University]

"Rather plump Indian girl sitting under tree at edge of bay or sea, with left hand upraised. Seems to be waving farewell to sailing vessel in distance." (Dichter & Shapiro, p. 75)

1851: My New England Home, L. Wade [Courtesy the Lester S. Levy Collection of Sheet Music, Sheridan Libraries, Johns Hopkins University]

The illustration depicts an American Indian couple looking at a ship anchored in the bay and pilgrims disembarking on land.

1851: Cora, The Indian Maiden's Song, Shirley Brooks & Alexander Lee [Courtesy the Lester S. Levy Collection of Sheet Music, Sheridan Libraries, Johns Hopkins University]

The cover indicates that the song is from "the New Burletta, The Wigwam." In *Grace Notes* (p. 282), Levy notes that several songs regarding Americans Indians such as this one were beginning to be sentimental and completely unrealistic. The cover illustration is different than the same song issued in 1845 (shown above); notably, instead of tepees in the background, we see a wood cabin.

1852: The Onondaga Polka, J. S. Jacobus [Courtesy the Lester S. Levy Collection of Sheet Music, Sheridan Libraries, Johns Hopkins University]

"Six nations claimed unity as brothers of Iroquoian stock. Among them were the Onondagas from upper NY State. The most famous member of the Turtle tribe, in the 1830s and 1840s, was the Head Chief, Ossahinta, who presided over the Onondaga councils for more than fifteen years. Shortly before his death in 1846 at the age of eighty-five, he was persuaded to sit for a portrait by a Syracuse artist. A few years later, a reproduction of this work was used by Napoleon Sarony and Henry B. Major, successful NY lithographers, as a title page for this sheet of spirited dance music. Wearing his tribal crown, surmounted by a feathery spray, with the sash of office draped across his chest and his tomahawk in hand, Ossahinta, Head Chief of the Onondagas, bears in his clear eyes and strong features an appearance not unlike a dark-haired Abraham Lincoln." (Levy, *Picture the Songs*, pp. 104-106)

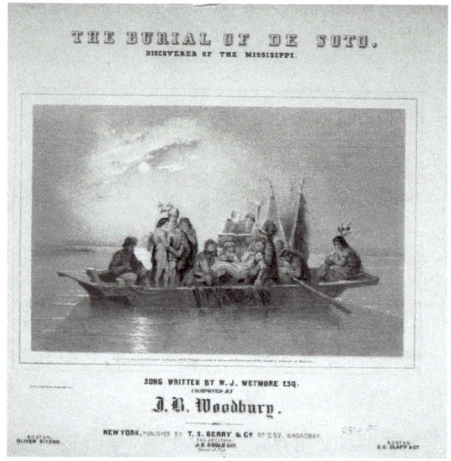   

1853: The Burial of De Soto, W. J. Wetmore and J. B. Woodbury [Courtesy the Lester S. Levy Collection of Sheet Music, Sheridan Libraries, Johns Hopkins University]

1855: Prairie Flower from Songs of the Prairies, Song No. 1, T. Elwood Garrett and Francis Woolcott [Courtesy the Lester S. Levy Collection of Sheet Music, Sheridan Libraries, Johns Hopkins University]

The other two songs listed on the cover are No. 2 Wenona, and No. 3 Ka-Loo-Lah. The cover features three vignettes, each featuring a lone American Indian.

1856: Clear the Way, Song of the Wagon Road, Stephen C. Massett [Courtesy the Lester S. Levy Collection of Sheet Music, Sheridan Libraries, Johns Hopkins University]

This song celebrates the extension of the railways to California. The illustration is dominated by the image of an oncoming railroad train, with figures of three American Indians watching as the train passes.

1856: Ho! For the Kansas Plains, James G. Clark [Courtesy the Lester S. Levy Collection of Sheet Music, Sheridan Libraries, Johns Hopkins University]

1856: Juanita, Hon. Mrs. Norton [Courtesy Sandy Marrone, top title trimmed]

The lithograph illustration by Ehrcott Forbriger & Co. is dated 1856. Neither the song lyrics nor the music are given attribution on the cover, but they are given for the 1866 version.

1856: Minnehaha or Laughing Water Polka, Francis H. Brown [Tinari collection]

"Indian girl sitting on rock with bare right foot in lake. Other Indians in background and in canoe. Lettering in title is drawn to represent Indian belt, feathers, spears, snow-shoes, arrows, etc. etc." (Dichter & Shapiro, p. 75)

1856. Minnehaha Schottisch, Charles Pape [Tinari collection]

This is one of the finest color lithographs with an American Indian theme. The color rendering is attributed to A. Hoen & Company, Baltimore. The description under the image reads: "Minnehaha (Laughing Water) is a beautiful Indian Girl portrayed by Longfellow in his celebrated poem 'Hiawatha.'"

1856: The Death of Minnehaha, Charles C. Converse with words from Longfellow's Hiawatha` [Courtesy Frances G. Spencer Collection of American Popular Sheet Music. Arts & Special Collections Research Center, Baylor University, Waco, Texas, and Courtesy Sandy Marrone]

The cover states that the song is based on Longfellow's poem that, "set in the Great Lakes area, has almost nothing to do with the historic figure of Hiawatha." (Kathryn A. Abbott in Hoxie, p. 245) "Indian girl standing before rocky scene, bow in hand, arrow slung over her back. Feather in head covering. Dress seems to be for winter. Tepees in background." (Dichter & Shapiro, p. 74) We include two sources of the cover lithograph image by J. H. Bufford. The Marrone sheet is trimmed at the top. The Baylor University digital image is more distinct and more colorful.

on the left, an Indian woman dancing for a group of seated American Indian men, with the small subtitle of Minna and, on the right, a white man playing a lute and gazing at a Christian altar, with the subtitle Be True to Me.

§

*1856: Poverty Ballad from Select Drawingroom Songs No. 11, E. Nicholls Crouch.

The illustration is the same as that of Wayside Spring.

1856: Wayside Spring from Select Drawingroom Songs No. 4, E. Nicholls Crouch [Courtesy the Lester S. Levy Collection of Sheet Music, Sheridan Libraries, Johns Hopkins University]

This is one of the composer's twelve songs, listed at the bottom of the cover. Crouch is noted as Lecturer and Professor of Music, Musical Director of the Philadelphia Oratorio and Madrigal Society. The main scene is of a meandering river surrounded by forest with mountains in the distance. The two smaller vignettes display,

1856: Land of Washington from National Songs of America, arranged for piano forte by Francis H. Brown [Courtesy the Lester S. Levy Collection of Sheet Music, Sheridan Libraries, Johns Hopkins University]

One of the multiple scenes depicted on the cover is an illustration of an American Indian man, bow and arrow on the ground beside him, kneeling and presumably weeping behind a white man who has raised his flag on the land.

1856: Sioux March and Waltz, Louis Wallis [Courtesy the Lester S. Levy Collection of Sheet Music, Sheridan Libraries, Johns Hopkins University]

Lithograph by E. Robyn of mounted U. S. troops attacking a Sioux camp. (Pisani, A Chronological Listing of Musical Works on American Indian Subjects) The illustration shows military men on horse and on foot chasing retreating American Indians.

1858: Dacota Waltz, Louis Wallis [Courtesy the Lester S. Levy Collection of Sheet Music, Sheridan Libraries, Johns Hopkins University]

"By mid-century, the pictorial evidence of the American Indian as gathered in the 1830s and later ... was well enough known to the general public so that the plains Indian came to be the standard popular image of all red men.... The ceremonial dance shown in the upper picture... is a hunt dance leading to the scene below." (Tatham, p. 122) The main illustration depicts American Indians hunting buffalo.

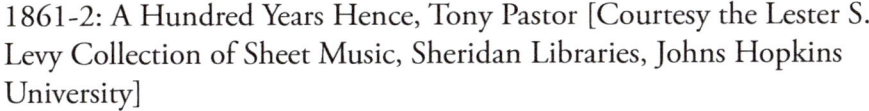

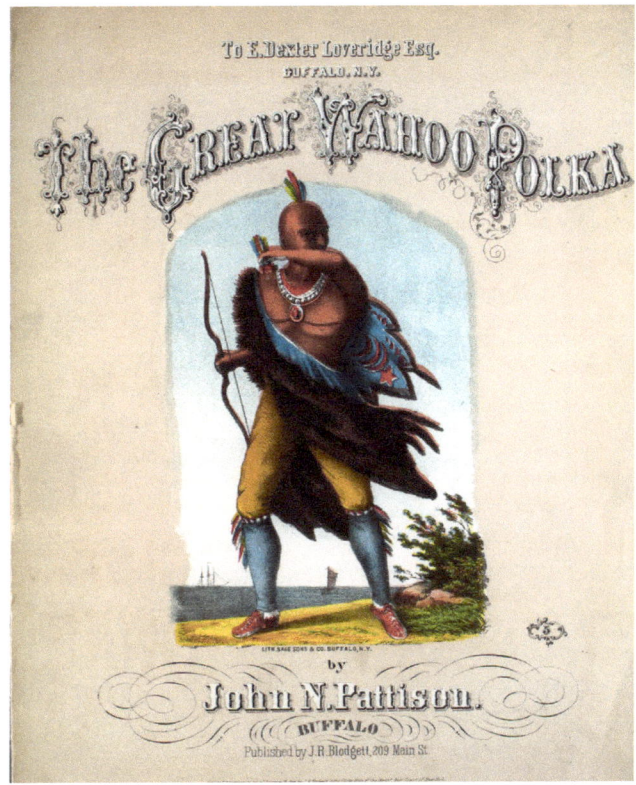

1861-2: A Hundred Years Hence, Tony Pastor [Courtesy the Lester S. Levy Collection of Sheet Music, Sheridan Libraries, Johns Hopkins University]

This is a one-page song sheet "sung by Tony Pastor, with great applause at the American Theatre, 444 Broadway, N. Y." "The Father of Vaudeville," Antonio Pastor (1837–1908), entertainer and theater manager, achieved acclaim when he appeared at the American Concert Hall at 444 Broadway (known as the "444") in April 1861, at the beginning of the Civil War, and closed his act with "The Star-Spangled Banner." Subsequently he became famous for his topical songs, the subjects of which were often derived from newspaper articles. (Tony Pastor: An Inventory of His Collection at the Harry Ransom Center, https://norman.hrc.utexas.edu/fasearch/findingAid.cfm?eadid=00106).

1864: The Great Wahoo Polka, John N. Pattison [Courtesy the Lester S. Levy Collection of Sheet Music, Sheridan Libraries, Johns Hopkins University]

"There were countless panaceas on the market . . . to cure every ill the body fell heir to. They were concocted in many localities. One of those which brought forth a musical tribute was a Buffalo, New York, product called 'Wahoo Bitters' [that] included some contribution from the wahoo plant (a shrub...), but the portion was not exactly overwhelming. The song's cover portrays a lusty Indian warrior, no doubt the Great Wahoo himself, and most piano performers could not have dreamed, or cared, that the Wahoo was a bush and not a brave." (Levy, *Grace Notes*, pp. 146, 148)

1866: Juanita, Mrs. Norton [Tinari collection]

The lithograph is by Ehrcott Forbriger & Co. Information given on the cover page is slightly different than the 1856 version. The song is attributed to Mrs. Norton but the Waltz, i. e., the music, is attributed to a melody by Schubert. This edition includes attribution to Richards as the transcriber. The publishing address is in New York whereas the earlier version shows Cincinnati as the publisher's location. Also, the music title page lists the arranger as T. Morton with a copyright date of 1866.

1866: John Ross, Francis De Haes Janvier, lyricist, and J. W. Jost, composer [Courtesy the Lester S. Levy Collection of Sheet Music, Sheridan Libraries, Johns Hopkins University]

Composed for the funeral of John Ross, Chief of the Cherokees, whose portrait is on the cover. Words by Francis DeHaes Janvier. (Pisani, A Chronological Listing of Musical Works on American Indian Subjects) The lyrics tell of the death of Ross, a great American Indian chief. It is not known if the lithographer 'Anglicized' the chief's features or if the chief did, indeed, have facial characteristics akin to those of a white man. Though portraits of this type were rare as song sheet illustrations, they were done as prints as early as 1710. (See Smithsonian Institution Press, *American Printmaking: The First 150 Years*, pp. 18-21) The unattributed lithograph was published by Porter Er. & Pr., Philadelphia.

1867: La Crosse Galup, J. Holt [Courtesy the Lester S. Levy Collection of Sheet Music, Sheridan Libraries, Johns Hopkins University]

We learn from several research articles cited in a *Wikipedia* article that lacrosse is based on games played by various American Indian communities as early as 1100 AD. By the 17th century, a version of lacrosse was well-established and was documented by Jesuit missionary priests in the territory of present-day Canada. In the traditional aboriginal

Canadian version, each team consisted of about 100 to 1,000 men on a field several miles (several kilometers) long. These games lasted from sunup to sundown for two to three days straight and were played as part of ceremonial ritual, a kind of symbolic warfare, or to give thanks to the Creator or Master. Those who participated did so in the role of warriors, with the goal of bringing glory and honor to themselves and their tribes. The French Jesuit missionary Jean de Brébeuf saw Huron tribesmen play the game during 1637 in present-day Ontario. He called it la crosse, "the stick" in French. Anglophones from Montreal noticed the game being played by Mohawk people and started playing themselves in the 1830s. In 1856, William George Beers, a Canadian dentist, founded the Montreal Lacrosse Club, and in 1860, codified the game, shortening its length and reducing the number of players to 12 per team. The color lithograph on the cover of this piece depicts a team of white men playing a team of American Indians.

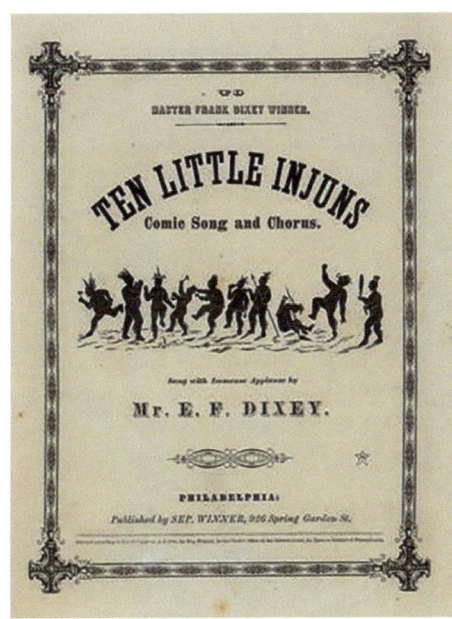

1868: Ten Little Injuns, Comic Song and Chorus, Septimus Winner. [Tinari collection]

The cover states: "Sung with immense applause by Mr. E. F. Dixey." The song was reprinted in 1896.

1869: The Indian Hunter's Bride (illust Lee), J. E. Carpenter and Stephen Ralph Glover [London] [Courtesy the Lester S. Levy Collection of Sheet Music, Sheridan Libraries, Johns Hopkins University]

1871: Old Betz, Song, J. H. Hanson and Frank Wood.

Old Betz (c. 1803–c. 1873), also known as Azayamankawin, Hazaiyankawin, Betsey St. Clair, and Old Bets, was one of the most photographed Native American women of the 19th century. A Dakota woman, she was well known in Saint Paul, Minnesota, where she once ran a canoe ferry service. Old Bets was said to have helped many women and children taken captive during the Dakota War of 1862. As biographer Mark Diedrich explains: "In the process of the awkward mingling of the Indian and white worlds, Betsey became a well-recognized figure to the early settlers. She was quite extroverted in personality, to the extent that she overcame the typical culturally-induced bashfulness and shyness of other Dakota women around white people. Betsey was also extremely industrious, even by Dakota standards. And furthermore, she was unabashedly straightforward when soliciting money or other goods."

1872: Kansas Pacific R. W. Grand March, George Schleiffarth [Courtesy the Lester S. Levy Collection of Sheet Music, Sheridan Libraries, Johns Hopkins University]

This is another piece hailing the progress of railways. Flanking the center illustration of a buffalo head are two depictions, one showing a buffalo running from an oncoming train, the other depicting an American Indian chief looking at a railroad train passing in the distance. The composer may have published using another name, perhaps a pseudonym; under his name, the name George Maywood is given in parentheses.

1872: Laughing Water, or The Enchanted Dell of Minnie-Ha-Ha. Song, J. H. Hanson and Frank Wood [Courtesy the Lester S. Levy Collection of Sheet Music, Sheridan Libraries, Johns Hopkins University]

The cover illustration is dominated by a large waterfall. The tiny figure of a maiden is on the bank flanked by trees.

1874: Hee-Lah-Dee – Mrs. S. R. Burtis [Tinari collection]

The cover lithography depicts an Indian woman standing on river stones with the water flowing below her. In 1832 at a Ponca village, George Catlin painted Hee-láh-dee, translated as Pure Fountain, Wife of The Smoke (oil on canvas), now seen at the Smithsonian American Art Museum. (Catlin, Letters and Notes, Vol. 1, No. 26, 1841; reprint 1973)

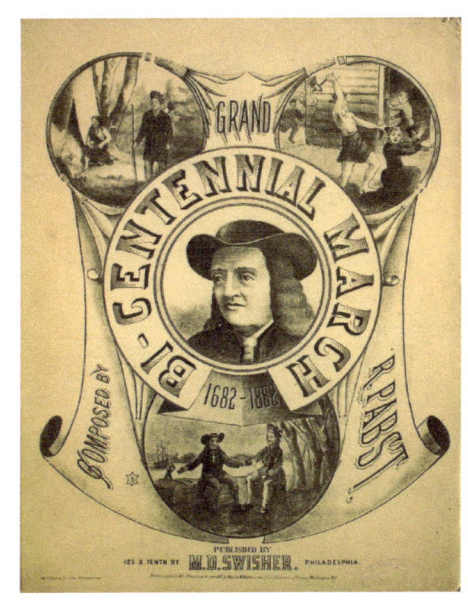

1876: Kissing Song, Edward E. Rice and J. Cheever Goodwin [Courtesy the Lester S. Levy Collection of Sheet Music, Sheridan Libraries, Johns Hopkins University]

The cover states: "from Rice and Goodwin's opera bouffe *Evangeline*" Encircling the main illustration of a woman, presumably Evangeline, are depictions of scenes from the performance. One such illustration depicts an Indian holding a knife in one hand and the scalp of a kneeling white man in the other.

1877: Black Hawk Waltz, Mary E. Walsh [Tinari collection]

The cover lithograph features a female dancing American Indian in princess-like headdress and dress, which has nothing to do with Black Hawk, the American Indian warrior. It is ironic to see that a waltz was named after Black Hawk, given that he proudly resisted and fought the continuing expansion of white people into his tribe's region, having been involved in some bloody battles. "After being imprisoned in Virginia for some months, he was sent back to his tribe in disgrace. He died in 1858." (Roger L. Nichols, in Hoxie, p. 78) See, also, the notes to the 1843 song sheet Black Hawk Quick Step.

1879: General Custer's Last March, A. R. Milner [Courtesy the Lester S. Levy Collection of Sheet Music, Sheridan Libraries, Johns Hopkins University]

"Its title page has a crude drawing of an Indian with raised tomahawk about to slay a fallen American soldier." (Levy, *Grace Notes*, p. 292) Most other song sheets dealing with Custer's last stand glorify his bravery and are illustrated with his portrait. Also, see Custer's Last Charge in the next chapter.

1879: Grand Bi-Centennial March, R. Pabst [Courtesy the Lester S. Levy Collection of Sheet Music, Sheridan Libraries, Johns Hopkins University]

The three inset illustrations depict what might be called, from a white man's perspective, the evolving relationship between the indigenous people and the European settlers. The first vignette shows a peaceful American Indian couple, the second an Indian about to scalp a victim, and finally the white man and red man sitting together and holding hands, with the American Indian holding a peace pipe.

1885: Little Bright Eye, George Cooper and F. A. Rothstein [Courtesy the Lester S. Levy Collection of Sheet Music, Sheridan Libraries, Johns Hopkins University]

This is one of the two pieces titled and depicted on the cover. Under the illustration of a costumed American Indian are the words: Kickapoo Indian Princess. The Kickapoo are an Algonquian-language people who likely developed as a people in a large territory along the Wabash River in the areas of modern Indiana and south of the Great Lakes.

1888: Oclemena, C. A. White [Tinari collection]

The music page title is written as Oc-Le-Me-Na. The color lithograph is from Sturn & Schmidt.

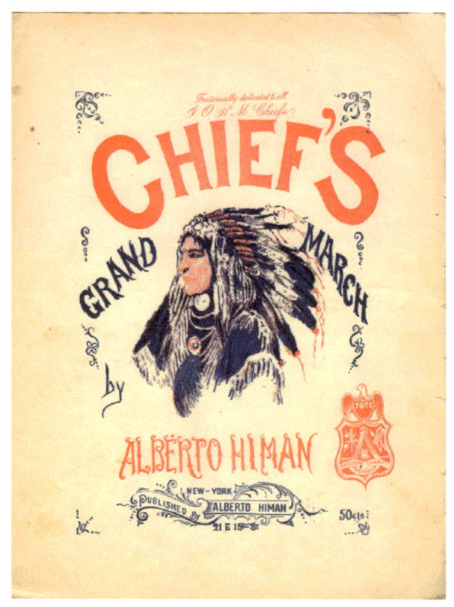

1893: Chief's Grand March, Alberto Himan [Tinari collection]

This is a self-published song sheet. Image of the bust of an American Indian is centered on the cover. Written above the illustration are the words: "Fraternally dedicated to the I. O. R M. Chiefs." The music title page lists the piece simply as Chief's March. It was composed for "The Improved Order of Red Men" that is claimed to be "America's Oldest Fraternal Organization Chartered by Congress" whose members have high regard for American history, temperance, and patriotism, and who promote freedom, friendship, and charity. The organization's founders trace their 1765 roots to the Sons of Liberty who disguised themselves as Indians for the Boston Tea Party. (http://www.redmen.org/redmen/info/)

1894. The Indian Sun Dance (illust H. Carter) – Edward J. Abram [U. S. Library of Congress, Music Division]

1894: The Indian Sun Dance (illust H. Carter) [London] – Edward J. Abram [sheetmusicwarehouse.co.uk]

The subtitle reads as follows: "Patrol Characteristique as played by all the leading Military Bands and orchestras. A small toy drum to be beaten throughout the entire piece." The cover uses the same illustration as the song sheet issued in the U. S.

§

*1894: Folk-Music of the Omaha Indians for Young Pianists, John Comfort Fillmore.

Includes three songs: Call to the Feast; Game Song; Poo G'thun Song.

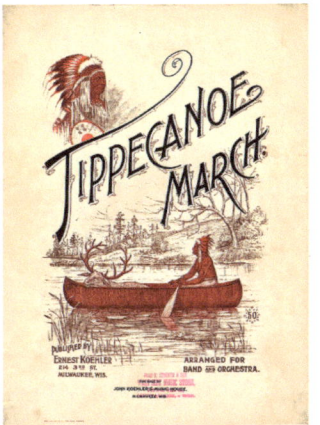

1895: Tippecanoe March, Ernest Koehler, a self-published piece [Courtesy Sandy Marrone]

1896: The Wild Indian Cherokee War Dance, C. T. DeCenial [Courtesy Sandy Marrone]

The inset illustration is of Little Bright Eye, an American Indian Princess. In 1885, a song was published entitled Little Bright Eye, listed previously.

 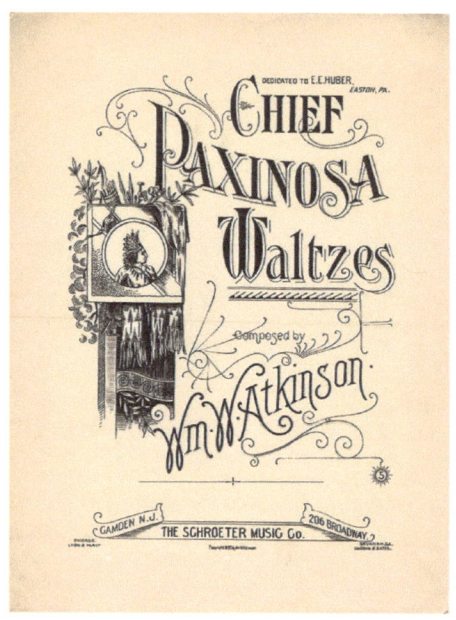  

1896: Ye Boston Tea Party, Arthur Willard Pryor [Courtesy Alex Hassan]

Though American Indians are depicted throwing boxes of tea into Boston Harbor, we know that they were disguised white colonial rebels objecting to King George's tea tax.

1897: Chief Paxinosa Waltzes, William W. Atkinson [Courtesy Sandy Marrone]

§

*1897: Anawanda, Louis J. Monico

Listed as a March and Two Step Dance, the cover depicts an American Indian, presumably of the named title. A song with the same title but different illustration was issued a few years later. See chapter 2.

1897: Fun with the Boys, G. R. Lampard (self-pub) [Courtesy John Paul Biersach]

Below the drawing of the Indian Chief "Oshkosh" we read: "The city of Oshkosh, Wis., (known as the place where you go to have "fun with the boys,") was named after this celebrated Indian Chief."

1897: The Chilkoot March, Alfred Roncovieri [Courtesy the Lester S. Levy Collection of Sheet Music, Sheridan Libraries, Johns Hopkins University]

A few other song sheets displaying Eskimo culture are presented in subsequent chapters.

1898: The Reading Sesqui-Centennial March, M. A. Althouse [Courtesy the Lester S. Levy Collection of Sheet Music, Sheridan Libraries, Johns Hopkins University]

The color illustration of this self-published piece includes two small, historical vignettes. The one on the left, labeled 1748, depicts two American Indians observing a covered wagon crossing their land.

2
AMERICAN INDIANS ROMANTICIZED

This chapter includes the bulk of American Indian illustrated song sheets, most of which were produced in the first two decades of the twentieth century. Deloria states that: "Tin Pan Alley cranked out Indian songs ... including 'Hiawatha' (1903), 'Blue Feather' (1909), 'In Tepee Land' (1911), 'Wahneka' (1912), 'Indi-Ana' (1915), and 'I'm an Indian' (1920), to name only a few." (p. 188) We should add that dozens are love songs (e.g., My Indian Maiden, My Prairie Song Bird), like those written in other genres, that had little to do with American Indian culture.

"The Indian song sheet covers are extraordinarily attractive. The cover artists seemed to take special pains with the Indian maidens, who more often than not graced the covers." (Westin, p. 54) In the late eighteenth century's Romantic era in European painting, "the powerful and compelling mood of noble sacrifice and profound sorrow, stoically endured, was partially subverted by the obvious voluptuousness of the female figures. This subcurrent of erotic interest in Indian women had strong echoes in America, where sexual contacts and occasional marriages between races had been taking place since the arrival of the first White settlers." (Parry, p. 72)

This was also a time when other 'exotic' genres captivated the attention of song writers, providing the public a means of escaping their day-to-day concerns, "music that far from attempting to affirm the composer's relation to his day and age is a deliberate attempt to liberate himself by evoking alien and exotic moods and atmosphere. The publishers' catalogues are full of Arab meditations, Persian dances, Hindu serenades, and countless similar attempts to get 'anywhere out of the world.'" (Taylor, p. 212) This escapism seems to have applied also to the many romanticized Indian song sheet covers of the early twentieth century.

Numerous titles of songs written during this period have familiar words that characterize the views of American Indians held by the public, words such as big chief, black hawk, feather queen, Indian girl, laughing water, wigwam, and others. "Many of the elements of the Indian sound that we hear today at baseball games and in Disney movies originated in the decades between 1890 and 1930—the founding years and the boom years for the sound of Indian." (Deloria, pp. 218-19)

A good number of these song sheets were produced both as musical pieces, often referred to as "intermezzos," and with lyrics, referred to as "songs." According to Tichenor, the "Indian intermezzo" was a "subcraze of the ragtime era which romanticized the American Indian." (p. ix) Westin observes the following:

> Baffling to me from the very beginning is the term "intermezzo." Webster's definition is, "a short, independent instrumental musical composition." But it seemed to be reserved almost solely for music pertaining to the American Indian. Silver Heels, Red Wing, Fawneyes, Morning Star, Red Man, Anona, Golden Arrow, Iola, Moon Bird, and other were published as Indian intermezzos. (p. 53)

   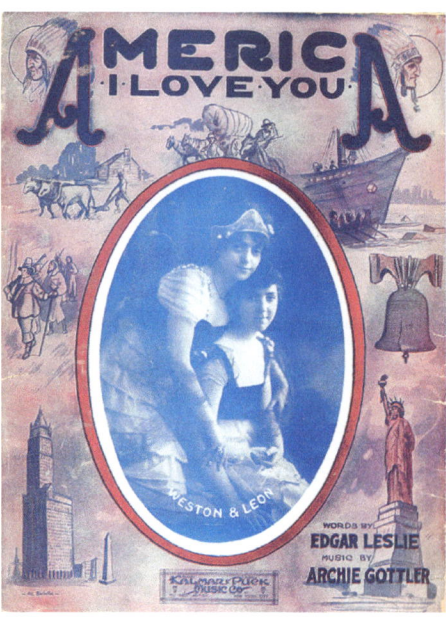

Ah-Wa-Ne-Da – B. Hartz 1903 [Tinari collection]

§

*Aisha (Indian Intermezzo) – John Lindsay 1920

Alameda Waltzes – Harry J. Lincoln 1908 [Tinari collection]

Algonquin – M. A. Marks Jr. 1905 [Tinari collection]

§

A-m-e-r-i-c-a – Greene and Francis 1917

America, I Love You (illust Barbelle) – Edgar Leslie and Archie Gottler 1915 [Tinari collection]

The song was issued featuring many other performers in the center oval. The song sheet cover is included in this book (the heads of two American Indians in full feather headdress are featured in the upper corners, along with other vignette drawings depicting aspects of American history) not because of any significant representation of American Indians but because of what it reveals about American cultural views at the time. In later editions, the vignettes no longer include American Indians on the cover.

America's "Appeal to the Great Spirit" – Ivers Louise Ashley 1929 ST [Tinari collection]

Cover photograph of a sculpture of an American Indian seated on his horse and praying. Permission to use was granted by the sculptor, Cyrus E. Dallin.

American Indian Rhapsody – Preston Ware Orem 1918

The cover illustration depicts an Indian blanket. The subtitle gives credit for the music's inspiration to Indianist composer Thurlow Lieurance.

Americana (Conservatory Edition) – Robert A. Keiser 1905 [Tinari collection]

Amerinda (An Occidental Incident) – Lee Orean Smith 1917 [Tinari collection]

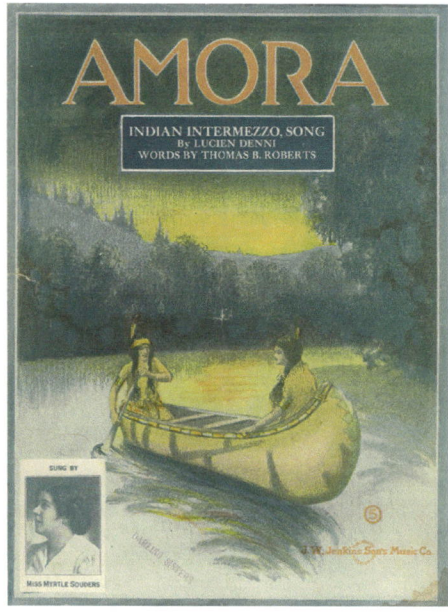

Amora – Lucien Denni and Thomas B. Roberts 1913 [Tinari collection]

§

*Anawanda – Louis J. Monico 1897

Anawanda March (illust Kiewitz) – Alois Merklin 1905 [Courtesy Sandy Marrone]

The composer's name is misspelled twice on the cover as Merklen.

Anona – Vivian Grey 1903 [Tinari collection]

The composer's name is a pseudonym for Miss Mabel McKinley, President McKinley's niece. Though a pseudo-Indian ballad, it was "one of the first in the field of songs about beautiful Indian maidens." (Levy, *Give Me Yesterday*, p. 192) This was the first "copycat" song with an Indian theme after the success of Hiawatha earlier in that year. (Amundson, p. 54) The composer's "singing in vaudeville helped to make the song popular." (Short, *Covers of Gold*, p. 138)

The song was also issued with a cover-filling photo of McKinley; it is not included in this book. Similarly, the song You're an Indian (1906) is not included in this volume because it features a photo of Stella Mayhew who sang it in the production of *Coming Thro' the Rye*.

Anowon (illust Emerson) – Paul Edwards 1904 [Courtesy Sandy Marrone]

Arizona (Indian Romance) – Oscar Haase, Mary Morrison and Clifford J. Werner 1908 [Courtesy Sandy Marrone]

Arizona (illust Bert Cobb) – Emily Smith 1901 [Courtesy Sandy Marrone]

Arranged and published by E. T. Paull. "It is one of the few monochrome covers to ever grace a first-run E.T. Paull published piece, and also attributed to a specific artist (Bert Cobb). A color version by the A. Hoen Company of Richmond, Virginia, was released in 1903 and again in 1912 in conjunction with Arizona's entry into the union, and stated as 'Rewritten' by E.T. Paull, rather than 'Arranged by' him as was often the case. There are some differences between the 1901 and 1903 editions, including additional repeats and transitions. It was enough to warrant a new copyright. Contained within either cover is a non-remarkable march celebrating what would become our 48th state in 1912, but was still clearly a part of the "wild west," as is indicated by the American Indian on the covers. In truth, the pictures appear to be more complimentary than the unfortunate stereotypes that were prevalent at the time." (Bill Edwards, RagPiano.com, http://www.perfessorbill.com/pbmusic_paull.shtml)

   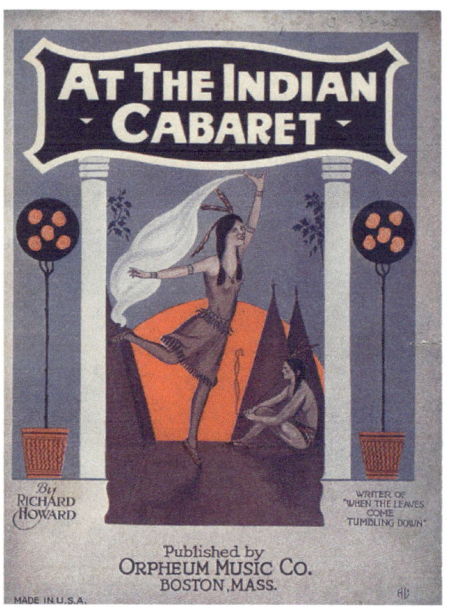

Arizona (illust Hoen: full cover litho; rewritten and arranged by E. T. Paull) – Emily Smith 1903 [Tinari Collection]

Arrah Wanna (illust De Takacs) – Theodore Morse 1906 [Tinari collection]

An Irish Indian combination, American Indian symbols cover green shamrocks as a beautiful maiden looks out from her tepee entrance. "Morse capitalized on the popularity of ethnically charged humor in the years before the Great War, producing songs that denigrated Jews…, Irish …, African-Americans…, and Germans." (Amundson, p. 83)

Arrah' Wanna (illust De Takacs) – Jack Drislane and Theodore Morse 1906 [Tinari collection]

This edition incorporates lyrics and has a different illustration depicting "an Irishman playing his bagpipes outside the tepee of the lovely maiden ArrahWanna. The cover is cleverly decorated with an Irish harp and shamrocks on one side, and Native American symbols on the other." (Short, *Covers of Gold*, p. 136) In the following year, the two song writers penned a sequel, Since ArrahWanna Married Barney Carney, listed later in this chapter.

At the Indian Cabaret – Richard Howard 1922 ST [Tinari collection]

 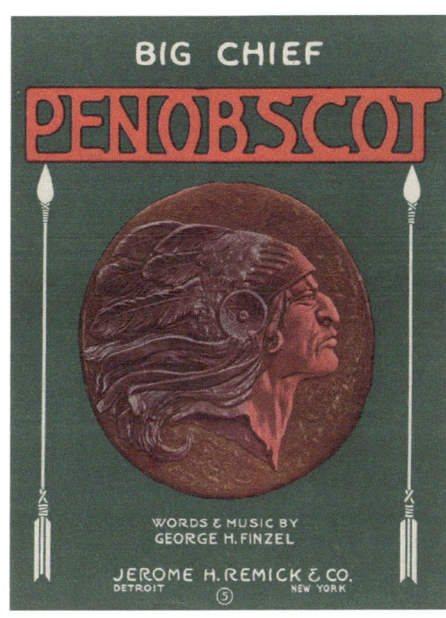  

Be the Sunlight of My Heart – Roy L. McCardell and Louis G. Muiz 1903 [Tinari Collection]

Big Chief Penobscot – George H. Finzel 1910 [Tinari collection]

Big Foot (inset: chief in full regalia) – Griffith Lewis Gordon 1909 [Tinari collection]

Big Pow Wow – Florence M. Pearce 1911 [Tinari collection]

A love song about Fawn, the chief's daughter, who is wooed by an American Indian man. The song Fawn-Eyes, published five years later, is listed later in this chapter.

Black Bead – Otto P. Ikeler 1911 [Courtesy Sandy Marrone]

Black Eyes – The Pit-Apat Song – Harry Rosenbush 1919 [Tinari collection]

Blue Beads (An Indian Legend) – Beth Slater Whitson and Leo Friedman 1909 [Tinari collection]

The lyrics tell of shy Blue Beads, as she gazes at her campfire, who is wooed by a "Paleface" shown hiding in the trees.

§

*Blue Eyes – Lee Onidas and Egbert Van Alstyne 1920

Blue Feather (illust De Takacs) – Theodore Morse 1909 [Tinari collection]

Jack Mahoney, the lyricist, is not listed on the cover though his name is on the sheet music." More love song than Indian song, the only clear connections are one line about an Indian maid and the … cover illustration [that] depicts a Caucasian-looking Indian girl…." (Amundson, p. 136)

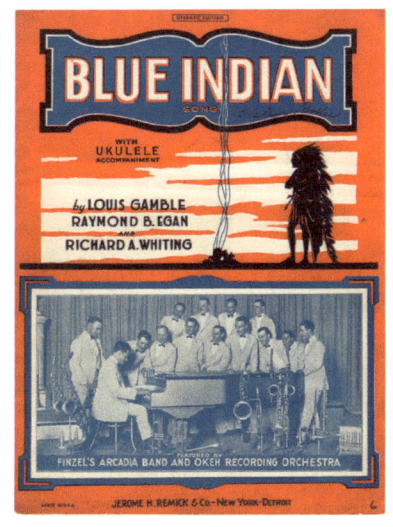

Blue Indian (photo: Finzel's Arcadia Band and Okeh Recording Orchestra) – Louis Gamble, Raymond B. Egan and Richard A. Whiting 1925 ST [Tinari collection]

Bow & Arrow – Walter S. Davis and Morris S. Silver 1909 [Tinari collection]

Buffalo Means Business (March Two-Step) – George L. Cobb and Louis C. Snyder 1909

A crude drawing of an Indian man holding a lasso and standing on the back of a buffalo is the cover illustration in a monocolor of white on a brown background. Here, the Indian image is appropriated to promote the city of Buffalo, NY.

By the Listening Willows I Wait – the second in Songs of Song-ah-tah, Four American Indian Songs – music by Homer Grunn, poems by Charles O. Roos 1923 ST [Tinari collection]

The song cover displays a pen and ink drawing of an Indian waiting at lakeside.

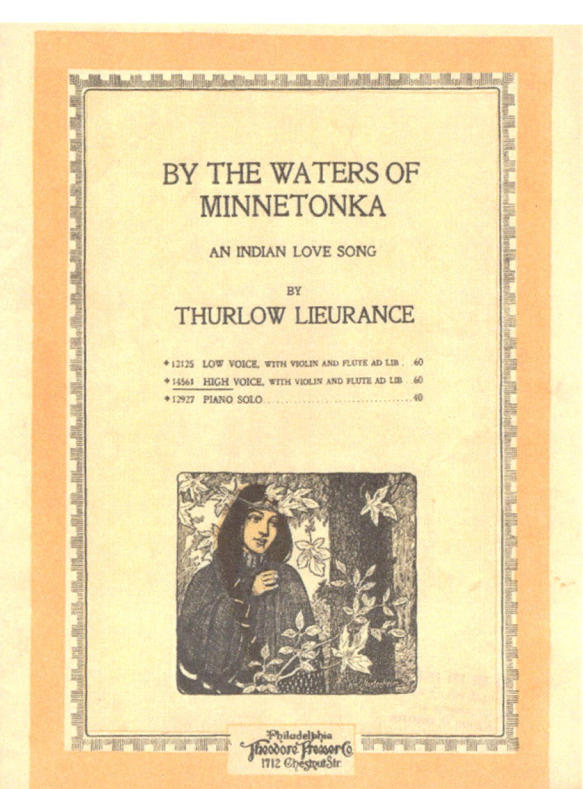

By the Waters of Minnetonka (illust Nortenheim) – Thurlow Lieurance 1917 ST [Tinari collection]

The cover illustration was used for various editions of this composition including vocal, piano, and concert editions. Lieurance (1878–1963), an authority on American Indian music, was a member of both the Indianist Movement of American composers and the Chautauqua Society that fostered adult education. He traveled in tent schools teaching music to American Indians while recording and transcribing their music and recorded about 1,500 American Indian tunes. This is one of several of his song sheets presented in this book.

By the Waters of Minnetonka – Thurlow Lieurance 1915 ST [Tinari collection]

This song's different cover features a quiet forest at the side of a lake, with a small depiction of an American Indian couple floating, as it were, in the air in the distance. The Concert Edition, consisting of eight pages and published in 1917 with the same cover image, includes a brief description of "The Legend of Minnetonka" on the inside front cover.

§

*Canoe Song of Hiawatha (The Ojibway) (see Ojibways' Canoe Song)

§

Cherokee (instrumental) – Leo Edwards 1906

Cherokee (Song) (illust Manning) – Sam Morris and Vaughn De Leath 1920 ST [Tinari collection]

Cherokee (illust IM-HO) (Indian Love Song) – Ray Noble 1928 ST [Tinari collection]

Cherokee Rose – Charles O. Roos and Claude Kelly Webster 1928

 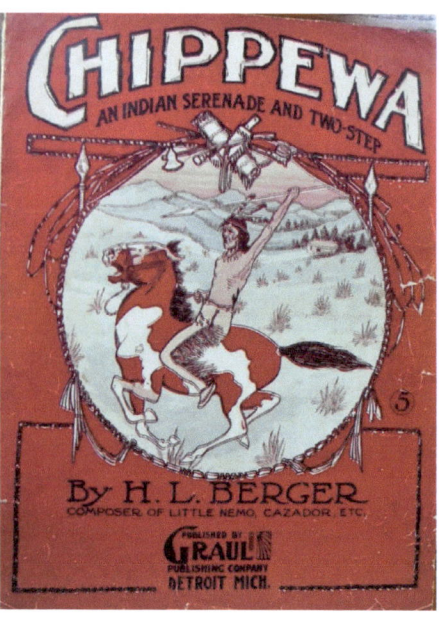  

Cherry Cherokee – Louis Weslyn and Neil Moret 1921

Moret was the pseudonym used by Charles Neil Daniels (1878–1943), a composer of many songs including the early classic Hiawatha, depicted in the next chapter.

Chippewa (An Indian Serenade and Two-Step) – H. L. Berger 1908 [Courtesy Mark Clardy]

§

*Chippewa Rag – Myrtle Hoy 1911

Cloud-Chief (illust Starmer) – J. Ernest Philie 1910 [Tinari collection]

Crazy Snake – Bobby Heath and Gus A. Benkhart 1909 [Tinari collection]

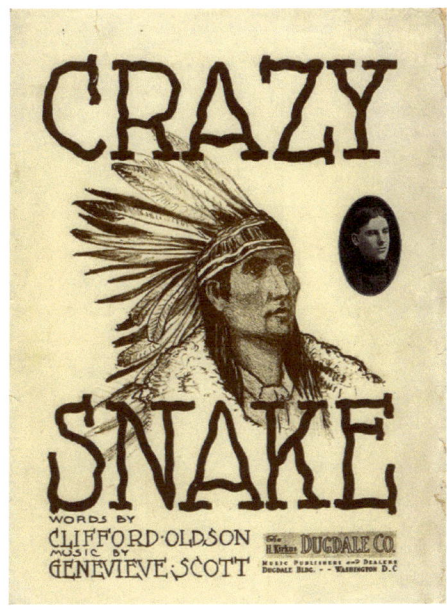   

Crazy Snake (inset photo: likely Oldson) – Clifford Oldson and Genevieve Scott 1913 [Tinari collection]

Crimson Arrow (Intermezzo) – Glen Hall 1910 [Tinari collection]

Custer's Last Charge (illust Starmer) – E.T. Paull 1922 ST [Tinari collection]

The inside of the front cover has a full-page explanatory article, rewritten from *the New York Evening Mail Newspaper*. As noted in Chapter 1's description of General Custer's Last Charge (1879), a portrait of General George Armstrong Custer is incorporated in the cover illustration.

Dancing Starlight (illust Pfeiffer) – Robert Roden and Jack Glogau 1910 [Tinari collection]

§

*Dancing Sunshine – Bartley Costello and Ted Snyder 1909

Quite unusual for a cover image is a Christian cross hanging around the neck of an American Indian maiden with flowing hair.

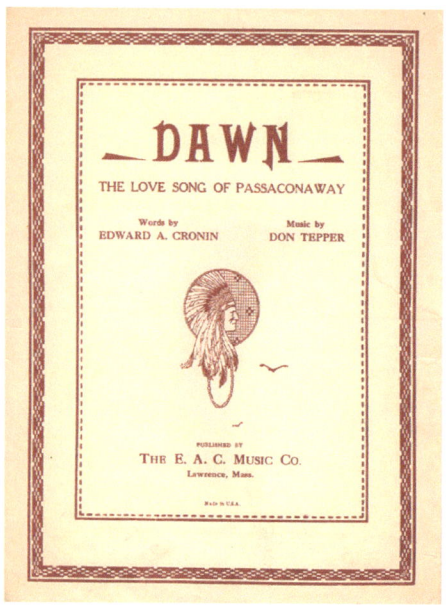   

Dawn (The Love Song of Passaconaway) – Edward A. Cronin and Don Tepper 1926 [Tinari collection]

The inside of the front cover gives background for this piece. Passaconaway is titled the Patron Indian Chief of Methuen (The Bashaba of the Merrimack). "Written Especially for the 200th Anniversary, Town of Methuen."

Deh-ge-wa-nus (The White Woman of the Genesee) (self-pub) – George L. Washburn 1914 [Tinari collection]

The lyrics deal with a woman whose American Indian name in the title was Pretty Maiden. Mary Jamison was taken captive and was adopted by an Indian family in Ohio. She lived with the Seneca Indians more than 70 years and was known for her close connection to the Genesee valley. The inside front cover gives a brief synopsis of her life.

Di-Wen-Da (illust Brown) – Sidney B. Holcomb and Will Carroll 1921 ST [Courtesy Sandy Marrone]

Down on the Lakes of Manitoba (illust Starmer) – Jack Caddigan and Chick Story 1914 [Tinari collection]

Eulah! Eulah! (My Indian Maid) – Max Hoffmann 1902 [Tinari collection]

The inset photo is of Miss Gertrude Hoffmann, most likely the composer's daughter.

Fallen Leaf (illust Van Doorn-Morgan) – Virginia K. Logan and Frederic Knight Logan 1922 ST [Tinari collection]

Falling Star (illust Starmer) – Benjamin Richmond 1903

The illustration depicts Princess Falling Star.

Falling Star – Benjamin Richmond c. 1914 [Tinari collection]

Later reissues of this piece, like this one and the next, are monochrome though they all use the same Starmer illustration that is in color on the 1903 original edition.

Falling Star (illustration of Princess Falling Star) – Benjamin Richmond 1924 ST [Tinari collection]

Fawn-Eyes (illust Henrich) – Charles L. Johnson 1908 [Tinari collection]

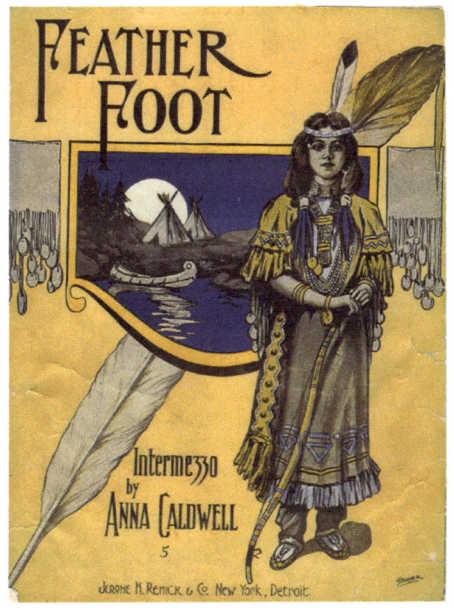   

Feather Foot (illust Starmer) – Anna Caldwell 1908 [Tinari collection]

Feather-Queen (illust Carter) – Mabel McKinley 1906 [Tinari collection]

A lovely maiden shades her eyes with her hand. A group of tepees sets the background. The cover of an initial version of this song, issued in 1905, is adorned by a large photograph of the composer. It is not included in this book. Also see the descriptive note for Anona.

Feather Queen – Arnold D. Scammell 1911 [Courtesy Sandy Marrone]

Feathers (illust Fisher) – Karl Lenox 1905 [Tinari collection]

§

*Firefly (My Pretty Firefly) (see My Pretty Firefly)

Firefly – Merle Kulow Sherrill
1924 ST [Courtesy Sandy Marrone]

Fleetfoot – Walter Rolfe 1910
[Tinari collection]

§

*Fleetfoot – George L. Cobb
1906

Flying Arrow (illust Carter) – Abe Holzmann 1906
[Tinari collection]

The composer "added the flavor of ragtime rhythm to this Indian intermezzo for piano. The action western cover [is] of a dashing brave on a charging horse shooting an arrow." (Short, Covers of Gold, p. 135)

Flying Bird – Warren Wainwright 1910 [Tinari collection]

The cover illustrates an American Indian woman walking by a body of water.

Genius of Ka-Noo-No, The (illust Redmond) – Frederick W. Jackson 1906 [Courtesy Sandy Marrone]

The inset photo is of an American Indian man. This was self-published. Official Musical Number, Carnival of 1907, Syracuse, NY.

Get the Safety Habit – J. D. M. Hamilton and George F. Root c.1900

The title on the music page is Rally 'Round the Safety Habit. The cover design consists of Navajo blanket art designs blatantly co-opted by the Sante Fe Railway in a song about railway safety. The tune is stated as "Rally 'Round the Flag." At the bottom of the cover is written: "The Battle Cry of Safety: Words by J. D. M. Hamilton, Claims Attorney Santa Fe System, and Dedicated to the Loyal Employees of the Santa Fe Railway Company."

Gleaming Star (illust Starmer) – Frederick W. Hager 1905 [Tinari collection]

§

*Glory of Jamestown-- James W. Casey 1907

The cover states that this is an 'Exposition March' and depicts an American Indian couple seeming to observe the Jamestown Settlement.

 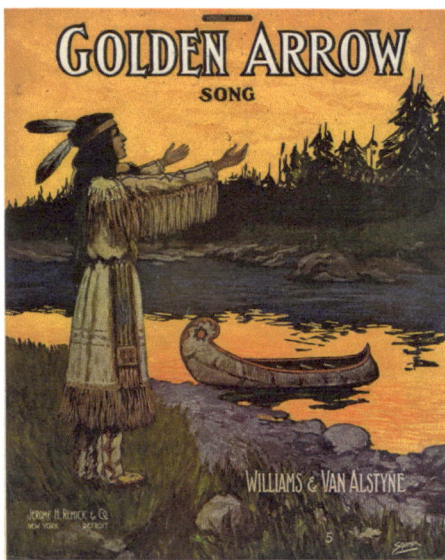  

Go-Wan-Go-Mohawk (Intermezzo) – Dewitt Bell 1911 [Tinari collection]

The piece was written in honor of Carolina "Go-Won-Go" Mohawk, "possibly the most famous celebrity from Edgewater..., an American Indian who was both an actress and a playwright, best known to the residents of Edgewater as a fixture in local parades, riding her horse Becky." (Hall, p. 119)

Golden Arrow (song) (illust Starmer) – Harry Williams and Egbert Van Alstyne 1909 [Courtesy Sandy Marrone]

In this song's lyrics, a "virile Sioux brave whispers his love to Golden Arrow. 'You've pierced my heart it's true. Pretty Sioux, take me to be your fallen sparrow.'" (Short, *Covers of Gold*, p. 132)

Golden Arrow (intermezzo two-step) (illust Starmer) – Egbert Van Alstyne 1909 [Tinari collection]

Like the song, the cover of this instrumental gives the lyricist's name Williams although his name is not on the sheet music.

Golden Deer (illust Starmer) – Harry Williams and Percy Wenrich (1887–1952) 1911 [Tinari collection]

The illustration depicts the face of an American Indian woman within a circular border colored in shades of red and blue. The song's lyrics tell of a young American Indian brave pining for his girl in yet another Tin Pan Alley love song clothed in American Indian apparel.

Golden Feather – Frank Choddy, Bernhard Stern and Harry De Costa 1909 [Tinari collection]

Golden Potlatch – Zellah Sanders Elwell 1911 [Tinari collection]

Good Bye, Red Man, Good Bye (illust Barbelle) – Ted Snyder, Edgar Leslie and Bert Kalmar 1916 [Courtesy Sandy Marrone]

§

*Hail Milwaukee – Thomas Shepherd and George M. Lipschultz 1920

A black and white depiction of the cover is reprinted in Corenthal, p. 212. Although the cover illustration depicts an American Indian with arms outstretched toward the city skyline, the lyrics profess how strong and prosperous is Milwaukee. Published by the Milwaukee Association of Commerce.

Grand Western Pageant – Frank McFarland (self-pub) 1914 [Tinari collection]

§

*Hail to the Blackhawk (see March of the Black Hawks)

Happy Hunting Grounds – Henry S. Sawyer 1909 [Tinari collection]

Pictured is a proud, stately American Indian, with a bison hunt in the distant background.

Heap Big Injun (illust Starmer) – Henry S. Sawyer 1908 [Tinari collection]

Heart of Wetona (photo: Norma Talmadge) – Sidney D. Mitchell and Archie Gottler (1896–1959) 1919 (war size) [Tinari collection]

Hello Miss Spokane (photo: Miss Marguerite Motie) – Frank Finney and Mayo Evans 1912 [Tinari collection]

From the back cover: "In private life, Miss Spokane, the inspiration for song and story and the ideal of the poet, is Miss Marguerite Motie. Weaving around her a beautiful Indian legend, the Spokane Ad Club has clothed her in picturesque Indian garb in keeping with the Indian name 'SPOKANE,' which, translated, means 'A Child of the Sun.'"

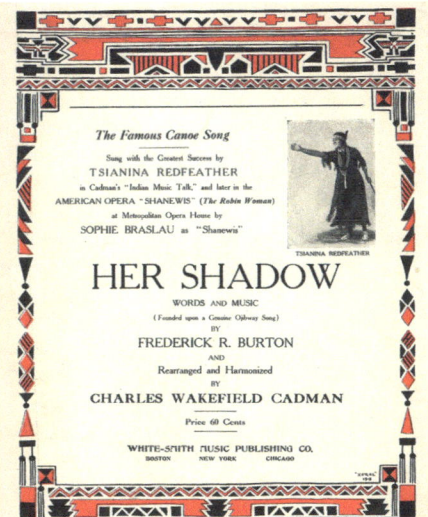

Here Come the Tribes – Laurena Van Valkenburg 1924 [Tinari collection]

Her Shadow – Frederick R. Burton 1918 ST [Tinari collection]

Lots of information is contained on the front cover including a photo of singer/performer American Indian Tsianina Redfeather who performed the song in Cadman's "Indian Music Talk." We also learn that Burton's song is "Rearranged and Harmonized by Charles Wakefield Cadman" and that the piece is "Founded upon a Genuine Ojibway Song."

Hiji (March Characterisque) – anonymous 1903 [Tinari collection]

The cover's words "Composed by a" are followed by a drawing of a baseball in the middle of a fan. That would explain the composer's initials listed on the music title page as A. B. B. F., which we believe stands for A Base Ball Fan. The illustration depicts an Indian facing right with his tepee off to the rear right.

Hollywood (illust Meggs) – Earle Fox and Lynn Cowan 1929 [Tinari collection]

This is one of the oddest American Indian song sheet covers we've encountered. The lower third depicts an American Indian family and a group of tepees, being approached in the distance by covered wagons. The middle section has a then-contemporary photo of lights shining skyward from the city of Los Angeles. The top section is an illustration of a motion picture being made. The word Hollywood is made to appear as smoke rising from the American Indian's pipe. The song lyrics bemoan the wreckage of American Indian culture, being replaced by jazz and syncopation. The back page compiles 107 numbered head shots of Hollywood personalities, but there is no listing of names associated with the numbers. At the bottom of the page is printed: "Compliments of Hollywood Boulevard Association."

Hotfoot (ragtime composer) – Archie W. Scheu 1906 [Tinari collection]

Another issue of this same song, not shown here, uses a different, less artistic illustration.

§

*How I Love That Man: That Kickapoo Indian Man [see That Kickapoo Indian Man]

Huckleberry Indians or It's Up to You (illust. Starmer) – Charles L. Van Baar 1903 ST [Courtesy Sandy Marrone]

§

*Hudson-Fulton March (compliments of Hearn Dry Goods) – L. Von Der Mehden 1909

§

*Humming Bird – Raybauld and Edwards 1912

Humoreskimo – Alfred Bryan, Pete Wendling and Henri Berchman 1928 ST [Tinari collection]

This is another love song telling of the singer pining for his love. See Chapter 5 for the Parisian version published with the same cover illustration.

I Left Her on the Shores of Minnetonka (illust Manning) – Robert Levenson and Abe Olman 1925 ST [Tinari collection]

Idaho (self-pub) – Louis Arden Schuch 1904 [Courtesy the Lester S. Levy Collection of Sheet Music, Sheridan Libraries, Johns Hopkins University]

§

*Idol Star – Borovsky 1909

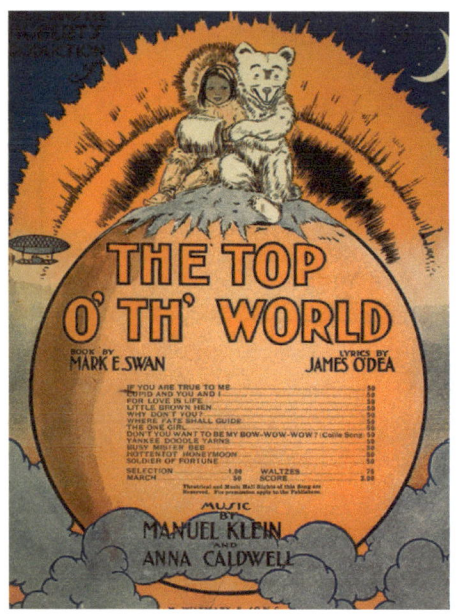

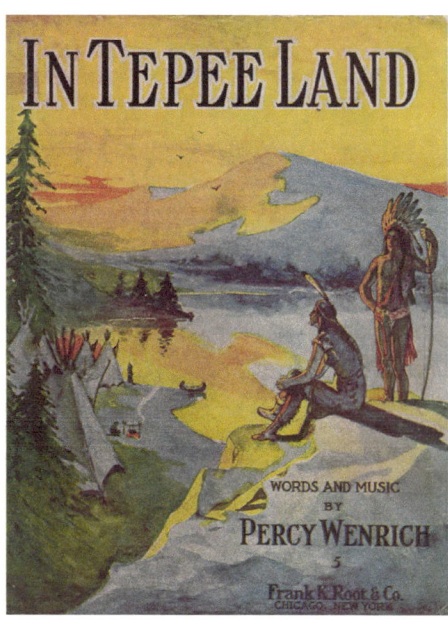

If You Are True to Me – Manuel Klein 1907 [Courtesy the Lester S. Levy Collection of Sheet Music, Sheridan Libraries, Johns Hopkins University]

This is a song from *The Top O' The World* theatrical production. Other songs from the show were published with the identical illustration.

Igloo Eyes (Love Lit Eyes) – Frank Peters 1924 ST [Tinari collection]

The cover is labeled "Introductory Copy."

In a Little Wigwam Built for Two – J. Rennie Cormack 1906 [Tinari collection]

In Tepee Land – Percy Wenrich 1911 [Tinari collection]

The lyrics tell "the story of Big Chief who loved a palefaced maid. He tries to woo her to live in his tepee after heap big wedding day. But she refuses his pleas, declaring her love for a cowboy bold, and the disappointed Chief comes to grief on the battlefield." (Short, *Covers of Gold*, p. 139)

In the Hills of Spavinaw (Indian Love Ballad) – Chief Bluejacket and Princess Jo Esther Bruner c. 1927 (self-pub) [Tinari collection]

Spavinaw is a small town in Oklahoma. Given the names of the lyricist and composer, this at first appears to be a piece composed by American Indians. But further research casts doubt on that conclusion. Regarding the music composer, a 1926 newspaper story states: "The Queen Esther Circle of the First Methodist church will meet Friday evening selections by Miss Josephine Bruner." (*Sapulpa Herald* (Sapulpa, Okla.), Vol. 11, No. 111, Ed. 1 Tuesday, January 12, 1926, p. 3.) Queen Esther is an Old Testament figure who helped save her Jewish people. About a year later, we find that Princess Jo Esther Bruner (Sapulpa) will give a solo piano performance of Chopin's "Third Ballade" at the banquet of the state convention of the Business and Professional Women's Club, April 23, 1927. (*The Wagoner Tribune* (Wagoner, Okla.), Vol. 7, No. 34, Ed. 1 Thursday, April 21, 1927) Thus, it is not known whether Josephine Bruner had American Indian blood, or for performance purposes added Esther as a middle name and used "Princess" because she was an unmarried member of the Queen Esther Circle. Regarding the lyricist's name, Louis Bluejacket was a surviving son in the 1920s of Chief Charles Bluejacket, after which the town Bluejacket was named. "Chief Charles Bluejacket and his wife located in 1870 on the farm now owned by the Chiefs only living son Louis Bluejacket who is still owner of his fathers farm. … Our Methodist church was built and dedicated in 1898 in memory of Chief. 'Bluejacket Memorial' is the name of our church of which he was a member and also a preacher. … This information was furnished us by Chief Bluejacket's daughter Mary Bluejacket Sharp of Bluejacket." (*The Craig County Gazette* (Vinita, Oklahoma), Vol. 27, No. 33, Ed. 1 Thursday, January 31, 1929, p. 1.) Thus, the lyricist could be American Indian and farm owner Louis Bluejacket with the pen name Chief Bluejacket, or Josephine Bruner could have assigned the chief's name to her own words for effect.

  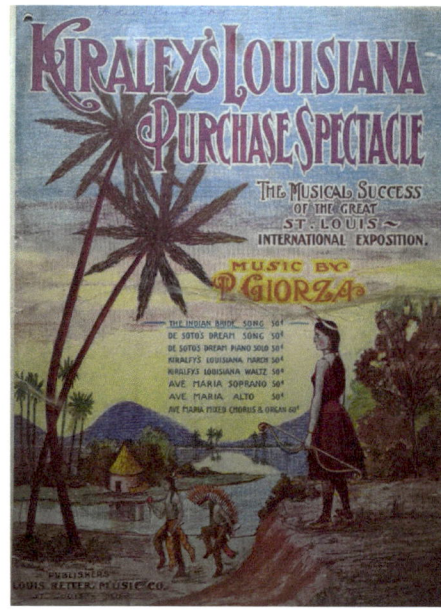 

Indian Blues (illust Travis) – Edwin McHugh and C. Perillo, Jr. 1918 ST [Tinari collection]

The Travis illustration differs substantially from the colorful Starmer cover depiction.

Indian Blues (illust Starmer) – Edwin McHugh and C. Perillo, Jr. 1919 ST [Tinari collection]

"A heart-broken American Indian warrior yearns for his squaw who ran away." (Short, *The Gold in Your Piano Bench*, p. 160)

Indian Bride Song, The – P. Giorza and John Curtis 1904

From Kiraley's Louisiana Purchase Spectacle "The Musical Success of the Great St. Louis International Exposition." The song title on the music page is Indian Bride, and it is one of four songs, with variations, composed for the show. The other tunes do not deal with American Indian subjects.

Indian Butterfly NAOMI (illust Barbelle) – Edgar Leslie, Henry Lodge and Billy Stone 1927 ST [Tinari collection]

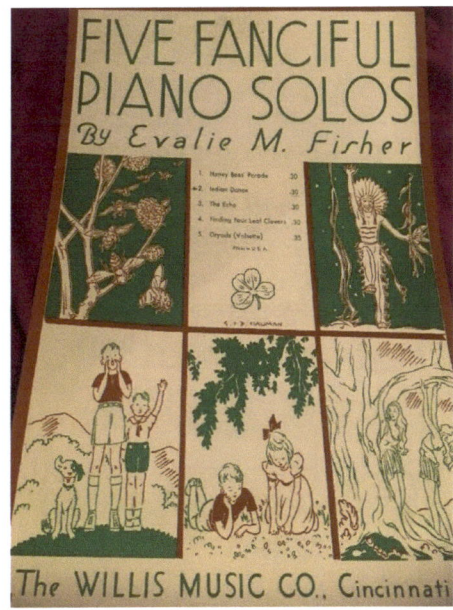

Indian Cradle Song – Charles Wakefield Cadman 1923 [Tinari collection]

Indian Cradle Song – Gus Kahn and Mabel Wayne 1927 ST [Tinari collection]

Indian Dance – Evalie M. Fisher 1917

Although an American Indian is not portrayed on the cover, we have included this piece because of the importance of its composer, whose photo graces the cover. It was published as a piano music lesson by the Art Publication Society (St. Louis), catalog number 732 in its Progressive Series Compositions. The song title is followed by these words: An idealization of a Pawnee Indian theme ("Kawas, the baby is crying") from the collection of Alice C. Fletcher. The inside front cover provides a biographical sketch of the composer, and the page that follows provides background information about the composition.

The cover lists five piano pieces, each with an illustrated vignette. The only piece related to American Indians is the Indian Dance, illustrated by a dancing American Indian man. This was part of The Willis Music Company's teaching pieces for piano students.

89

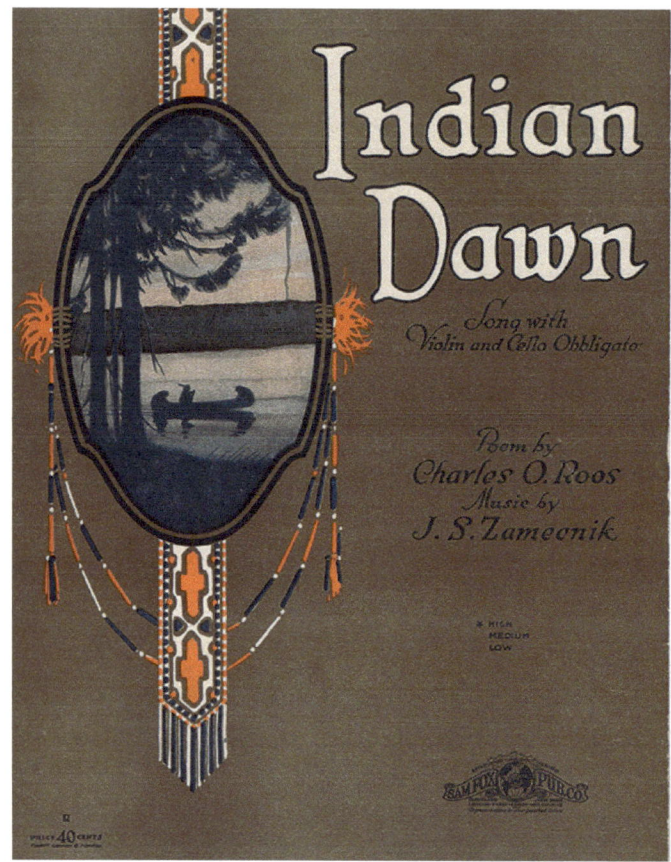

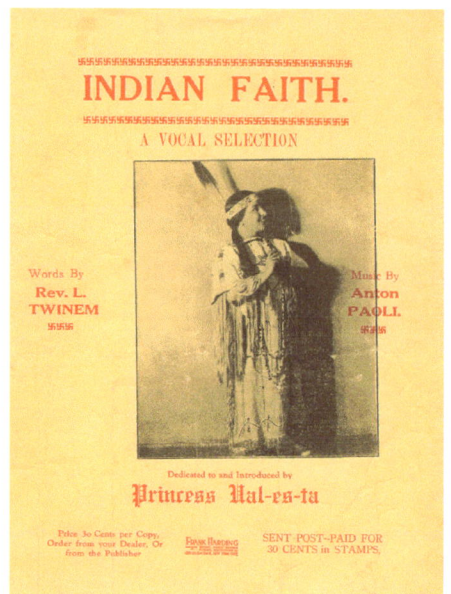

Indian Dawn – Charles O. Roos and John S. Zamecnik 1924 ST [Tinari collection]

Indian Faith – Rev. L. Twinem and Anton Paoli 1927 [Tinari collection]

Indian Girl – Frank Loewenstein 1911 [Tinari collection]

In this book we list three song sheet covers of popular songs composed by Zamecnik. Deloria writes: "In 1913, John Zamecnik, a composer who had studied under Dvorak, put together a collection of music to be played for silent films. Included in his array were ... the Indian sound– with pounding tom-tom beats ... and a four-part battle sequence, with plenty of the bugle-call imagery so characteristic of film cavalry charges." His collection "reflects the consolidation of a number of stereotypical expectations into simple sonic short hands. Zamecnik's was only one of the many collections available, and most theaters had their own libraries of various musical accompaniments." (p. 221)

"Dedicated to and Introduced by Princess Val-es-ta." The Princess was a Menominee singer named Isabella Erdlitz, who held a monthly dance for the local American Indian community at her New York City studio. The swastika symbol, used by the Navajos for good luck, is placed across the top of the song title and below the composers' names.

  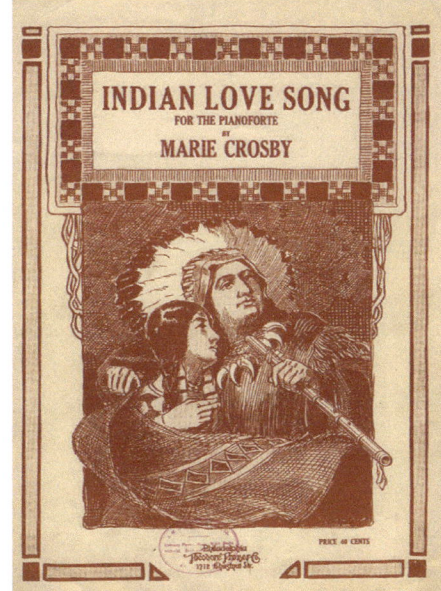 

Indian Lament – Anna Priscilla Risher 1923 ST [Tinari collection]

Indian Love Moon (illust Manning) – Wm. J. McKenna, Christian Sinding and Frederic Watson 1924 ST [Tinari collection]

The cover image is unusually simple compared to most of Manning's color-filled illustrations.

Indian Love Song – Marie Crosby 1914 [Tinari collection]

§

*Indian Love Song, An – Hudson and Buckley 1913

Indian Lover's Serenade – Charles J. Wilson 1905

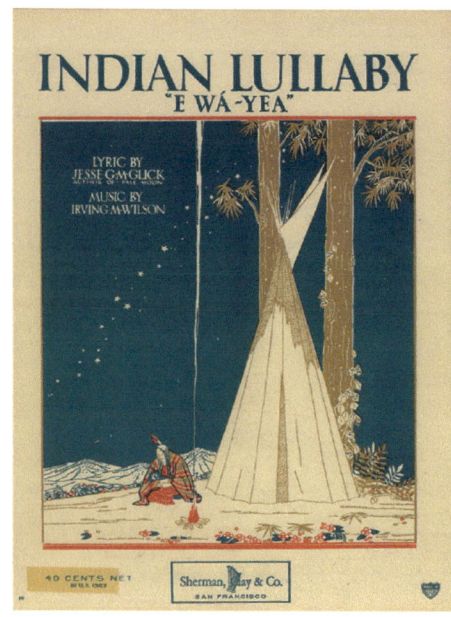   

Indian Lullaby – Jesse G. M. Glick and Irving M. Wilson 1925 ST [Tinari collection]

Indian Patrol – Howard Whitney 1904 [Courtesy Sandy Marrone]

Indian Reverie – Cecil Kappey 1922 ST [Tinari collection]

Indian River Dance – E. Langdon Thurston 1904 [Courtesy Sandy Marrone]

§

*Indian Rag – Seymour Brown and Nat D. Ayer 1912

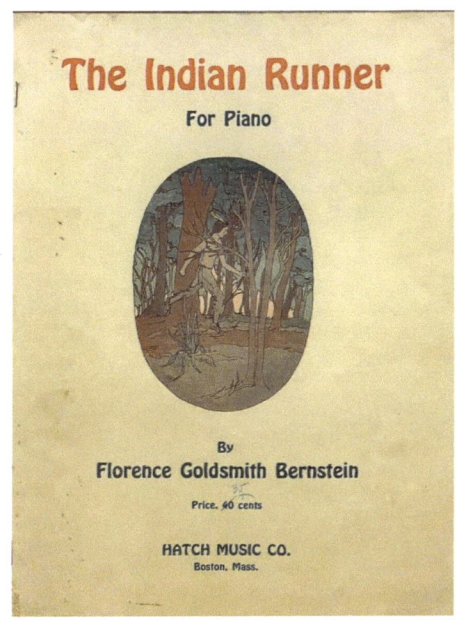   

Indian Runner, The – Florence Goldsmith Bernstein 1923 ST EPP

Indian Sagwa (illust Starmer) – Thomas S. Allen 1915 [Courtesy Sandy Marrone]

Indian Smoke Dance – Theodore A. Metz 1919 ST [Tinari collection]

The border of the illustration is filled with Indian designs and pictographs.

Indian Snake Dance – Mrs. L. Rottanzi Steffani 1910

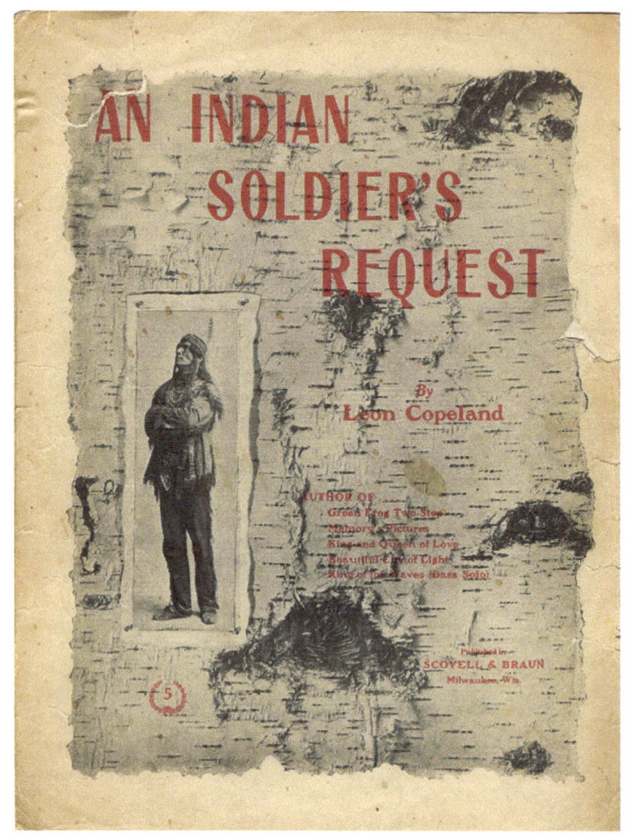

Indian Soldier's Request, An – Leon Copeland 1903 [Courtesy Sandy Marrone]

Indian Spring Bird (Ski-Bi-Bi-La) – Thurlow Lieurance 1920 ST [Courtesy Sandy Marrone]

Indian Two Step, The (Dedicated to the Detroit Indians) – Fred S. Stone 1895 [Courtesy Sandy Marrone]

From the composer: The incident which gave rise to this song, happened during the late Cuban war, and the lake of which our Indian soldier speaks is the well-known lake Mo-No-No near the capital city of Wisconsin. The story of the song was related to the author, by a brother of Men-Do-Ta, the hero of the song.

Indi-Ana (illust Henrich) – George Stevens 1906 [Tinari collection]

Intermediate to advanced "Redowa" scoring--Czech leaping waltz dance. This is odd for an American Indian piano solo.

Indi-Ana (Intermezzo) (illust Barbelle) – M. Kay Jerome 1915 [Tinari collection]

Indianola (Patrol-Two Step) – B. Hartz 1903 [Tinari collection]

Indianola (color, w/o lyrics) (illust Starmer) – S. R. Henry and D. Onivas 1917 [Tinari collection]

S. R. Henry was the alias of Henry R. Stern, and Onivas the alias of classically trained composer Domenico Savino. (Amundson, p. 181) Another version was published using green instead of red ink.

*Indianola (with lyrics) (illust Starmer) – S. R. Henry, D. Onivas and Frank H. Warren 1918 ST

This is an example of a song sheet reduced to standard size. Amundson (p. 182) notes that publishers conserved by reducing the amount of color, evident in this cover. "World War I song tells of Chief Bug-a-Boo who begs Indianola to be his bride before he leaves for France to 'help Yank man win war, and scalp old Kaiser Bill.'"(Short, *Covers of Gold*, p. 134) Warren's lyrics created an international hit "by capitalizing on America's growing involvement in the Great War, anti-German sentiment, and the continued popularity of Indian stereotypes of the warrior and the Big Chief as well as the Indian love song legacy." (Amundson, p. 181)

Indian's Serenade, An (self-pub) – Luther A. Clark and Alice L. Beardsley 1925 ST [Tinari collection]

§

Injun Gal (Novelty Indian Intermezzo and Two-Step) – Ellis R. Ephraim 1905

The unlabeled inset photo is presumably that of the composer.

Injun Gal ("Novelty Indian Song") – P. C. Mason and Ellis R. Ephraim 1905 [Courtesy the Lester S. Levy Collection of Sheet Music, Sheridan Libraries, Johns Hopkins University]

Iola (illust Merrian) – Charles L. Johnson 1906 [Tinari collection]

Iola represents the effort by songwriters to spin off another hit within the American Indian love song genre. (Amundson, p. 86)

Iola (Song) (illust DeTakacs) – James O'Dea (1871–1914) and Charles L. Johnson 1906 [Tinari collection]

This song was issued with inset photos of different performers including Della Fox.

Iolanthe – W. C. Powell 1903 [Courtesy Sandy Marrone]

Irish Indian, The (illust Starmer) – B. Hartz 1904 [Courtesy Sandy Marrone]

Iroquois Fox Trot (illust Pfeiffer) – Louis G. Castle 1915 [Tinari collection]

It's a Pontiac (automobile promotion) – Porter E. Potts 1928 ST [Courtesy Sandy Marrone]

§ § §

*Iroquois ("Characteristic March and Two-Step") – Herbert Williams 1905

*Iroquois (Waltz) - M. Davis c. 1924

The cover image is in color and is the same as Here Comes the Tribes which is monochrome.

*Kachina-Hopi Girl's Dance – Albert Van Sand and Arthur Green 1914

Kalooka – John Martin 1904 [Tinari collection]

Ka-Noo-No Maid (Dedicated to the Mystique Krewe of Ka-noo-no) (self-pub) – Daisy M. Davis 1912 [Courtesy Sandy Marrone]

Katunka (illust Starmer) – Lee Orean Smith 1904 [Tinari collection]

The cover states: "Also published as a song." It likely has the same or very similar cover illustration.

  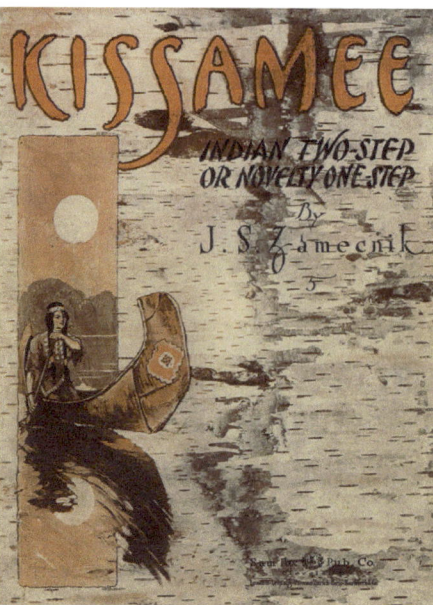 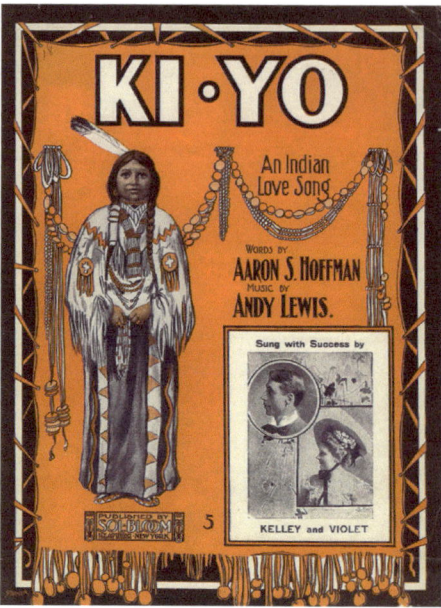

Kiowana – Leo Pevsner and Bob Miller 1928 ST [Courtesy Sandy Marrone]

Kiss-I-Mee (self-pub) – Ester Ruth Magbee and A. D. Magbee 1909 [Tinari Collection]

Kissamee – John S. Zamecnik 1914 (see note under Indian Dawn) [Tinari collection]

Ki-Yo (illust Starmer) (inset photo: Kelley and Violet) – Aaron S. Hoffman and Andy Lewis 1903 [Tinari collection]

La Owna (Serenade) (illust Smith) – R. Hamilton McLain 1909 [Tinari collection]

La Santa Fe (The Holy Faith) – Jesse Click and Irving Wilson 1926 ST [Tinari collection]

Subtitled an "Indian Love Song," the photo credit reads: "Sung with great success by Princess Tsianina." Information about the Princess is presented under Mulberry Moon.

§

*Lackawanna (An Indian Love Song, Story from Florida) – Eugene Francis Deas and Eugene Francis Mikell 1912

Laughing Eyes – Charles H. Musgrove and E. Clinton Keithley 1908 [Tinari collection]

Laughing Eyes (My Omaha) – H. B. Binner 1911 [Courtesy Mark Clardy]

The cover illustration shows a cowboy entreating an American Indian woman. The inset photo is of band leader Arthur Hahn.

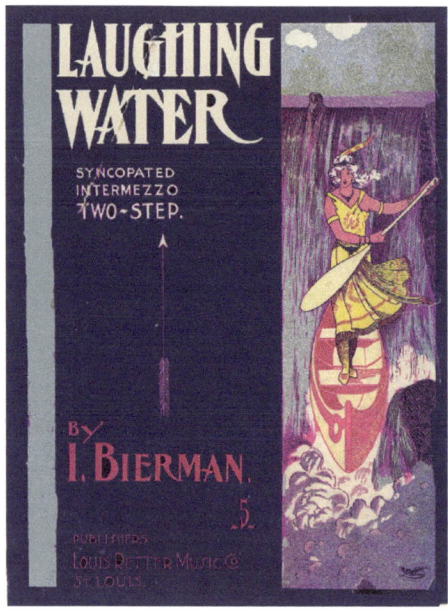   

Laughing Water – Irene A. Bierman 1903 [Charles H. Templeton, Sr. sheet music collection. Special Collections, Mississippi State University Libraries]

Laughing Water (illust Starmer) (full face American Indian woman) – Frederick W. Hager 1903 [Tinari collection]

Laughing Water (illust Starmer) – George Totten Smith and Frederick W. Hager 1903 [Tinari collection]

The illustration is of an American Indian couple. As sung and featured by Harry Bulger in "Mother Goose."

Laughing Water! Ha, Ha, Ha (photo: unnamed American Indian woman) – Eugene West and Joe Gold 1919 ST [Tinari collection]

102

Laughing Water, Stop Your Crying (illust Barbelle) (inset photo: featured by Arthur Nealy, tenor) – Alfred Bryan, Pete Wendling and Francis Wheeler 1928 ST [Tinari collection]

Laughing Waters (Intermezzo) (illust ZUS) – H. Engelmann 1903 [Tinari collection]

Lawana (illust Nuyttens) – Louis Robinson and Harry I. Robinson 1911 [Tinari collection]

Robinson's Intermezzo (1911) also was illustrated by Nuyttens.

§

*Lenore Song – Gus Kahn, Charles Besche and Johnson 1921

A beautiful woman is illustrated, looking upward, against a dark oval backdrop. Though she wears an Indian head band, her features are not particularly American Indian.

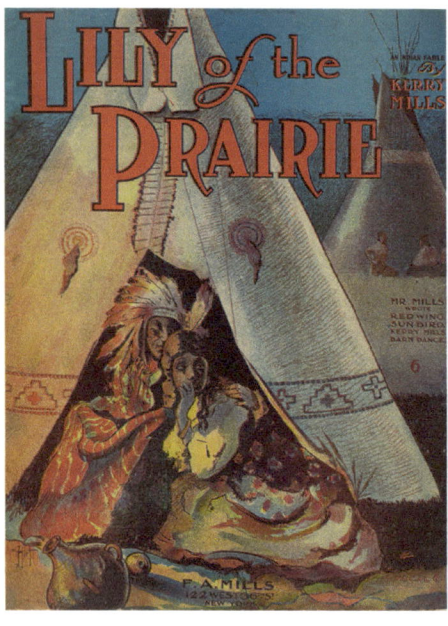

Lily of the Prairie (illust Hirt) – Kerry Mills 1909 [Tinari collection]

"This song fable is about a warrior, brave and bold, who confesses his love to a pretty little prairie girl. He asks her to wed and join him in his 'wigwam nice and cosy, a little nest for two.'" (Short, *Covers of Gold*, p. 134) Frederick Allen "Kerry" Mills was a trained violinist, successful song writer and music publisher. He composed major hits in vaudeville, and published George M. Cohan songs. In 1904 he wrote the music for *Meet Me in St. Louis, Louis*. (Amundson, p. 98)

Linganore (song) – Ammon E. Cramer (self-pub) 1910 ST

Little Indian, A (March) – Charles Henlein 1912 ST [Tinari collection]

Little Indian (Characteristique for the Pianoforte) – Walter Wallace Smith 1921 ST [Tinari collection]

The cover illustration depicts an American Indian holding his bow and standing proudly on a rock overlooking the scenic forest below. The back cover depicts the first line of each of nine "pleasing piano pieces for the average player," the publisher being Theodore Presser of Philadelphia.

   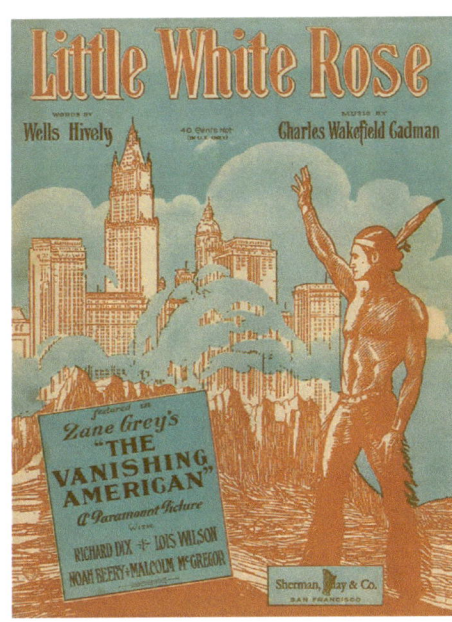

Little Indian Chief – L. Strickland 1919 ST [courtesy Mark Clardy]

Theodore Presser issued this piece, depicting a young teenage American Indian with two feathers in his hair.

Little Indian Maid – Samuel Lehman 1904 [Tinari collection]

This is a New York issue, but it was originally copyrighted in England. According to Pisani, the piece was: "Also published as a vocal: My little Indian Maid. Words by Maurice Stonehill. New York: T. B. Harms, 1904."(Pisani, A Chronological Listing of Musical Works on American Indian Subjects)

Little Min-Ne-Ha Ha (Be My Little Injun Squaw) – Bert Kalmar and Harry Ruby 1921 ST [Tinari collection]

Little White Rose – Wells Hively and Charles Wakefield Cadman 1925 ST [Tinari collection]

The tune was featured in Zane Grey's *The Vanishing American* film. "Richard Dix's (1894–1949) strong portrayal of a Native American hero in *The Vanishing American* has been praised as the best performance of his career. The movie showed the irony of a Native American fighting in World War I for his country, while his lands and crops were being despoiled by government agents. A great deal of historical background about

Native Americans' subjugation is included in this highly-regarded silent movie." (Short, *From Footlights to "The Flickers,"* p. 129)

Little White Rose – Wells Hively and Charles Wakefield Cadman

Published by Sherman, Clay and Co., San Francisco, the cover features an American Indian man sitting alone at his campfire, outside his tent, dreaming of a woman, whose face is symbolically shown in the large white moon.

Lo-Nah – Bud Green and Sam H. Stept 1926 ST [Tinari collection]

The photo byline states: successfully introduced by Lillian Bernard. Variations feature the photos of other performers such as Edward Albano and Adele Rowland.

Lost Arrow (An Indian Romance) – E. Clinton Keithley and Thompson 1914 [Courtesy Sandy Marrone]

Lost Phase, The (illust Dittmar and Furman) – Harry J. Lincoln 1907

Love Bird – Joseph A. Burke and Joseph T. Dempsey 1911 [Tinari collection]

The grid background is filled with an American Indian design that looks like the Nazi swastika symbol.

Love Song (From the Red Willow Pueblos) – Thurlow Lieurance 1917 [Tinari collection]

This is one of four song sheets issued under the theme "Four Indian Songs," all with the identical cover layout and illustration. All are small, war-size sheets. Edna Dean Proctor is listed on the inside music title page; we assume she did the arrangement for women's voices. Also, on the music title page is written the following: "The melody is one of the Red Willow ceremonial songs and the Text is from an Omaha Legend. The young Indian, when he feels the spring of love dawn, mounts the hill overlooking the valley where the camp is located, and calls upon his flute to his love."

§

*Lovelight (illust Meserow) (instrumental) – Theron C. Bennett 1909

Lovelight (illust Meserow) (song) – Theron C. Bennett and Hal Harrett 1909 [Tinari collection]

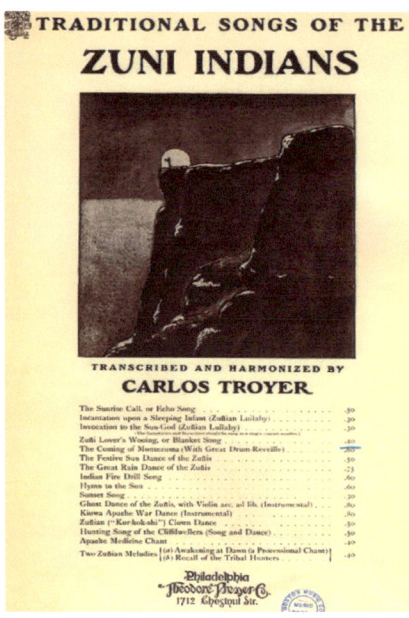

Lover's Wooing, one of Traditional Songs of the Zuni Indians – transcribed and harmonized by Carlos Troyer 1913 [Courtesy Sandy Marrone]

Each of the sixteen songs was printed individually and includes a fairly lengthy description of the song and the related dance ceremony.

Maid of the Midnight Moon – Dave Reed Jr. 1912 [Tinari collection]

The photo depicts Theresa Bluford; the inset photo byline states: sung with great success by Carter and Bluford.

Maiden America (photo: Gail Kane, silent movie star) – Lee Orean Smith 1916 [Tinari collection]

Manisot (illust Dewey) – T. P. Brooke (Bandmaster, Chicago Marine Band) 1900 [Courtesy Sandy Marrone]

This piece was also issued without color, in black ink on white.

Division of Stutz Motor Car Company of America, Inc., Indianapolis". The black and white illustration is a respectful and relatively realistic tribute to American Indians. By the end of the 1920s, the market for prestige cars like the Stutz was falling. The company decided to introduce a more affordable line of cars, but with the Stutz name minimized, something other manufacturers also did. As a result, Stutz established a separate marque called "Blackhawk."

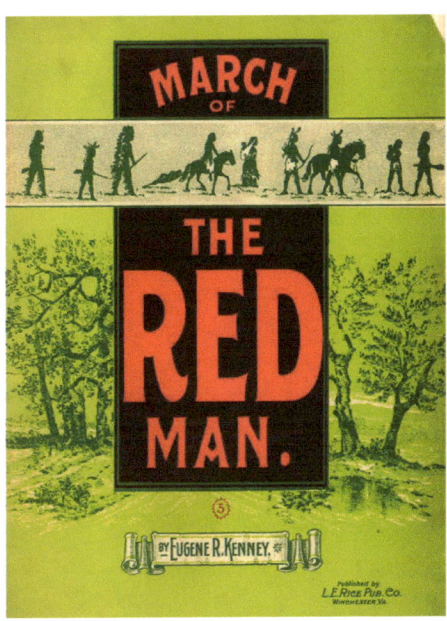

Mar-An-Da (My Irish Indian Maid) – Stewart and Vernette 1908 [Courtesy Sandy Marrone]

The cover photo appears to be a Caucasian woman.

§

*March of the Black Hawks – George Irish c. 1929

The cover has a different title (Hail to the Blackhawk) than the music, and states "A Tribute to the Blackhawk Companion Car to Stutz. Presented to you with the compliments of Blackhawk

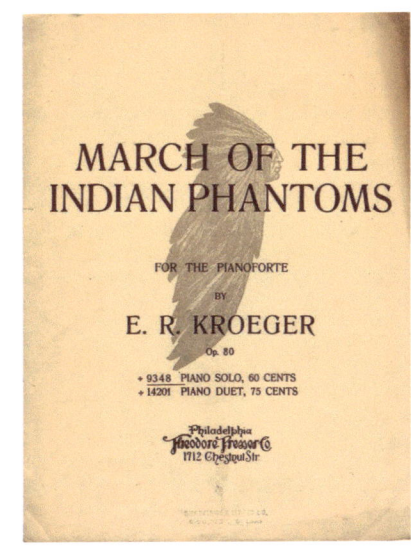

March of the Indian Phantoms – E. R. Kroeger 1912

March of the Red Man – Eugene R. Kenney 1908 [Tinari collection]

§

*March of the Redmen – Frederick H Groves 1904

March of the Santa Fe Trail – G. Holcombe 1927 ST [Tinari collection]

Printed with the music: "This composition represents a tribe of Indians marching homeward. Begin very softly. Imitate their approach by gradually increasing the sound."

§

*Meadow Lark – Howard Dalton 1910

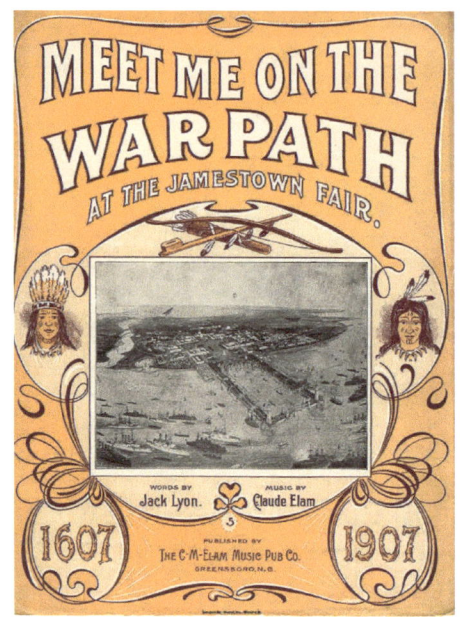

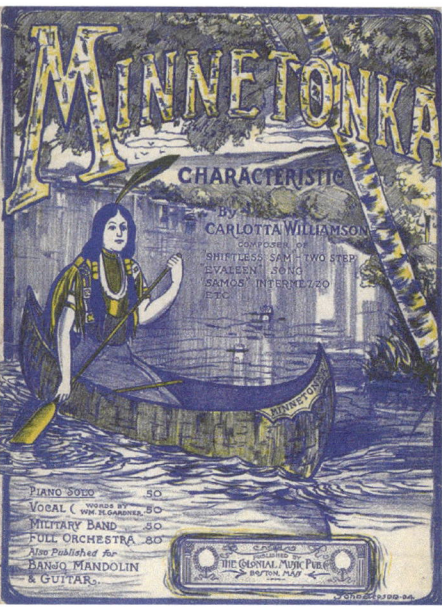

Meet Me on the Warpath at the Jamestown Fair – Jack Lyon and Claude Elam 1907 [Tinari collection]

This was likely self-published. Another song about the Jamestown founding, Scouting on the New Warpath, is displayed later in this chapter.

Minnetonka – Carlotta Williamson 1904 [Courtesy Sandy Marrone]

Minnie Ha Ha Ha, The – Eugene E. Noel and Earl E. Crooke 1916 [Courtesy Sandy Marrone]

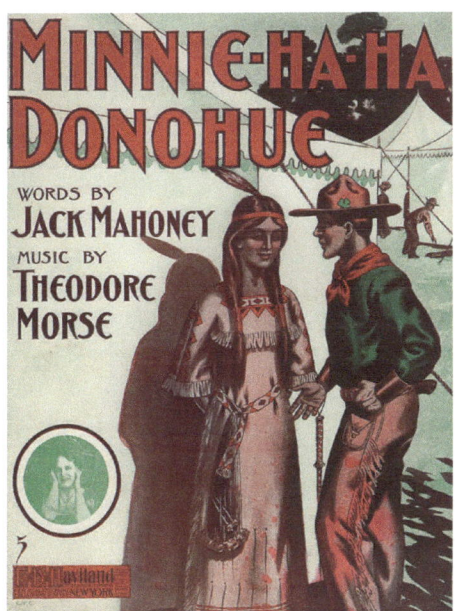

Minnie-Ha-Ha Donohue (illust E. P. C.) – Jack Mahoney and Theodore Morse 1908 [Tinari collection]

The inset photo is of Eleanor Wisdom. The title page subtitle is: An Irish Indian Love Affair.

§

*Minnie-Waha – Edward Campbell 1906

Missoula (Meeting of the Waters) – John J. Scull (self-pub) 1906 [Tinari collection]

§

*Moccasin Blues – E. Stanelli

An image of the British edition of this song is presented in Chapter 5.

Moccasin Maiden (An Indian Intermezzo) – Will H. Lewis 1908 [Tinari collection]

§

*Moccasin Rag – W. R. and C. H. Garton 1913

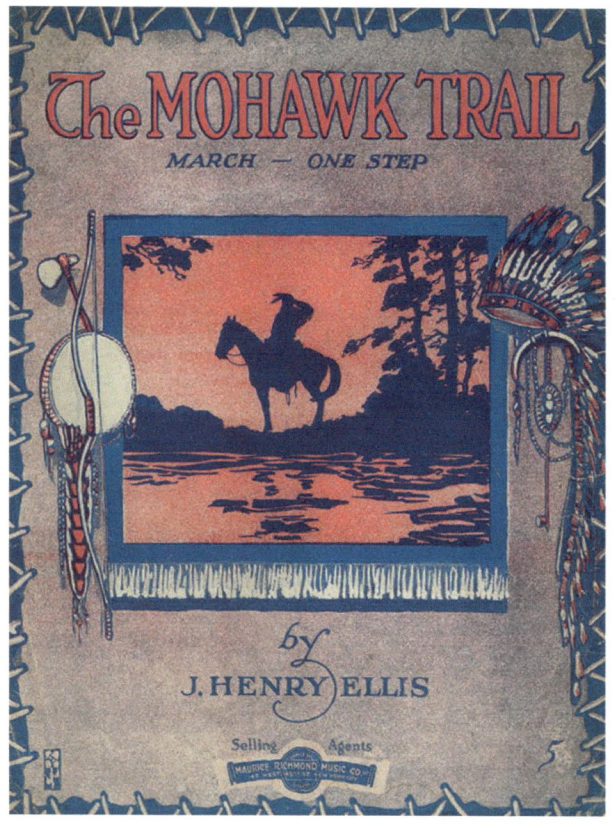
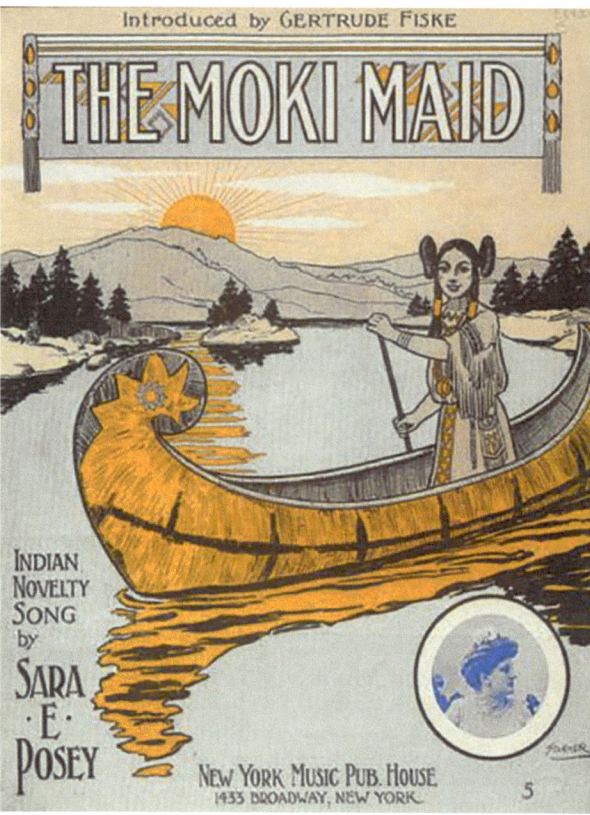
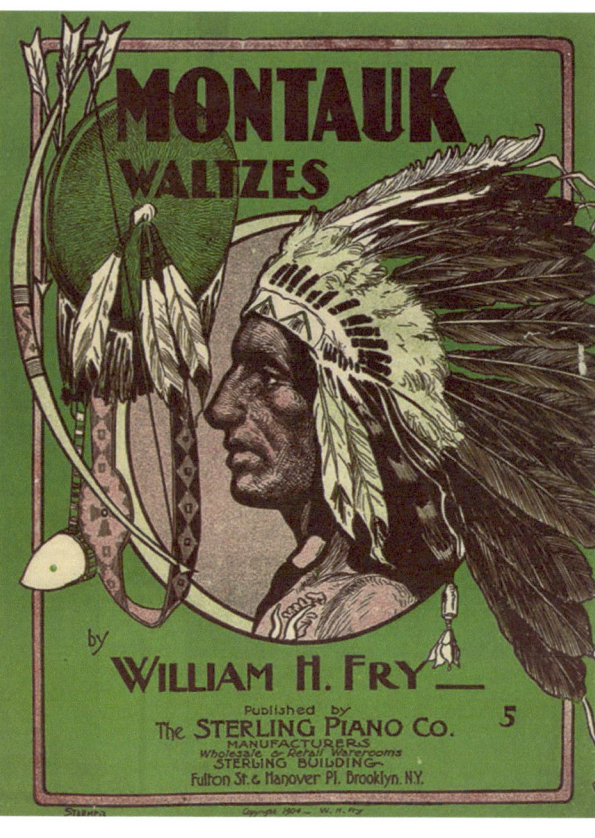

The Mohawk Trail (illust Rose) – J. Henry Ellis 1917 [Tinari collection]

The Moki Maid – Sarah E. Posey 1906 [Courtesy Frances G. Spencer Collection of American Popular Sheet Music. Arts and Special Collections Research Center, Baylor University, Waco, Texas]

Montauk Waltzes (illust Starmer) – William H. Fry 1904 [Tinari collection]

Moon Deer (illust Cameron) – Raymond B. Egan, Richard A. Whiting and Neil Moret 1925 ST [Courtesy Sandy Marrone]

Moonbeam (Indian Love Song) (illust Vance) – Arthur C. Wilson 1913 [Tinari collection]

§

*Moon-Bird (illust Young) – Johann C. Schmid 1909

Moon-Bird (An Indian Love Song) (illust Young) – J. F. Dempey and Johann C. Schmid 1909 [Tinari collection]

#

Moonlight Dear (illust Starmer) –W. A. Murchison and Hodge 1909 [Courtesy Sandy Marrone]

Moonlight Waltz – Victor LaSalle 1912 [Tinari collection]

Morning Star (illust Young) – Neil Moret and James O'Dea 1907 [Tinari collection]

§

*Morning Star – Neil Moret 1906

2-148. Mulberry Moon (An Indian Tango) (illust De Takacs) – Frederick W. Hager and C. M. Denison 1916 [Courtesy Sandy Marrone]

The inset photo depicts Red Feather, a Native American woman. Born at the end of the nineteenth century, the Creek singer Tsianina Redfeather was a leading performer in Cadman's Indian Music Talk that criss-crossed America in the second decade of the twentieth century. Cadman's opera *Shanewis* was based in large part on Tsianina's life. (Deloria, pp. 210-14) On the cover of this sheet and several others, the woman's name is printed as Red Feather rather than Redfeather.

Multnomah (an Oregon Indian Tale) – Ernest Traxler 1910 [Historic Sheet Music Collection, Oregon Digital, University of Oregon Libraries]

"Dedicated by permission to the Portland Rose Festival" There is a pink Portland Rose Festival rose in lower right corner and a photograph of R. M. Emmerson in the lower left corner.

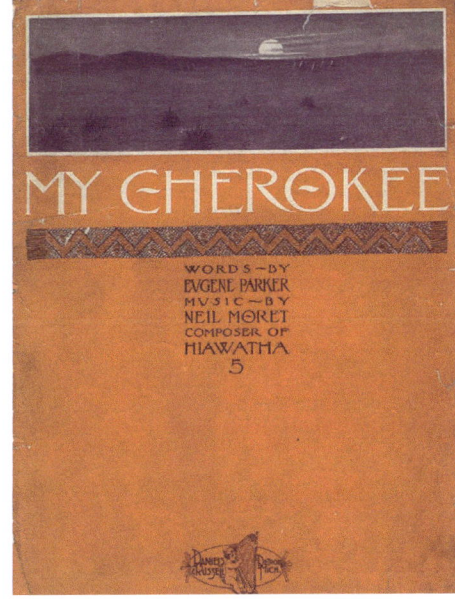

My Black Papoose – H. L. Kann 1899 [Courtesy Frances G. Spencer Collection of American Popular Sheet Music. Arts and Special Collections Research Center, Baylor University, Waco, Texas]

The cover illustration depicts a variety of Indian items including moccasins, headdresses, knives, and peace pipes, among others. The papoose in the center reveals the face of an African American baby.

My Cherokee – Neil Moret and Eugene Parker 1904 [Courtesy Sandy Marrone]

115

  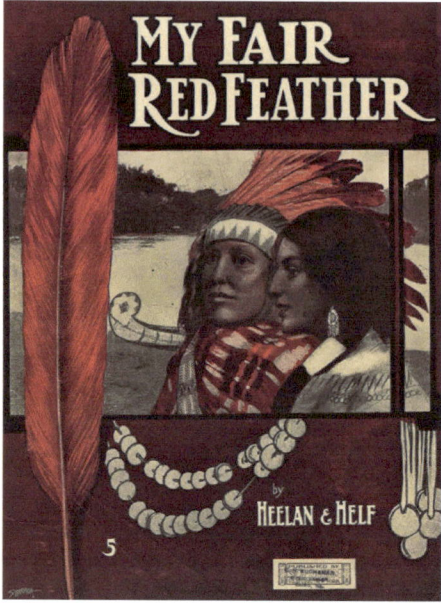 

My Chippewa – Dave Reed Jr. 1907

My Copper Colored Squaw – Peter S. Clark 1909 [Duke University Digital Collections]

The cover illustration depicts an Indian maid pleading with her father the chief to let her go with the white cowboy who is shown walking away. The lyrics' first line is: Big Chief heapee wild, white man love him child.

My Fair Red Feather (illust Starmer) – W. A. Heelan and F. J. Helf 1904 [Tinari collection]

See the note regarding Red Feather under Mulberry Moon.

My Forest Flower Red Skin Rose (illust Starmer) – Francklyn Wallace 1909 [Tinari collection]

My Indian Maid – H. Federoff; lyrics adapted by Everett J. Evans 1913 [Courtesy Sandy Marrone]

My Indian Maid – Marion Raybould and H. Federoff 1914 [Tinari collection]

Inset photo: Featured by Herman Dick. A smaller inset photo of the musical composer Federoff is placed below his name. Although the music title page states the piece is an intermezzo, it actually is a song with full lyrics that are different from the 1913 issue. Moja indianka is its Russian title.

My Indian Maiden (illust Eddy) – Harry Wilson and Edward J. Coleman 1904 [Tinari collection]

The inset photo depicts Miss Genevieve Day in *A Venitian Romance*; Supp. to the *NY American and Journal,* Sept. 18, 1904.

My Indian Queen (Sacajawea) – H. W. Hayes and Fred Brownold 1904 [Courtesy Frances G. Spencer Collection of American Popular Sheet Music. Arts and Special Collections Research Center, Baylor University, Waco, Texas]

The photo is of Harriet Burt. "From Kiralfy's Wonderful Spectacular Production of *Louisiana*"

   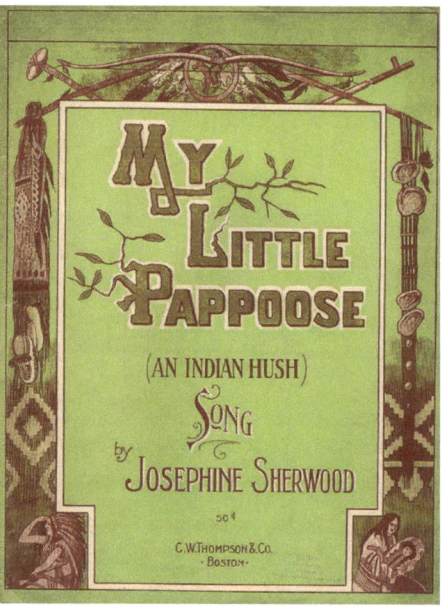

My Irish Indian (inset photo: Hattie Williams) – Jean Schwartz and William Jerome 1905 [Courtesy Sandy Marrone]

My Irish Prairie Queen (illust Stillmunk) – J. W. Walsh and Charles P. Shisler 1919 [Tinari collection]

My Kickapoo (illust Hirt) – Harry Von Tilzer (July 8, 1872 – January 10, 1946) 1904 [Courtesy Sandy Marrone]

The same song with words was issued as My Pretty Little Kickapoo, listed below.

§

*My Little Indian Maid – Louis Blake 1904

My Little Pappoose (An Indian Hush) – Josephine Sherwood 1908 [Courtesy Sandy Marrone]

This sheet was also issued with all lettering and illustration in green on a white background.

§

*My Little Indian Maid (song) – Samuel Lehman and Maurice Stonehill 1904

See Little Indian Maid, above.

My Love, My Lark (Characteristic) – Thurlow Lieurance 1918

This was one of two songs in a set for voice and piano, the other being O'er the Indian Cradle: Yankton Sioux Lullaby, issued under "Where the Papoose Swings." (Pisani, A Chronological Listing of Musical Works on American Indian Subjects)

My Moonbeam (An Indian Serenade) – Ren Shields and Joseph Santley 1910 [Charles H. Templeton, Sr. sheet music collection. Special Collections, Mississippi State University Libraries]

My Morning Rose (illust Etherington) – Arthur Longbrake and Edward Edwards 1910 [Tinari collection]

"This ballad tells of a proud chieftain who falls in love with a fair maiden known as Morning Rose. She avows her love for him, creeps to his tepee, and becomes his bride." (Short, *Covers of Gold*, p. 134)

My Prairie Maid – Carl Olson and Amos Edwards 1908 [Courtesy Sandy Marrone]

§

*My Prairie Queen – Edward Rose and Ted Snyder 1904

119

 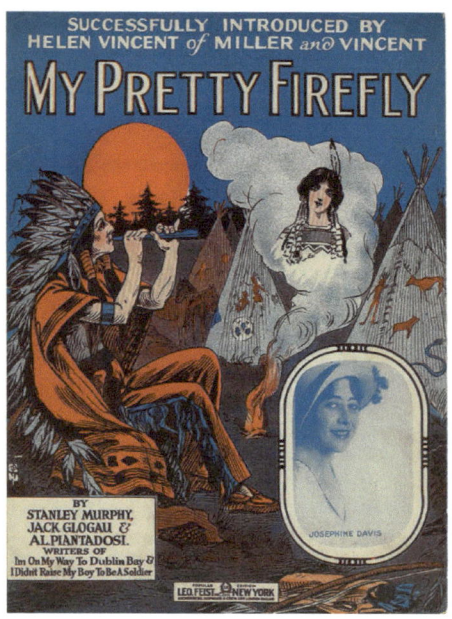  

My Prairie Song Bird (illust E.P.C.) – Jack Drislane and George W. Meyer 1909 [Tinari collection]

This version is actually an Intermezzo with the music title page listing only Meyer. The song issued with words by Drislane has the same cover illustration.

§

*My Pretty Indian Maid (illust Fisher) – R. M. Kane and J. L. Chandler 1912

§

*My Pretty Little Indian Maid – M. J. Fitzpatrick 1915

My Pretty Firefly (illust Rose) – Stanley Murphy, Jack Glogau and Al Piantadosi 1915 [Tinari collection]

The music title page gives the song title as Firefly (My Pretty Firefly). Though the inset photo is of Josephine Davis, the cover states: "Successfully Introduced by Helen Vincent of Miller and Vincent". There may be another version with a photo inset of Vincent; we have seen a copy with an inset photo of Mae Francis.

My Pretty Little Kick-Apoo (illust Hirt) – Andrew B. Sterling and Harry Von Tilzer 1904 [Tinari collection]

The inset photos are of Von Tilzer and Daisy Dumont. "Song writers usually endowed each maiden with the name of the Indian nation to which she belonged. In 1904 one of the best-known teams in the field of popular music, Andrew B. Sterling and Harry Von Tilzer wrote 'My Pretty Little Kickapoo,' a boy-and-girl love song with a heavily contrived Indian atmosphere." (Levy, *Give Me Yesterday*, p. 174)

My Ramapoo (illust Starmer) (An Indian Love Song) – Frederick W. Hager 1910 [Tinari collection]

   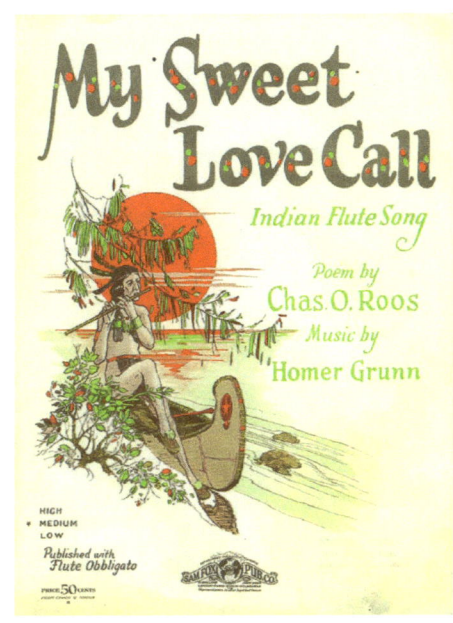

My Silver-Throated Fawn (Sioux Love Song) – Thurlow Lieurance 1917 [Tinari collection]

This is one of four song sheets issued under the theme "Four Indian Songs," all with the identical cover layout and illustration. All are small, war-size sheets. Karl Jones is listed on the inside music title page; we assume he did the arrangement for women's voices. Also, on the music title page is written the following: "Melody sung by 'Frank Double the Horse.' The Sioux Indians have music of perfect intervals and their love songs are the most melodious of all."

My Sweet Dakotah Maid – Hiram W. Hayes, William John Halland and Anton Heindl 1904 [Courtesy Frances G. Spencer Collection of American Popular Sheet Music. Arts and Special Collections Research Center, Baylor University, Waco, Texas]

The photo is of Atherton Furlong as Pontiac. "Musical Gems from *Louisiana*. The World's Fair Historical Extravaganza as produced at Delmar Garden, St. Louis, 1904"

My Sweet Love Call – the first in Songs of Song-ah-tah, Four American Indian Songs – music by John Homer Grunn (1880–1944), poems by Charles O. Roos 1923 ST [Tinari collection]

The song cover displays a pen and ink drawing of an Indian playing a flute. This song and three others were issued in a dark brown, thick paper cover that has elevated gold-toned lettering and a colorful illustration of an American Indian woman. See songs of Song-ah-tah listed later in this chapter.

My Sweet Love Call (Indian Flute Song) – Charles O. Roos and Homer Grunn 1923 ST [Tinari collection]

Publisher Sam Fox produced a separate issue featuring a color illustration of the previously listed song.

My Tom Tom Man – Egbert Van Alstyne and Gus Kahn 1915 [Tinari collection]

My Tom Tom Man (photo: Al Jolson) – Egbert Van Alstyne and Gus Kahn 1915 [Courtesy Sandy Marrone]

§

*My Wigwam Queen – James O'Dea and H. B. Blanke 1903

My Wild Deer (Dear) – Alfred Bryan and Ted Snyder 1908

The insert photo is a head shot of Princess Chinquilla with a full headdress of feather, beads and braids, but the lyrics tell of a Pawnee maiden who gets educated and decides to leave the tribe.

Na-Gar-Ah (illust Brewster) (self-pub) – Clifford W. Walsh 1910 [Tinari collection]

Dedicated to the "Sachema of Na-Gar-Ah," Oneida, NY. Carnival of 1910.

Na-Jo – Rudy Wiedoeft, Walter Holliday and George O'Neil 1921 ST [Tinari collection]

§

*Naoma – Willis Frets and Archie W. Scheu 1909

Napanee – William S. Genaro and W. R. Williams 1906 [Tinari collection]

Cover page states: "It 'Scalps' All Other Indian Songs" and "or My Pretty Little Indian Napanee." Displayed is a photo of a Native American couple in a canoe, with copyright 1905 by A. E. Young. The music title page subtitle reads: A Song Founded on Actual facts." There exists a somewhat different cover version with the identical photograph, but which states at the bottom of the cover page: As Sung in the Comic Opera Success "The Royal Chef."

Natoma (An Indian Love Song) (illust Rickert) – William Held and William C. Welzel, Jr. 1911 [Courtesy Sandy Marrone]

The message of the song is that marriages between Indians and non-Indians would be subject to cultural dissonance and irreconcilabilities. It is interesting to note that in the same year, one of the three Indian operas to grace the stage was Joseph Redding and Victor Herbert's *Natoma*. (Deloria, p. 228) Since Herbert is not credited with this song, it could have been inspired by the plot or just the name of his opera.

Nat-U-Ritch (illust Frew) – Theodore Bendix 1906 [Tinari collection]

This piece is labeled as an Intermezzo from the play *The Squaw Man*; the photo of an actress has an illegible signature (research of the theater listing does not include a feasible name). See the discussion of The Squaw Man (later) for more details about the play and the subsequent DeMille films.

§

*Nat-U-Ritch (An Indian Idyll) (from the film *Squaw Man*) – Theodore Bendix 1914

Stubblebine (*Cinema Sheet Music*, p. 367) relates that the cover of this piece features Red Wing whose real name was Lillian St. Cyr. She was born into the Winnebago Tribe on the Winnebago Reservation (Nebraska).

Navajo (illust Starmer) ("Indian Characteristique") – Egbert Van Alstyne 1903 [Tinari collection]

The cover illustration depicts "a Native American woman standing in a forest at the base of some snowy mountains. The clothing ... is not a traditional dress worn by Navajo women. ... Similarly, the tepees in the center of the image are not the traditional Navajo abode, the hogan, but a generic type of temporary Plains Indian dwelling." (Amundson, p. 60) The song version with lyrics by Harry Williams was published in 1904 with a full photo of performer Marie Cahill who sang the song in "the musical comedy success 'Nancy Brown.'" The song "is a love story between a Navajo woman and an African American man. Although Marie Cahill made *Navajo* a hit on stage, over the next few years recording artists made it a national hit that transformed the genre, propelled its composers to stardom, brought songs about the West to a wider audience, and made lyrics featuring racial stereotypes common practice in western music." (Amundson, p. 58) Because the song version does not feature an American Indian, it is not included in this book. According to Pisani, the piece was "arranged also as a "March and Two-Step" published by Shapiro, Bernstein, and Co., New York. Arranged for military band, 1905." (Pisani, A Chronological Listing of Musical Works on American Indian Subjects)

§

*New Mexico March – John Philip Sousa 1928

Nippinittic – Robert L. Howard 1913 [Courtesy Sandy Marrone]

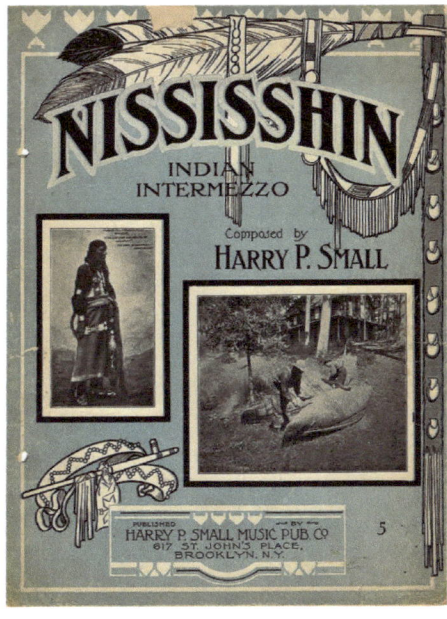

Nississhin – Harry P. Small 1907 [Courtesy Sandy Marrone]

There are two inset photos: one shows an American Indian man with notes regarding his dress; the other depicts two laborers (possibly American Indians) making a canoe constructed of wood and animal skin.

Nokomis (illust Marashiel) – J. Bodewalt Lampe 1903 [Courtesy Sandy Marrone]

The North American – Marie Louka 1904

Obeja (photo: American Indian woman) – Eugene R. Kenney 1904 [Tinari collection]

Ogalalla (Indian Love Song) (illust Frew) – Vincent Bryan and Ted Snyder (1881–1965) 1909 [Tinari collection]

The inset photo is of Mabel Hite, and the description states: As featured by Mabel Hite and Mike Donlin. "A cowboy, riding into Mexico from the North, meets Ogalalla, an 18-year-old redskin Queen. He is smitten by her charms and begs her to go away with him before the Big Chief makes war. A tribal redskin discovers the lovers and as his war cries echo across the prairie, the cowboy takes her bridle rein and madly gallops to safety." (Short, *Covers of Gold*, p. 135) The song uses "racist broken English attributed to Native Americans." (Amundson, p. 148) Pisani lists a self-published intermezzo titled O-ga-lal-la by Snyder dated 1910. (Pisani, A Chronological Listing of Musical Works on American Indian Subjects) But we have not seen it nor its cover illustration.

O-Gal-La-La (Sioux) – Evans Lloyd 1905 [Courtesy Sandy Marrone]

It could be that the spelling of the title is a variation or even a corruption of the proper spelling for one of the Sioux nations, the Oglala Sioux.

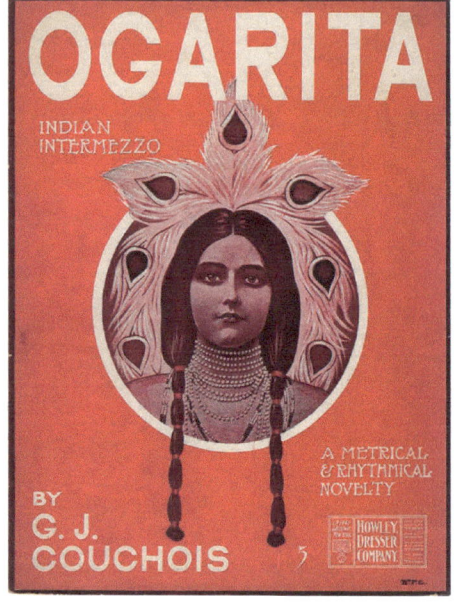

Ogarita (Indian Intermezzo) – G. J. Couchois 1904 [Tinari collection]

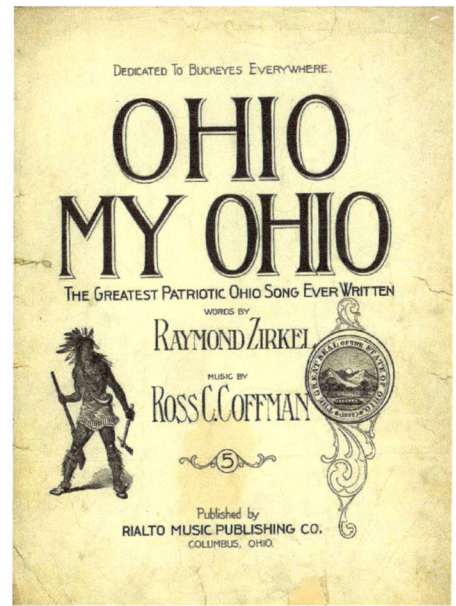

Oh That Navajo Rag (illust Starmer) – Harry Williams and Egbert Van Alstyne 1911 [Tinari collection]

"The cover image clearly represents an appeal to the general public's stereotypical notion of an Indian rather than a Navajo man's clothing exhibition. The buckskin tunic, fringed leggings, moccasins, and trailer war bonnet better resemble the clothing of Northern Plains tribes like the Lakota Sioux or Crows than the Navajo's velvet shirts and cloth headbands." (Amundson, p. 168) "Shake your moccasin and roll your eye, Tear my blanket, make my feathers fly" and similar lyrics emphasized dancing to a rag, rather than anything authentically related to American Indians.

Ohio My Ohio (Ohio, My Ohio! as written on the music title page) – Raymond Zirkel and Ross C. Coffman 1913 [Tinari collection]

A patriotic song about Ohio and some of its great figures, with a cover design that includes the figure of an Indian man. American Indians called the nut from a regional tree "hetuck" meaning the eye of a buck. The buckeye word was used in Harrison's presidential campaign, and it stuck in the mind of the public: Ohio is known as the buckeye state and its state tree is the buckeye.

Ojibways' Canoe Song (self-pub) – J. E. Whitney 1905 [Tinari collection]

The music title page reads: Canoe Song of Hiawatha (The Ojibway).

Oklahom (illust Walton) –Harry H. Williams and Don C. Cowell 1908 [Tinari collection]

The cover illustration shows two American Indian men looking up to what appears to be a shooting star; a third Indian in a chief's headdress is seated.

Oklahoma Indian Jazz (illust Perret) – Ray Hibbeler, T. J. Johnsen, J. W. Barna, J. J. Murrin and T. Guarini 1923 ST [Tinari collection]

The inset photo is of Jules Herbuveux and his Guyon's Paradise Orchestra.

Ola (illust Hayward) – Charles B. Weston 1916 [Tinari collection]

The subtitle of this piece is My Sweet Hawaiian Love. It is included here because the mixed-message cover illustration depicts, against a backdrop of palm trees, an American Indian woman with the swastika-like symbol on her clothing.

Old Loves Are Best (An Indian Love Ballade) (illust the composer) – Wilson MacDonald 1907 [Courtesy Sandy Marrone]

On the Rainbow Trail (illust Miska) – Coleman Goetz, May Singhi Breen and Peter De Rose 1930 ST [Courtesy Sandy Marrone]

On a Cloud I Will Ride – music by Homer Grunn, poems by Charles O. Roos 1923 ST [Tinari collection]

This is the fourth in Songs of Song-ah-tah, Four American Indian Songs. The song cover displays a pen and ink drawing of an American Indian on horseback viewing clouds and flying eagles.

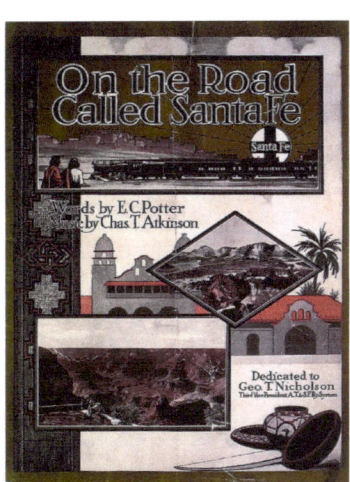

On the Road Called Santa Fe – E. C. Potter and Charles T. Atkinson 1907 [Courtesy the Lester S. Levy Collection of Sheet Music, Sheridan Libraries, Johns Hopkins University]

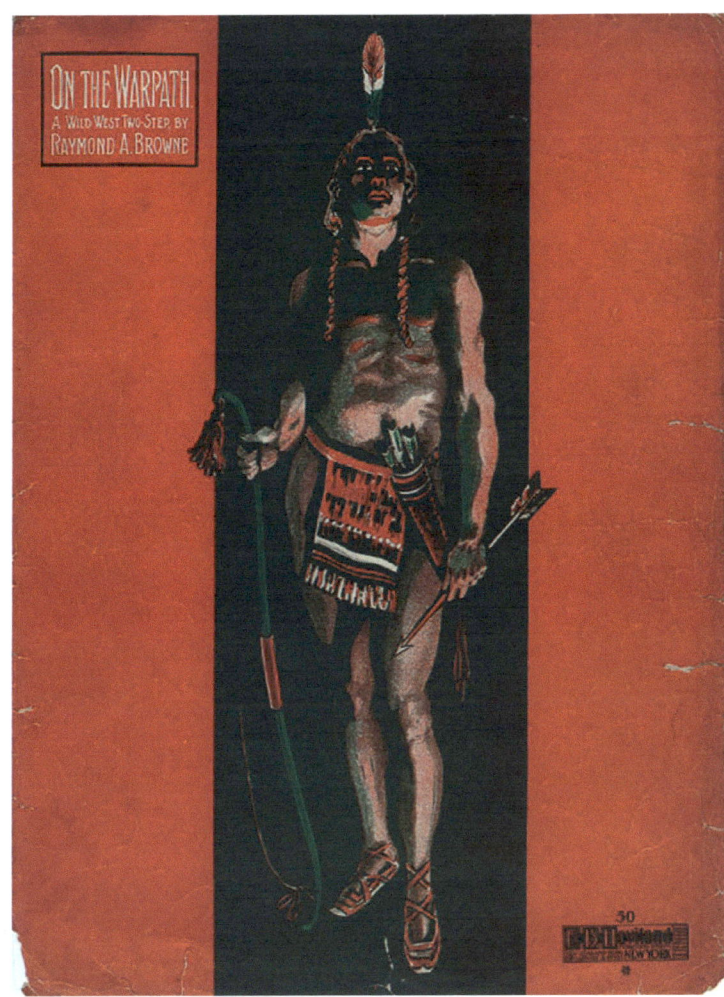

On the Warpath (A Wild West Two Step) – Raymond A. Browne 1904 [Tinari collection]

Onawa (illust Fisher) – E.L. Sutton 1904 [Tinari collection]

Onawa (Intermezzo) (self-pub) – Bert R. Anthony 1928

In the distance are two American Indians outside their tepee around a campfire, illustrated in a stylized silhouette.

Onawanda (Wigwam Dance) – Dox Cruger 1906 [Courtesy Sandy Marrone]

Oneonta – Glen Ashleigh 1904 [Tinari collection]

Oneonta – Charles E. Bray 1904

The cover illustration depicts what appears to be a window view of a banked canoe, with an American Indian and perhaps an Indian boy on the banks of a river. The figures are very small and somewhat indecipherable.

Ontario – John B. Lowitz and Alfred Solman 1906

Ooh La La (illust Bazant) – Ring Hager 1904 [Tinari collection]

Oraibi (Antelope Dance) (illust Frew) – Ted Snyder 1910 [Courtesy Sandy Marrone]

Opechee (Robin) (illust De Takacs) – Robert F. Roden and Jack Glogau 1909 [Tinari collection]

On the music title page, the subtitle is given as Song-Bird.

Origin of the Rainbow, The (An Indian Legend; words Anonymous) – Laura Sedgwick Collins 1908 [Courtesy Sandy Marrone]

Oriole [illust Fung] – Harold Weeks 1921 ST [Tinari Collection]

Osceola (illust Crews) – George L. Spaulding 1904 [Tinari collection]

§

*Os-ka-loo-sa-loo (Indian Love Song) – Henry S. Sawyer and Jeffrey T. Branen 1906

Also issued as a Characteristic Indian March and Two-Step by Sawyer. (Pisani, A Chronological Listing of Musical Works on American Indian Subjects)

Ottawah (Ottawa) (illust DeTakacs) –J. Wesley Ossman and T. Jay Flanagan 1915 [Tinari collection]

Over the Mohawk Trail (self-pub) – Hattie M. Guilford and Jeannie Munro 1917 [Tinari collection]

§

*O-Wah-Hoo!! (A War Whoop from the Wild Wooly West) – K. Kennett and Lyn Udall 1900

O'Wahneta – Henry Clay Smith and Sam Lewis 1905 [Courtesy Sandy Marrone]

Owatonna (Indian Song) (illust DeTakacs) – Harry Williams and Egbert Van Alstyne 1906 [Courtesy Frances G. Spencer Collection of American Popular Sheet Music. Arts and Special Collections Research Center, Baylor University, Waco, Texas]

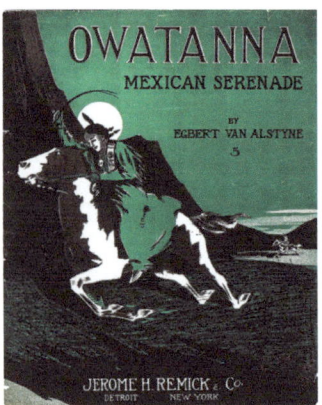

Owatanna (Mexico Serenade) –Egbert Van Alstyne 1906 [Courtesy Mark Clardy]

Pale Moon (An Indian Love Song) (concert edition, illust Van Doorn-Morgan) – Jesse G. M. Glick and Frederic Knight Logan 1925 [Tinari collection]

The copyright date is 1920, but it is not known if it was issued at that time.

Papoose (illust Starmer) – Thomas J. Lyle 1910 [Tinari collection]

§

*Paleface (American Indian ghost following cowboy) – Monroe H. Rosenfeld and Harry Gregg 1909

§

*Papoose (self-pub) – Rolland V. Meeks 1907

§

*Papoose Dance. Danse des Enfants. Marche Indienne. – Adolph Lindstedt (Arranged by Hugo O. Marks) 1904

§

*Passing of the Dakotahs, The – Bernice Frost 1912

"The Dakotas were a group of seven tribes in the northern plains Sioux nation. They have been described as brave and spirited with great integrity of character, proud of their war exploits, tall and stately with colorful dress. They lived in tepees, and were nomadic and nonagricultural following the great buffalo herds." (Short, *Covers of Gold*, p. 134)

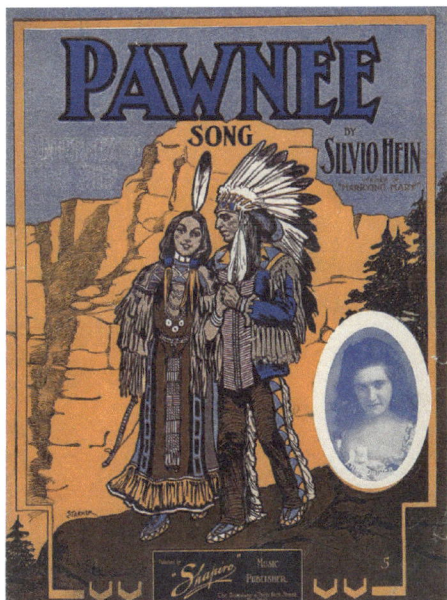

Passing of the Red Man (Indian Characteristic) – K L. King 1916 [Tinari collection]

The music title page states: To my esteemed friend Col. Wm F. Cody "Buffalo Bill"

Pawnee (Song) (illust Starmer) – Silvio Hein 1906 [Tinari collection]

The inset photo is of Anna Driver. "The Pawnees are one of the oldest Native American cultures in North America. They lived in earth lodges, planted, and harvested maize, and hunted the Great Plains bison herds twice a year for meat and skin. This song with a ragtime lilt is sung by a brave to a Pawnee miss asking her to become his bride and change her tribe to Shawnee." (Short, *Covers of Gold*, p. 133)

Pawnee (Intermezzo – Two Step March) – Silvio Hein 1906 [Tinari collection]

"On the colorful title page is a lovely young woman, shading with her hand her big brown eyes, a group of tepees nestled among the pines behind her." Levy (*Give Me Yesterday*, p. 175)

  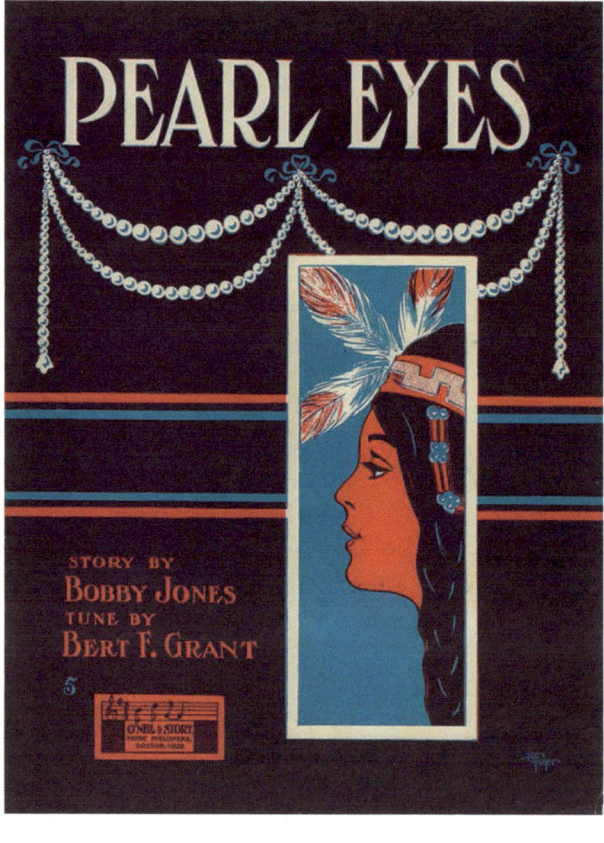

Pawnee Dear (illust Vance) – Terry Sherman 1913 [Tinari collection]

Pawnee Queen (illust Miller) – Grace Heller 1911 [Courtesy Sandy Marrone]

Pearl Eyes (illust Fisher) – Bobby Jones and Bert F. Grant 1911 [Tinari collection]

§

*Paxinosa – Ella Disbrow Jones 1906

A musical composition about Chief Paxinosa was published in 1897 (see Chapter 1).

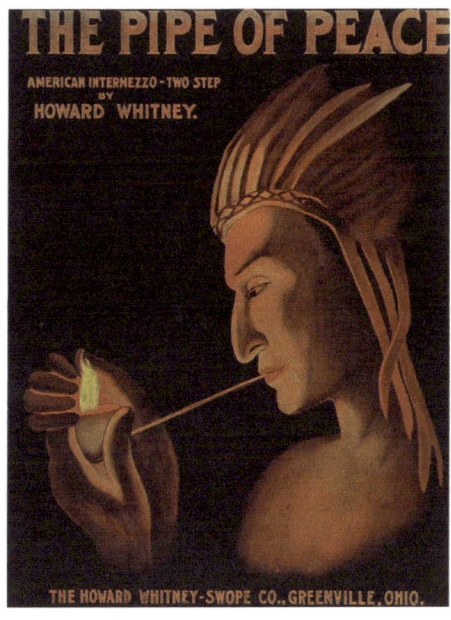

Pipe of Peace, The (illust Pfeiffer) – Howard Whitney 1906 [Tinari collection]

Pliney Come Out in the Moonlight (illust Starmer) – Bob Cole and J. Rosamond Johnson 1914 [Tinari collection]

The insert photos show the composers. The song is from *The Red Moon* musical production, written in 1909 and listed later in this chapter.

Powhatan's Daughter March – John Philip Sousa 1906 [Courtesy the Lester S. Levy Collection of Sheet Music, Sheridan Libraries, Johns Hopkins University]

The inset photo appears to be Sousa but is unattributed.

§

*Prairie Echoes – Benjamin Richmond 1910

§

*Prairie Rose – Al Dubin and Morris Siltmitzer 1909

This was prolific composer Dubin's first published song.

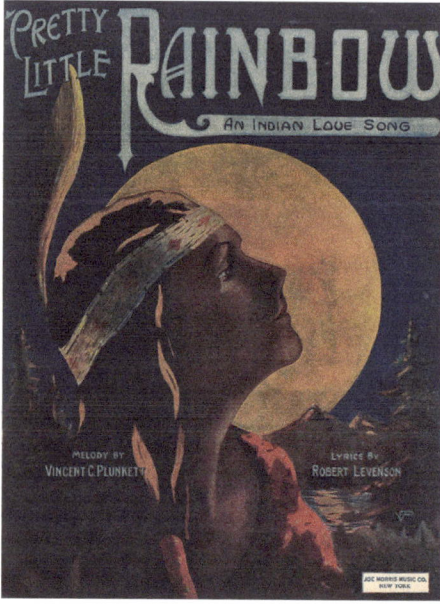

Pretty Little Maid of Cherokee (illust Starmer) – W. R. Williams 1909 [Tinari collection]

The inset photo displays Marie Roslyn in feathered headdress. Another issue features Will G. Frey and Sue Marshall dressed in American Indian garb in the inset photo. We have seen yet another variation, in grey tone instead of red, showing singing performer John Baxter in the inset photo.

Pretty Little Rainbow (An Indian Love Song) (illust Plunkett) – Vincent C. Plunkett and Robert Levenson 1919 [Tinari collection]

Published by Joe Morris Music, NY, in 1911. Revised and republished in 1919. (Pisani, A Chronological Listing of Musical Works on American Indian Subjects)

Pretty Little Rainbow (pub D. W. Cooper Music Co.) (illust Plunkett) – Vincent C. Plunkett and Robert Levenson 1919 [Tinari collection]

It appears that the Cooper Company acquired the copyright and re-issued the song sheet with this much plainer version of the original cover illustration.

§

*Queen of the Cherokees – Harry S. Joseph 1909

The cover depicts a head-and-shoulders view of an American Indian woman with long flowing hair.

§

*Queen of the Everglades – C. D. Paxton 1912

Depicted is a meeting of two American Indian women in their respective canoes.

§

*Rainbow (An Indian Intermezzo) – Percy Wenrich 1908

The viewer is left to decipher the message intended by the illustrator of this image in which the bust of an American Indian floats in the clouds below a rainbow.

§

*Rain-Flower – Leo Robin and Massard Kur Zhene 1930 ST

The cover image is identical to Song of the Waters, shown later in this chapter.

Rainbow (illust De Takacs) – Alfred Bryan and Percy Wenrich 1908 [Tinari collection]

"Despite the lyrics suggesting a setting under a palm tree, the sheet music covers for both the intermezzo and the song depict a forest locale." (Amundson, p. 127) The song was very popular and was recorded by several vocalists.

§

*Rally 'Round the Safety Habit (see Get the Safety Habit)

Ramona (self-pub) – Lee Johnson 1903 [Tinari collection]

The photo is of an American Indian woman. This composition was written for the musical *Roly-Poly*. (Klamkin, p. 143) The play was preceded by Helen Hunt Jackson's romantic novel of the same title in 1884 (Berkhofer, p. 106), and a stage play of the same name by Ina Dillaye in 1887.

Ramona (Intermezzo) – Lee Johnson 1916 [Courtesy Frances G. Spencer Collection of American Popular Sheet Music. Arts and Special Collections Research Center, Baylor University, Waco, Texas]

*Ramona's Dream – Florence C. Seward Fisher 1915

The illustration in the center of the cover depicts an American Indian woman holding a hunting bow. The song title is placed in a banner across the top with hand-crafted Indian jewelry-like decorations hanging on both sides of the center illustration. The decorations include the well-known Nazi-like symbol.

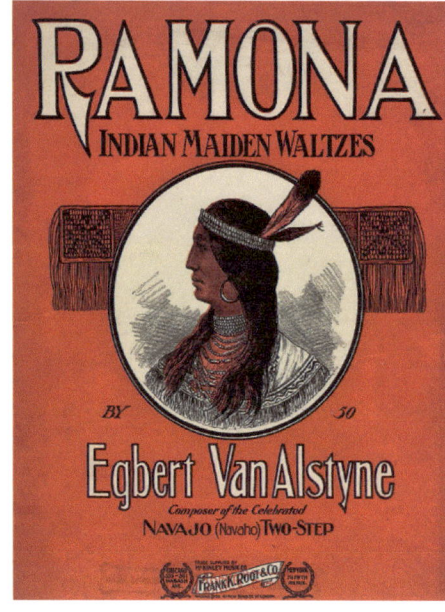

Ramona – Indian Maiden Waltzes – Egbert VanAlstyne 1904 [Tinari collection]

§

*Ramona – Fred Gensler 1904

Real, Live, Regular Town, A (The Official Cadillaqua Song) (illust Clarke) – Earle C. Jones and Charles N. Daniels 1912 [Tinari collection]

Unlike for many of his other songs, Daniels used his real name rather than Neil Moret.

Red Cloud (An Indian Love Affair) (illust Bryant) – W. A. Lang and A. Fred Phillips 1904 [Tinari collection]

§

*Red Deer – Otto Porter Ikeler 1911

§

*Red Feather – Frederick W. Hager and C. M. Denison 1916

Red Feather (illust Jewell) – Stanley Church 1924 ST [Tinari collection]

"Second Prize First Week Popular Group, The Chicago Daily News Music Contest." As noted in the description of the song Mulberry Moon earlier in this chapter, Red Feather was an American Indian woman. This sheet's illustration features an American Indian man whose headdress includes red-tipped feathers.

Red Fern (illust Fullam) Eddie Eckels and Leroy Stover 1909 [Tinari collection]

The inset photo is Charles Ledegar as sung with His Nine Red Path Napanees. The music title page indicates that Stover alone did both the words and music.

Red-Man (Indian Reverie) – Henry Longboat 1914 [Tinari collection]

The illustration of a male rider on his horse looks more Arabian, with palm trees in the background. The original was published in 1909; this is a revised edition.

*Red Man, The – John Philip Sousa 1910

This song is Part 1 of the composer's *Dwellers of the Western World* suite. Pisani reports that this is the first movement of a three-movement suite, the others titled *The White Man* and *The Black Man*. Band and orchestra arrangements were published in 1911 and 1916, respectively. (Pisani, A Chronological Listing of Musical Works on American Indian Subjects)

142

Red Moon (inset photo: Those Three Boys) – Eddie Dustin and Charles Humfeld 1908 [Tinari collection]

The same cover illustration is found on the Humfeld instrumental song sheet.

§

*The Red Moon (illust American Indian couple by Starmer) (inset photo: composers) – Bob Cole and J. Rosamond Johnson 1908

The Beineke Club of Yale University has a photo of "Rosamond Johnson in Iroquois attire upon being made a sub chief of the Iroquois tribe in 1920 to honor his respectful portrayal of Native Americans in *The Red Moon*. Chief Clear Sky of Quebec, Canada named Johnson 'Io no kwen ta ra o tsi to,' or 'Red Star.'" (*The Songs of Cole and Johnson Brothers*, p. 10) Of the ten songs from the show that are listed on the cover, two deal with American Indian themes: The Red Shawl and Bleeding Moon. Pisani lists as an Indian song, The Big Red Shawl. (Pisani, A Chronological Listing of Musical Works on American Indian Subjects)

§

*"The Red Moon" – Bob Cole and J. Rosamond Johnson 1909

The inset photo is of the composers. The illustration of an American Indian couple is different than the 1908 issue. Of the six show songs listed on this cover, none deal with American Indian themes.

§

*Red Skin, The – Frank W. McKee 1917

p. 97) The song was among the first to be promoted by means of projected slides accompanied by a performance of the piece. For "the exploitation of" this song, "eleven hundred sets of colored slides were used." (Goldberg, p. 129)

There was a real Princess Red Wing who worked professionally in the movie industry. Deloria reports that she worked with James Young Deer "to make the critical 1912 films *The Prospector and the Indian*, *The Squawman's Revenge*, and *Red Eagle the Lawyer*." Redwing's career was heating up, and she starred, in those years, in *Little Dove's Romance* (1911), *A Redskin's Appeal* (1912), *The Unwilling Bride* (1912), *The Penalty Paid* (1912), and quite likely several others.... (p. 228)

§

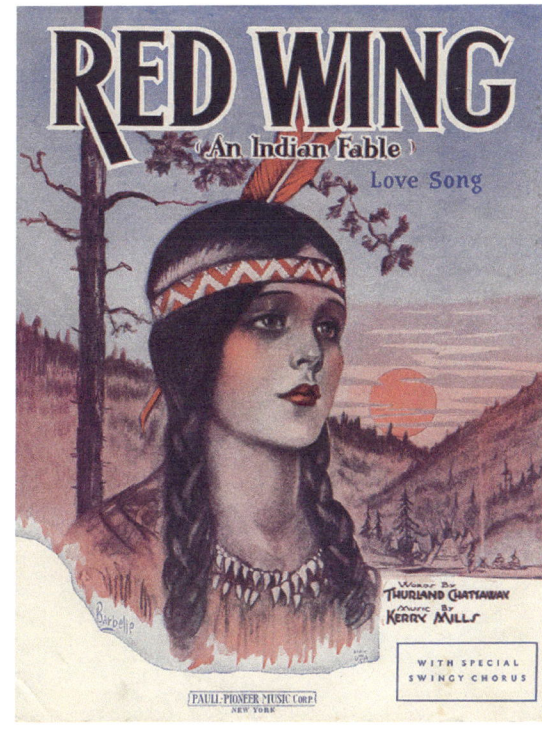

Red Wing (An Indian Intermezzo) (illust Hirt: American Indian woman facing left) Kerry Mills 1907 [Tinari collection]

*Redwing (illust Artemio) - Kerry Mills 1907 [displayed in Chapter 5]

Red Wing (An Indian Fable) (illust Barbelle: American Indian woman facing right) – Kerry Mills and Thurland Chattaway 1907 ST [Tinari collection]

The cover image is another Hirt illustration that has more color and 'movement' than most. Deloria writes that this suggestive cover "evoked the romance attached to the figure of the Indian princess–fusing familiar cultural expectations to the music inside." (p. 189) "By far the most popular Indian love song ever, the melody ... actually got its start almost six decades earlier as 'The Happy Farmer Returning from His Work' in composer Robert Schumann's *Album for the Young*." (Amundson,

The song was issued in 1939 in standard size. "The best loved Indian song of all time is, I believe, 'Red Wing.' Its first publication date was 1907; the composers were Kerry Mills and Thurland Chattaway. A resurgence of popularity in 1932 was responsible for its reissue at that time. This could be one of the first examples of a Tin Pan Alley era song revival." (Westin, p. 54)

Redskin (from *Redskin* film) – Harry D. Kerr and John S. Zamecnik 1929 (see note under Indian Dawn) ST [Tinari collection]

Redskin (from *Redskin* film; photo: Richard Dix and co-star) [Eng.] – Harry D. Kerr and John S. Zamecnik 1929 ST [Tinari collection]

"The brilliantly colored cover ... shows Richard Dix done up as a Native American in this movie about a Navajo who is caught between the prejudices of the white man and the American Indian. This was one of Paramount's last basically silent movies, but it had some sound and music effects added. Mr. Dix was later honored with an Academy Award nomination for best actor in the prestigious movie production *Cimarron*, but lost out to Lionel Barrymore." (Short, *From Footlights to "The Flickers,"* p. 130)

Regarding Hollywood's early cinematic treatment of American Indians, Deloria says "As silents became talkies in the early 1930s, music remained central to films, aural cues to the impending conflicts to be found on western ridges silhouetted with saddled warriors. Such westerns as *In Old Arizona* (Fox, 1929; the first sound western), *The Big Trail* (Fox, 1930), *Cimarrom* (RKO, 1931), and the Eddie Cantor spoof *Whoopie!* (United Artists, 1930) all had Indian-music soundtracks warning viewers that Indians were 'up there in them hills,' plotting attacks or preparing to fall in love with whites." (pp. 221-2)

Reed Bird (The Indian's Bride) (illust Hirt) – Dave Reed Jr. 1908 [Tinari collection]

Reed, who was the son of Dave Reed, a pioneer minstrel singer, composed many songs including several Indian songs: My Kickapoo Queen, My Chippewa, and Maid of the Midnight Moon. (Amundson, p. 91)

Reindeer (Intermezzo Two-Step) (illust Henrich) – Robert P. Skilling 1906 [Tinari collection]

The Indian-Eskimo Song version has lyrics by James O'Dea (1871–1914).

Round Up, The (illust Staubach) – J. C. Halls 1911 [Tinari collection]

On the right, the full face of an American Indian chief is depicted, loosely surrounded by lariat rope. To the left are depicted two cowboys on horseback.

Rowena (A Characteristic Indian Love Song) (inset photo: Gay Errol) –James Tim Brymn 1904 [Courtesy Frances G. Spencer Collection of American Popular Sheet Music. Arts and Special Collections Research Center, Baylor University, Waco, Texas]

Sacajawea Lullaby – Ziporah Harris 1903 [Courtesy Sandy Marrone]

The title on the inside music page is given the possessive Sacajawea's Lullaby.

Sagamore (illust Pfeiffer) – Eva Williams and Joe Maxwell 1920 [Tinari collection]

The cover illustration depicts a pretty girl with an American Indian in the background.

Sagawana (Conservatory Ed.) – Katherine Gray 1905 [Tinari collection]

Subtitled: A Wigwam Episode, but there are no lyrics.

 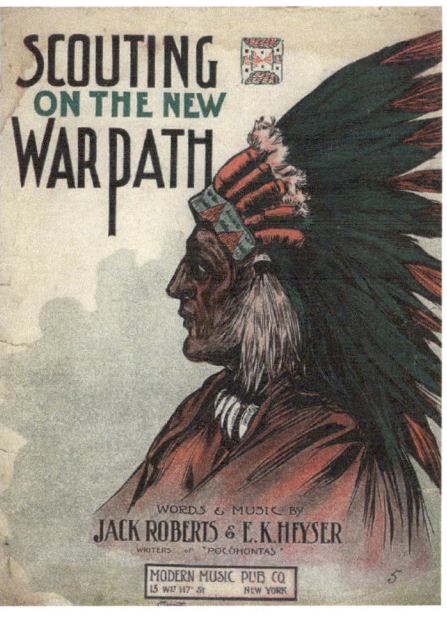  

Samos (illust Fisher) – Carlotta Williamson 1904 [Courtesy Sandy Marrone]

§

*Screeching Eagle – Bernhard Stern and Dan Capece 1906

Scouting on the New Warpath (illust Etherington) – Jack Roberts and E. K. Heyser 1907 [Tinari collection]

"This song was written for the Jamestown Terventennial exposition to celebrate the founding at Jamestown, Virginia, of the first permanent English-speaking settlement in America. Most of the states of the union as well as the federal government and many foreign nations took part in the festivities." (Short, *Covers of Gold*, p. 135) The lyrics tell of the Indian savages wielding their axes on the warpath.

Seattle – Walter Augustyne 1909 [Courtesy Frances G. Spencer Collection of American Popular Sheet Music. Arts and Special Collections Research Center, Baylor University, Waco, Texas]

In this love song, Pocahontas says goodbye to her Chief Seattle as he departs for battle.

Seenah (Indian Love Call) – Wm. J. Schmidt 1928 ST [Tinari collection]

The cover depicts an outdoor scene of an Indian chief standing on a rocky ledge next to a seated woman playing the harp.

Seminola (inset photo: Billy Burton and His Orch.) (An Indian Love Song) – Robert King and Harry Warren 1925 ST [Tinari collection]

This song sheet, as presented by Crew (Florida Sheet Music) was issued at least twenty-one times, each featuring a different orchestra. (pp. 125-26)

Seminole (illust Buck) – Egbert Van Alstyne 1904 [Tinari collection]

"Again a little Indian girl was introduced to remind American pianists of the Seminole tribe, her great nation. Egbert Van Alstyne, a prolific composer who had a short while previously scored a hit with his 'Navajo,' in 1904 brought out a bright march and two-step called 'Seminole.' On the title page is the picture of a stunning Indian girl, drawn by Gene Buck, a gifted composer himself." (Levy, *Give Me Yesterday*, p. 175)

Seminole (illust Starmer) – Harry Williams and Egbert Van Alstyne 1904 [Tinari collection]

The inset photo is of Emma Carus. Other covers were published with an inset photo of Blanche Ring, Edna Hopper, Louise Henry, and other popular performers. Crew (Florida Sheet Music) displays fourteen versions.

§

*She-Boy-Gan – Moe Goldberg and Robert Dailey 1918

The cover depicts the busts of an American Indian man and woman seemingly floating in the rising smoke of a campfire.

§

*Shining Star – Jack Drislane and Theodore F. Morse 1908

§

*Silent Enemy, The (see Song of the Waters)

Shanewis (*The Robin Woman*; American opera produced at the Metropolitan Opera House): Spring Song of the Robin Woman – Nelle Richmond Eberhart and Charles Wakefield Cadman 1918 ST [Tinari collection]

The inset photo is of Tsianina. Other songs include Her Shadow, listed previously, and Amy's Song. "Cadman used perhaps twenty idealized themes in *Shanewis*, ranging from the Osage powwow song, to existing concert pieces, to newly worked Indian music." (Deloria, p. 186)

Shawondasee Waltz (The South Wind) – Harold A. Thompson 1910 [Courtesy Mark Clardy]

Silver Bell – Edward Madden and Percy Wenrich 1910 [Tinari collection]

The cover illustration for this song and the intermezzo version (by Wenrich) is the same, presenting a proud chieftain warrior with his faithful bride. The song's "sheet music reads like the other Indian love songs of this period. There are few references to specific Indian items except for a 'lonely little Indian maid' and 'chieftain longing to woo' while 'paddling his tiny canoe.'" (Amundson, p. 153)

Silver Cloud (Intermezzo) – H. Sylvester Krouse 1910 [Courtesy Frances G. Spencer Collection of American Popular Sheet Music. Arts and Special Collections Research Center, Baylor University, Waco, Texas]

§

*Silver Heels [see Silverheels]

Silver Star (Intermezzo) (illust Chilberg) – Charles L. Johnson 1910 [Courtesy Sandy Marrone]

Silver Star (Song) (illust Chilberg) – Charles L. Johnson and William R. Clay 1911 [Courtesy Sandy Marrone]

The "choice of title, lyrics, and recording artists looks like a clear attempt to capitalize on the popularity of the earlier song [Silver Bell]." (Amundson, p 160)

Silver Star (illust Starmer) – Roy C. Phillips 1913 [Tinari collection]

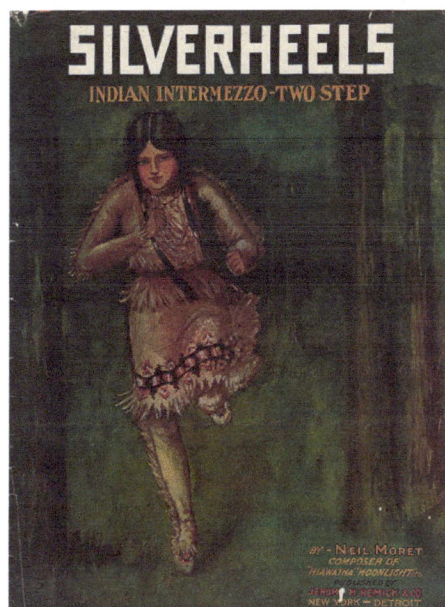

Silver Water – Lucien Denni and Gwynne Woolworth 1909 [Courtesy Sandy Marrone]

Silver Water (illust Barbelle) – George Kershaw and Harry Von Tilzer 1920 ST [Tinari collection]

Silverheels (illust Bertha Young) – Neil Moret 1905 [Tinari collection]

The inside music page gives the title as Silver Heels. The cover illustration depicts a dancing American Indian woman. The "love story between an 'Indian brave' and the 'sweetest and neatest little girl' clearly has overtones of assimilation and domesticity. ... [but] the song's use of 'fake Indian speech' in lines such as 'heap much kissing' suggests a derogatory attitude toward Native Americans rather than Moret's purported admiration." (Amundson, pp. 75-76)

Silverheels (illust Young) – Neil Moret and James O'Dea 1905 [Tinari collection]

The inside music page gives the title as Silver Heels. The cover depicts the face of an American Indian woman.

Since Arrah Wanna Married Barney Carney (illust E.P.C.) (inset photo: Pierce and Roslyn) – Jack Drislane and Theodore Morse 1907 [Tinari collection]

Little is known about the illustrator E.P.C. who created the colorful cover artwork for this and other songs by publisher F. B. Haviland. (Amundson, p. 101) This is one of those rare sequel songs, continuing the saga of marriage between an Irishman and an American Indian woman. The back cover promotes the song, ArrahWanna, published in the previous year.

Singing Bird (illust Myers) (Indian Intermezzo) – Edward Edwards 1909 [Courtesy Sandy Marrone]

§

*Sioux Song – Harry Williams and Egbert Van Alstyne 1905

The illustration is yet another of an American Indian couple traveling in their canoe. The instrumental by Van Alstyne was published in the same year.

Singing Bird (illust Myers) (Indian Song) – Arthur Longbrake and Edward Edwards 1909 [Tinari collection]

§

*Singing Water – C. K. Denison and Anna G. Berg 1911

Sitka – Harry W. Jones 1909 [Tinari collection]

The music title page states, "A Northern Romance" and the song lyrics refer to the Yukon.

 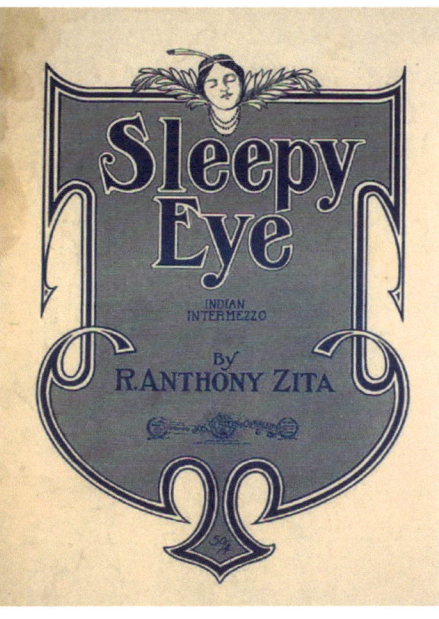 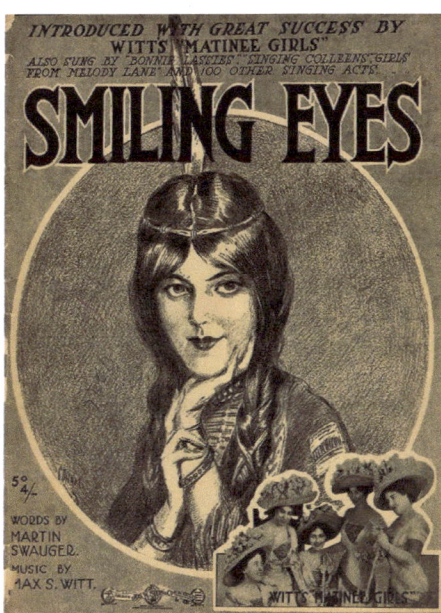 

Skowhegan (Indian Waltz Song) – Walter R. Gage (self-pub) 1925 [Tinari collection]

The pictured copy has a sticker at bottom indicating that the song sheet is a reprint as part of the Skowhegan [Maine] Sesquicentennial. We are not aware of the original issuance of the song.

Sleepy Eye (Indian Intermezzo) – R. Anthony Zita 1908 [Courtesy the Lester S. Levy Collection of Sheet Music, Sheridan Libraries, Johns Hopkins University]

§

*Sleepy Eye (litho) – Mark Hawkins and Hal Paris 1909

Smiling Eyes (illust Caagat or Chagat, inset photo: Witt's "Matinee Girls") – Max S. Witt and Martin Swauger 1909 [Courtesy Sandy Marrone]

Smiling Star (illust Hirt) – Jack Drislane and Theodore Morse 1908 [Tinari collection]

Snow Bird (illust Wohlman Studios) – Robert Schafer, Bert. Brosseau and Louis H. Alfred 1920 ST [Tinari collection]

Snow Deer (illust Starmer) – Percy Wenrich and Jack Mahoney 1913 [Tinari collection]

Snow Deer is a Mohawk maiden who is urged by her cowboy lover to elope with him to his ranch before the tribe gets wind of the tryst.

Snowbird (Buck and Lowney Art Dept) – Theodore B. White and Clair Van Lynden 1916 [Tinari collection]

The music title page gives the title as Snow Bird.

Song of Mo-ha-ve (illust Elder) – Meyer Witepski and Clay Smith 1926 ST [Courtesy Sandy Marrone]

§

*Song Bird – Harry L. Alford 1909

This was also published as a vocal with words by Arthur Gillespie. (Pisani, A Chronological Listing of Musical Works on American Indian Subjects)

Song of the Waters (theme song of *The Silent Enemy* film) – Sam Coslow and Newell Chase 1930 ST [Tinari collection]

This may be the earliest song sheet of a "talkie" film focusing on American Indians. Another song sheet from this movie, Rain-Flower, uses the identical image.

Songs of Song-ah-tah.

This is the dark brown cover with colorful illustration that contains four songs, each listed in this chapter under their titles.

Sowania (March and Intermezzo) Milo Benedict 1907 [Tinari collection]

Inspiration for this instrumental piece appears to have come from the verse printed on the cover:

"Cried the fierce Kabibonokha,
Who is this that dares to brave me?
Dares to stay in my Dominion,
When the Wawa has departed,
When the Wild Goose has gone Southward."

 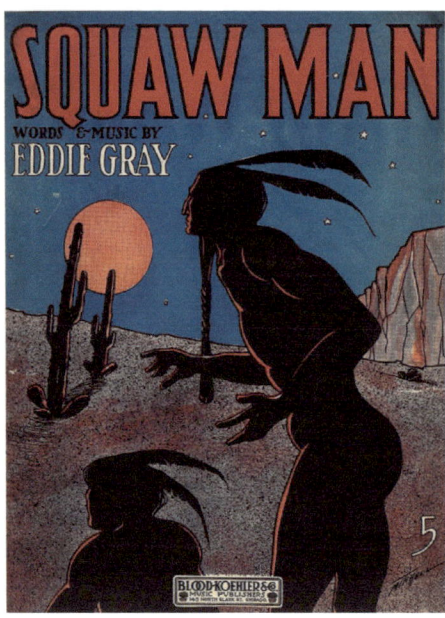 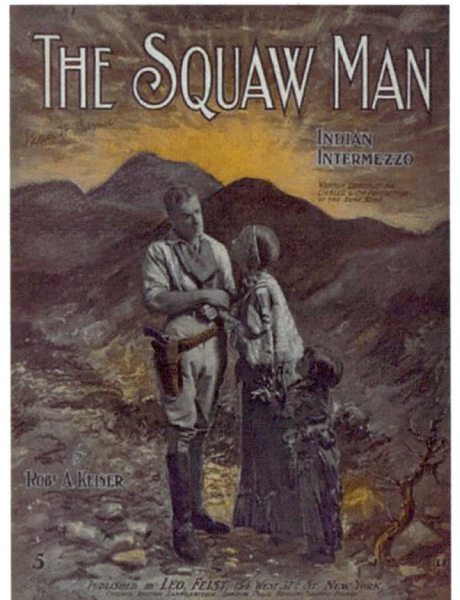

Sparkling Eyes (illust Starmer) – William L. Livernash 1911 [Tinari collection]

§

*Spring Song of the Robin Woman (see *Shanewis*)

Squaw Man (illust Mitchel R.) – Eddie Gray 1911 [Tinari collection]

Squaw Man, The (Indian Intermezzo) – Robert A. Keiser 1905 [Courtesy Frances G. Spencer Collection of American Popular Sheet Music. Arts and Special Collections Research Center, Baylor University, Waco, Texas]

The cover states: "Written especially for Liebler and Co.'s. production of the same name." The show was a Broadway Western/Drama Stage Play starring William Faversham. The cover depicts his Indian wife Nat-u-ritch and their son Little Hal. The marriage between a white man in his social position and an Indian woman played by Mabel Adrienne Morrison is deemed scandalous. Cecil B. DeMille's subsequent film *The Squaw Man* is a first and a last. The 1914 version is widely regarded as the first feature film made in Hollywood. DeMille made the final film under his MGM contract with a 1931 Talkie of the oft-told tale. DeMille lensed a second silent version in 1918 about a British outcast in the West, his American Indian bride and events that shatter their happiness. The films vary greatly. The first is packed with events—a horse race, a brawl with a Scotland Yarder, a shipboard fire, a night in New York—that foreshadow DeMille's ambitious narrative reach. The second focuses on the tender and ultimately heartbreaking familial relationship. Same story. Same filmmaker.

§

*Star and the Flower, The – Raymond Hubbell 1900

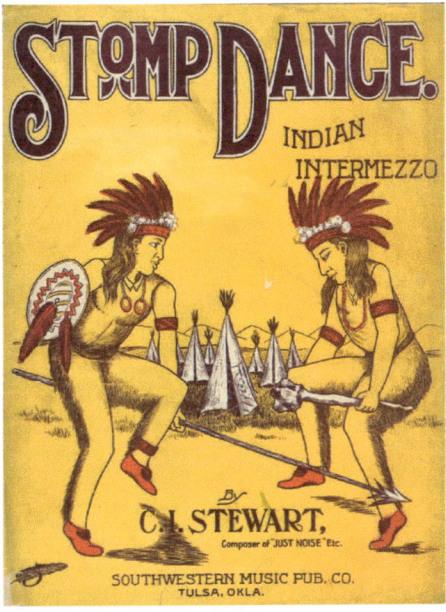

Starlight Sioux (An Indian Idyll) – Ernie Erdman and Aubrey Stauffer 1910 [Courtesy Sandy Marrone]

The composition is without words and, thus, without credit to lyricist Stauffer.

§

*Starlight Sioux – Ernie Erdman (1879–1946) 1910

Stomp Dance – C. I. Stewart 1907 [Courtesy Sandy Marrone]

Storm Cloud – M. M. Redding, G. M. Koockogey and Charles A. Roth 1909 [Tinari collection]

Strongheart (Intermezzo-Two-Step for piano) – Will E. Dulmage 1906 [University of Maine Parlor Salon Sheet Music Collection, Score 73, Digital Commons]

Actor Robert Edeson is featured on the cover. His photo is flanked by Indian-designed banners hanging from a peace pipe.

Sun Bird (An Indian Intermezzo) (illust Hirt) – Kerry Mills 1908 [Tinari collection]

One of the most artistic of the Indian maiden covers. "Hirt's impressive, colorful paintings of beautiful women are represented on the cover …." (Wenzel and Binkowski, *I Hear America Singing*, p. 135) The song issue by Mills and lyricist Thurland Chattaway uses the same cover illustration.

Sun Dance, The (illust Havelka) – Leo Friedman and George Totten Smith 1903 [Courtesy Sandy Marrone]

Issued a couple of years after the original instrumental by Friedman, this song sheet has a much more dramatic and colorful illustration. On the inside music page, the composers are listed as Friedman and Hugh Willing. Deloria states that several years later, in 1913, Indian writer and activist Zitkala-Sa collaborated with William Hanson on the Indian opera *The Sun Dance*. (p. 228)

Sunbeam – W. C. Powell 1909 [Tinari collection]

§

*Sun Dance, The (Indian Characteristic) – Leo Friedman 1901

Overall, the illustration is quite indistinct, but does show Indian figures dancing in the distance.

Sunlight (Song) – Olive L. Frields and Harry L. Newman 1909 [Tinari collection]

The photo inset is of Newman. The music title page has the subtitle "An Indian Serenade." For Newman's "Indian Intermezzo," the cover image and the inset photo are the same as that of the Song.

Sunray (A New Indian Intermezzo) – Al. Dubin and Charles P. Shisler 1909 [Tinari collection]

Sunset Dreams (Waltz) – James W. Casey 1918 [Tinari collection]

Sunset Song, one of Traditional Songs of the Zuni Indians – transcribed and harmonized by Carlos Troyer 1913 [Courtesy Sandy Marrone]

Each of sixteen songs was printed individually and includes a lengthy description of the song and the related dance ceremony.

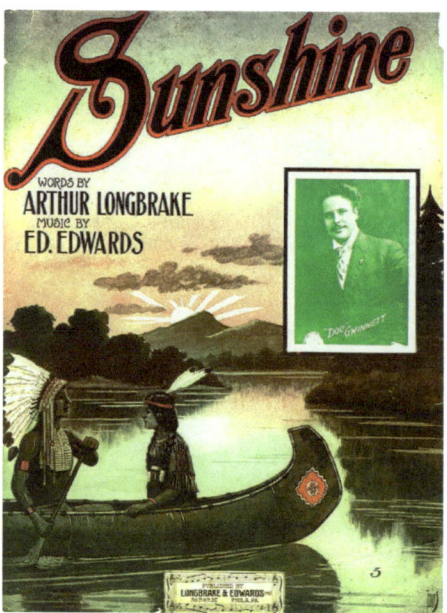

Sunset Trail, The – Charles Wakefield Cadman 1925 [The International Music Score Library Project (IMSLP) / Petrucci Music Library]

"An operatic cantata depicting the struggles of the American Indians against the edict of the United States Government restricting them to prescribed reservations." Poetic settings of Gilbert Moyle consisting of 68 pages. Although not a single song sheet, which is the focus of this book, the cover is interesting enough to include here, particularly because of the extensive work by Cadman in attempting to create Indian-based and Indian-inspired music for popular consumption. As listed by Pisani: "First performed San Diego. Expanded from a series of pieces for mixed choir under the same title. (1920)" (Pisani, A Chronological Listing of Musical Works on American Indian Subjects)

Sunshine (illust Jenkins) – Arthur Longbrake and Edward Edwards 1911 [Tinari collection]

The inset photo presents performer 'Doc' Gwinnett. The author also owns a version in which Harold Hill is featured. In this love song, the American Indian man woos his female companion while rowing his canoe.

Sure Fire Rag – Henry E. Lodge 1910 [Tinari collection]

"Almost nothing is known of Lodge, one of the most talented and prodigious composers in the idiom [of ragtime]." (Tichenor, p. ix)

*Swaying Willow (An Indian Love Song) (illust Hauman) – Bernard Hamblen 1928

Depicted are tepees on a river shoreline with the front of a canoe in the foreground as it passes a weeping willow tree.

Sweet Little Caraboo (illust Starmer) – Edward Laska and Thomas Kelly 1904 [courtesy Mark Clardy]

Talking to the Moon (inset photo: Shwas-Nee-Sehee-Noo, The Indian Bard) – George Little and Billy Baskette 1926 ST [Courtesy Sandy Marrone]

Tepee for Two, A – W. N. LaMance (self-pub) 1937 ST [Tinari collection]

Tepee Just for Two, A (Indian Love Song) – Laura Mason Crisp 1927 ST [Tinari collection]

Printed in parentheses after the composer's name is Starlight who is very likely the woman featured in the inset photograph. The cover states: Dedicated to the Girls Scouts and Boy Scouts of America and the Camp Fire Girls of America.

That Indian Rag (contains several songs in folio) – Marvin Lee and Donald Bestor (1889–1970) 1911 [Tinari collection]

That Kickapoo Indian Man (illust Starmer) – Robert J. Adams and James O'Dea 1904 [Courtesy Sandy Marrone]

The title is also listed as How I Love That Man: That Kickapoo Indian Man. The cover features an Indian woman looking at a departing man who is not an American Indian but African American in Native garb and a top hat. We learn from the lyrics that the man is from a medicine show in which he poses as an American Indian. The inset photo is of Artie Hall, a performer in blackface. In the mid- to late-1800s, "the few White men who repeatedly put on full Indian costumes, including war-paint and feathers, were eastern actors treading the boards in one 'Indian' melodrama after another." (Parry, p. 159) We surmise that this illustration published in 1904 was a very late comer to that tradition. The same song and cover were issued with at least one other performer, Madge Fox.

§

*That Tom Tom Tag (illust Cooney) – Fred C. Noble and John L. Golden 1915

That Tomahawk Rag (illust Bodine) (inset photo: Downing) – Earl Downing and Allen Spurr 1912 [Tinari collection]

There's a Land Beyond the Rainbow (Where There's Room for You and Me) (illust Pfeiffer) –Gilbert C. Tennant 1916 [Tinari collection]

The cover illustration exhibits the classic Indian romanticism of the era, depicting an American Indian couple in a canoe with a glowing sun in the distant rear.

Thunder Cloud (Indian Characteristic March) – G. Leroy Lowell 1904 [Tinari collection]

Tip-Tip-Tippy Canoe – Ballard Macdonald and James F. Hanley 1920

The cover is a highly stylized illustration of an American Indian couple in a canoe against the backdrop of a large sun.

  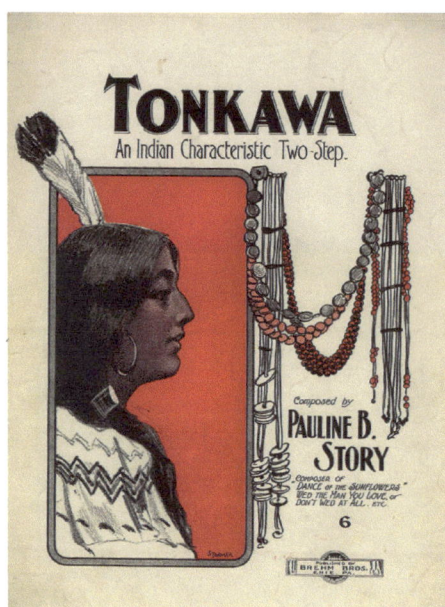 

Tishomingo (Indian Love Song) (illust Herse) – Philip Henry Hale 1920 ST [Courtesy Sandy Marrone]

There was a Chief Tishomingo of the Chickasaw Indians of the South in the late eighteenth century. Counties, parks, and institutions also bear the Tishomingo name.

Tonawanda (illust Cornwell) (self-pub) – A. F. Marzian 1913 [Tinari collection]

Tonkawa (illust Starmer) – Pauline B. Story 1903 [Tinari collection]

Topeka (Two-Step Intermezzo) (illust Henrich) – Henry W. Jones 1907 [Tinari collection]

The artistic cover is set in the muted colors of autumn, featuring an American Indian gazing in thought. Henrich did several other Indian song sheet covers displayed in this book.

Topeka (song) (illust De Takacs) – James O'Dea and Henry W. Jones 1908 [Tinari collection]

"Topeka is a Cherokee girl who is courted by a copper colored brave who hoped to make her his own, but he 'fell to the might of the paleface in the fight.' Now, often in the misty shadows the maiden hears the sad ghost dance refrain of 'My own Topeka, my sunflow'r bride.'" (Short, *Covers of Gold*, p. 136) Lyricist O'Dea also wrote the words to Hiawatha, Silver Heels, and Iola.

Trailing the Trail (A Promenade March) – George L. Spaulding 1905 [Tinari collection]

In this cover illustration, the chief's war bonnet and gun lead us to conclude that the riders are heading toward a fight. In Coen's book we read of a similar artistic line in a Frederick Remington painting, The Trail of the Shod Horse (1907): "In this painting, a band of Indians has come across the tracks of a lone horseman. ... The Indians know he is a white man, for only white men's horses were shod." (p. 58)

Uncle Sam's Chief – Harry E. Stupp 1904 [Courtesy Sandy Marrone]

Underneath the Harvest Moon – William J. Robertson 1929 ST [Tinari collection]

  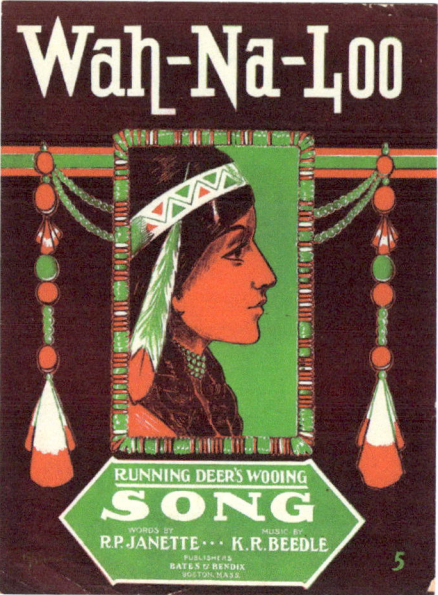 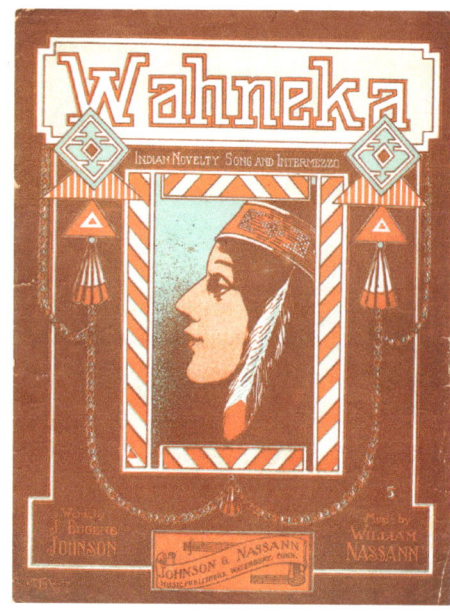

Up on the Top of the Hill (illust Elder) – Susie Kerin and George Roberts 1927 ST [Tinari collection]

Valley Flower (illust De Takacs) – Kerry Mills 1910 [Tinari collection]

Wah-Na-Loo (illust Fisher) – K. R. Beedle and R. P. Janette 1908 [Courtesy Sandy Marrone]

Wahneka (illust Fisher) "Indian Novelty Song and Intermezzo." – William Nassann and J. Eugene Johnson (self-pub) 1912 [Courtesy Sandy Marrone]

  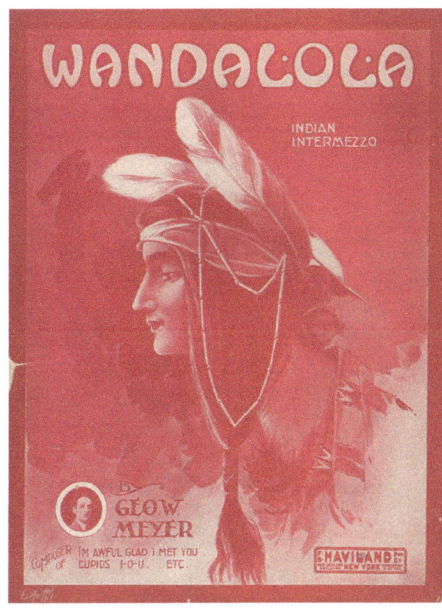 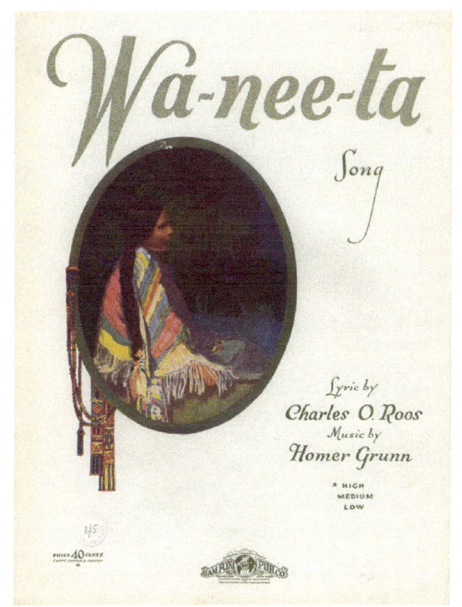

Wait No More for Me – the third in Songs of Song-ah-tah, Four American Indian Songs – music by Homer Grunn, poems by Charles O. Roos 1923 ST [Tinari collection]

The song cover displays a pen and ink drawing of an Indian with bow and arrow aimed at a bear in the distance.

Walla Ki-Ki (Jungle Two Step) – Josephine Baker 1911 [Courtesy John Paul Biersach]

§

*Wan-a-tea (illust Starmer) – Richard K. Moritz 1906

§

*Wanda Waltzes – E. Roy Smith (self-pub) c. 1900

Wandalola (illust Pfeiffer) – George W. Meyer 1910 [Tinari collection]

Wa-nee-ta – Charles O. Roos and Homer Grunn 1930 ST [Tinari collection]

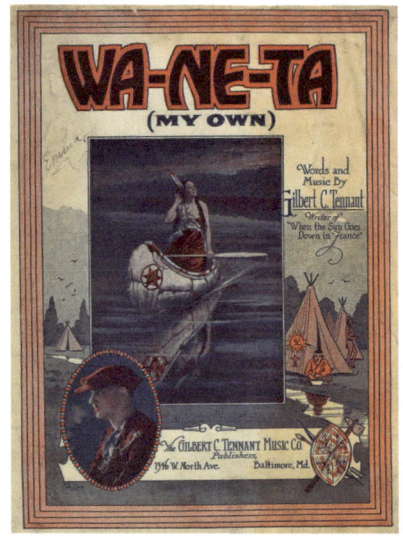

Wa-Ne-Ta (My Own) (inset photo: composer) – Gilbert C. Tennant 1920 ST [Courtesy Sandy Marrone]

Wanita (illust Beck) – Lora Lee 1903 [Tinari collection]

Wa-Pa-Tee-Tah (Yankee Man) – Letha Layton Willet and Jean Walz 1921 ST [Tinari collection]

168

Waters of Muscle Shoals, The or The Indian Chieftain's Lament – W. R. McKerrall and Albert E. Orrendorf 1927 ST [Courtesy Sandy Marrone]

A lamentation by a Cherokee native of his lost environment due to the construction of Alabama's Wilson Dam, a photo of which is given on the back cover.

Waters of the Perkiomen (illust Starmer) – Al Dubin and F. Henri Klickmann 1925 ST [Tinari collection]

The song was one among several featured in On With the Show, a 1925 British production, though that song sheet did not feature any American Indian images. None of its other songs, popular tunes of the day, are Indian-related. The 1929 Hollywood color movie having the same title did not include the song.

Waupanseh (illust Thompson) – Clarence M. Chapel 1903 [Courtesy Sandy Marrone]

§

*Wenona (An Indian Intermezzo) (illust Buck) - Percy Wenrich 1903

Another of the many "Indian Intermezzos," the center illustration depicts an American Indian woman in a canoe. The name Wenona was used for past musical compositions including a piece published in 1855 (see the listing under Prairie Flower in Chapter 1). Also, see the two issues of Winona, listed later in this chapter.

Wenonah (An Indian Intermezzo) (illust Buck) – Percy Wenrich 1903 [Tinari collection]

This version features a photo of Winona Winters, to whom the song is dedicated. The music title page spells the piece Wenona, revealing that it is the same tune as the piece titled Wenona. This issue places Winters' photo over the original illustration.

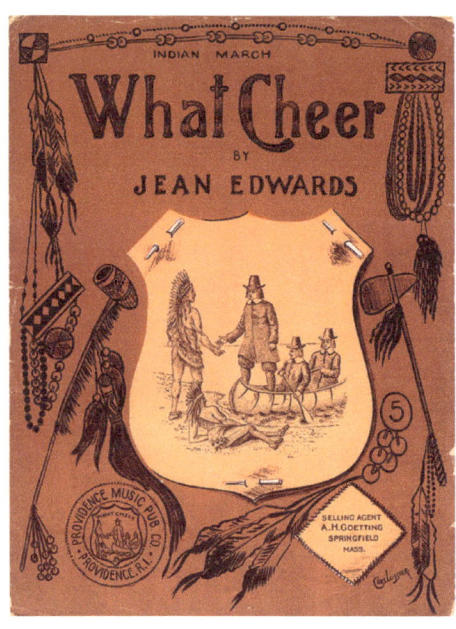  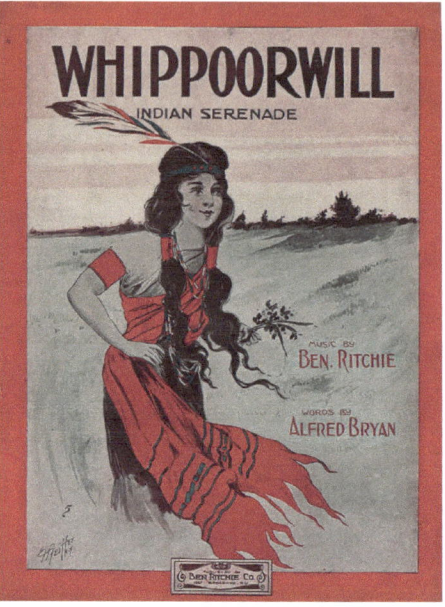 

What Cheer (illust Lussier) – Jean Edwards 1904 [Tinari collection]

§

*Where the Papoose Swings (see My Love, My Lark)

While the Tom-Tom Plays (illust Starmer) – C. P. McDonald and Walter Coleman Parker 1905 [Tinari collection]

Whippoorwill (Indian Serenade) (illust Pfeiffer) – Benjamin Ritchie and Alfred Bryan 1912 [Tinari collection]

Whippoorwill (Indian Song) – Hans Von Holstein and Richard W. Pascoe 1914 [Courtesy Sandy Marrone]

§

*Whistling Squaw, The – Robert Recker 1904

§

*White Bird (illust Pfeiffer) – Frederick W. Hager 1916

The cover presents a small illustration of an American Indian.

White Dove (illust Barbelle) – M. Kay Jerome and Jack Stern 1915 [Tinari collection]

White Feather (An Indian Croon) – Lyle Weaver Sparks 1911 [Courtesy Frances G. Spencer Collection of AmericanPopular Sheet Music. Arts and Special Collections Research Center, Baylor University, Waco, Texas]

The cover depicts an American Indian woman whose head band holds a single white feather. She is standing outside her tepee.

White Wings – James Dempsey and J. C. Schmid 1909 [Tinari collection]

Wigwam Courtship, A (self-pub) – Sadie Koninsky 1903 [Tinari collection]

Wigwam Dance (A Reservation Innovation) (illust Keller) – Leo Friedman 1903 [Tinari collection]

Wild Flower – George Martens and Mary Earl 1920 [Tinari collection]

This beautiful illustration is by the Hayes Litho Co., Buffalo, NY. The title page includes, in parentheses, the subtitle Tsianina.

Wildflower (illust Starmer) – E. Ray Goetz and Louis A. Hirsch 1908 [Tinari collection]

The instrumental issue has a red background; the vocal issue is tan.

Wild Rose (illust Young) – Katherine Donart and Harry S. Webster 1909 [Tinari collection]

§

*Winnebago – L. J. Vaughan and Phillip A. Laffey 1908

Wild Rose (newspaper suppl., *Inter Ocean*, Sunday Morning, March 10, 1912) – Katherine Donart and Harry S. Webster 1912 [Tinari collection]

Winona (illust Werner) (A Wigwam Wooing) – Isidor Heidenreich 1903 [Courtesy Sandy Marrone]

In the traditional Dakota language, Winona is not a personal name but a general term for a first-born female child. Winona or Wenonah, a Dakota Sioux, is said to have leaped to her death from a high precipice rather than marry a suitor she did not love. Winona's father is sometimes said to be Chief Wabasha (Wapasha) of a village identified as Keoxa, now known as Winona, Minnesota, or perhaps Chief Red Wing of what is now Red Wing, Minnesota. The story is very similar to the apocryphal legend of a young Cherokee woman of Noccalula Falls Park in Gadsden, Alabama, as well as events in James Fenimore Cooper's *The Last of the Mohicans*. (Wikipedia)

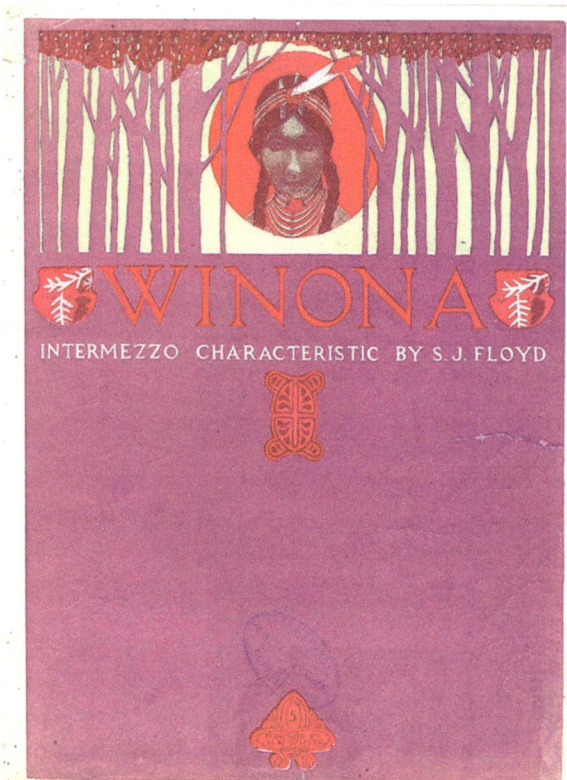

Winona (Intermezzo Characteristic) – S. J. Floyd 1903 [Tinari collection]

The top third of the cover image includes, at its center, a colorful head illustration of an American Indian woman within a stylized red moon, flanked by stylized tree trunks. The remainder of the artwork consists of the song title, accompanied by several American Indian symbols.

Winona (An Indian Love Song) (illust Pfeiffer) – James Stanley Royce and F. W. Vandersloot 1927 ST [Tinari collection]

Perhaps not coincidentally, an opera of the same title by Alberto Bimboni was produced in 1926.

Wooing of Sha-Wah-Wah, The (illust Stone) (self-pub) – William E. Dulmage 1903 [Courtesy Sandy Marrone]

Wyandotte (self-pub) – M. B. Mawhorter 1904 [Tinari collection]

Yahola (Indian Intermezzo) – Minnie Smith 1914

The woman in the photograph on the cover is presumably the composer.

Yellow Moccasin, The (March & Two-Step) – Clara Saile 1904 [Courtesy Joh Paul Biersach]

You are the One and Only (inset photo: Kummer) (sung by Sallie Fisher, photo, in Native American wear) – Clare Kummer 1913 [Tinari collection]

Yo-Kum-Kee (My Indian Maiden) (illust Stump) – Clyde Hager and Walter Goodwin 1916 [Tinari collection]

This cover illustration is unique in its use of Art Deco styling.

*Youlianna (My Indian Maid) – Russell Webb 1906

Young Warriors March, The – Julian Edwards 1917 ST [Tinari collection]

This was copyrighted by the B. F. Wood Music Co. in both the USA and England.

Zuni Lover's Wooing, or Blanket Song, one of Traditional Songs of the Zuni Indians–transcribed and harmonized by Carlos Troyer 1913 [Courtesy Sandy Marrone]

Each of the sixteen songs was printed individually and includes an extended description of the song and the related dance ceremony.

3
NOTABLE NAMES

Song sheets that are included in this part have on their covers either a photo of a known chief or princess, or an illustration of an historical American Indian.

At the End of the Sunset Trail (photo of Princess Fawn-Eyes and Co.) – Ralph Waldo Emerson and Ethwell "Eddie" Hanson 1924 ST [Tinari collection]

Black Hawk Waltz (Conservatory Edition) – Mary E. Walsh 1902 [Courtesy the Lester S. Levy Collection of Sheet Music, Sheridan Libraries, Johns Hopkins University]

Black Hawk Waltz (The Artist's Edition) – Mary E. Walsh 1907 [Tinari collection]

Black Hawk Waltz – Mary E. Walsh 1919 [Tinari collection]

Among the various published versions of the song, this colorful and appealing cover features a head-and-shoulders illustration of an American Indian man in full feather headgear.

Black Hawk Waltz – Mary E. Walsh 1919

This colorful cover presents a full-body illustration of an American Indian in a feathered head piece and holding a decorated staff. The background is a stylized white sun. Published by the same McKinley Music Company as the next listed sheet, this edition has "No. 110" printed in the lower left corner.

§

*Black Hawk Waltz (illust Barbelle) – Mary E. Walsh 1924

Black Hawk Waltz (illust Frew) (Edition De Luxe) – Mary E. Walsh c. 1924 [Tinari collection]

181

Black Hawk Waltz, The [UK] – Mary E. Walsh (erroneously listed as M. A. Walsh) 1930s [Tinari collection]

Black Hawk Waltzes (illust Frew) ('Beaux Arts Edition') – Mary E. Walsh 1926 ST [Tinari collection]

Copies of this song sheet were also issued in black instead of blue ink. All of the preceding Black Hawk Waltz song sheets are reissues of the original issued in 1877, described in Chapter 1.

Call of the First American – Laura S. Duvall and Chief He-Wan-Jee-Cha 1931 [Tinari collection]

   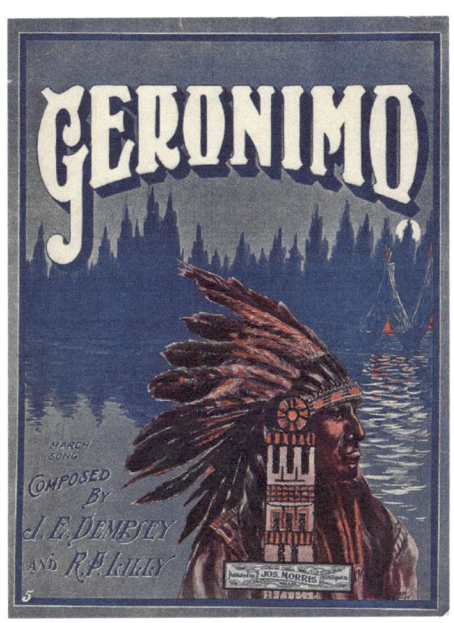

Chief Joseph of the Nez Perce Indians (educational piano piece) – Nell Wait Harvey 1951 ST [Courtesy Sandy Marrone]

First American, The (inset photo: Dedicated to Haske Naswood, Indian Baritone) – Merrill E. Seeber 1930 ST [Courtesy Sandy Marrone]

Forest Queen (illust De Takacs) – J. Brandon Walsh and Charley Straight 1913 [Tinari collection]

Cover states: "Sung with great success by Chief Caupolican" who is shown in the inset photo.

Geronimo (illust Gilliam) – J. E. Dempsey and R. P. Lilly 1905 [Tinari collection]

Born Heinmot Tooyalakekt in 1841, Chief Joseph later resisted the U.S. government's continual reduction in his native lands and was eventually captured. Having some command of English, he visited Washington, DC, for permission to return to his beloved Pacific Northwest. After years of negotiations and speechmaking, his efforts were successful in moving the Nez Perce to their Northwest reservation, though he was never permitted to settle with them. (Otis Halfmoon, in Hoxie, pp. 309-11) This song sheet is the only one known by the author to use Chief Joseph's name.

After his capture, the fearless fighter Geronimo (c. 1823–1909) was imprisoned and later became a personality at various events. He was never allowed to return to his tribal homeland, yet his legend as a warrior survives. In 2011, the U.S military operation that eliminated Al Qaeda leader Osama bin Laden was code named "Geronimo." (bookmark issued by the National Museum of the American Indian, www.AmericanIndian.si.edu)

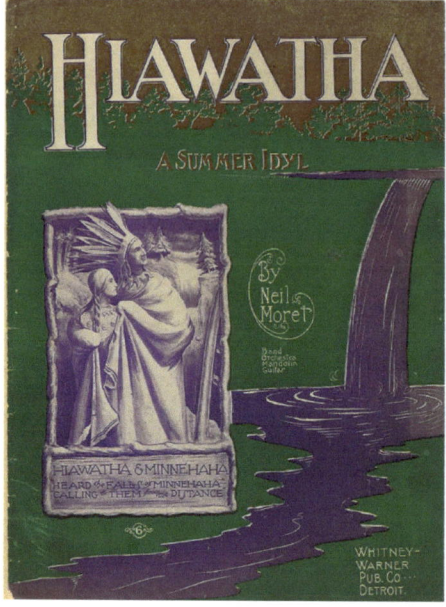 

Geronimo's Own Medicine Song (inset photo: Geronimo in 1886 on the warpath) – Carlos Troyer 1917 [Courtesy Mark Clardy]

Geronimo had been in Omaha for the 1898 Trans-Mississippi and International Exposition, in Buffalo for the 1901 Pan-American Exposition, and in the 1904 Louisiana Purchase Exposition in Saint Louis, and had ridden on horseback in Theodore Roosevelt's 1905 inaugural parade. (Deloria, p. 147) The cover is striking because it features a photograph of Geronimo riding his horse, and it displays the American Indian swastika-like symbol in the upper left corner.

Hiawatha (A Summer Idyl) – Neil Moret 1901 [Tinari collection]

The cover depicts Hiawatha and Minnehaha who "heard the falls of Minnehaha calling to them from the distance."

Hiawatha (A Summer Idyl) – Neil Moret 1901 [Tinari collection]

The cover illustration is of a seated American Indian woman. "Within a year, the sheet music sold more than a million copies." (Amundson, p. 51)

The Hiawatha song sheets were preceded by literature and dramatizations of the story of Hiawatha, e.g., the play *Hiawatha* by A. L. Warner in 1889, and before that, *Hiawatha, a Long Song of the Longfellow* by E. E. Rice in 1880. However, unlike the character presented in the romanticized story by Longfellow, the historic figure of Hiawatha was key founder of the Five Nations of the Iroquois in the middle of the fifteenth century.

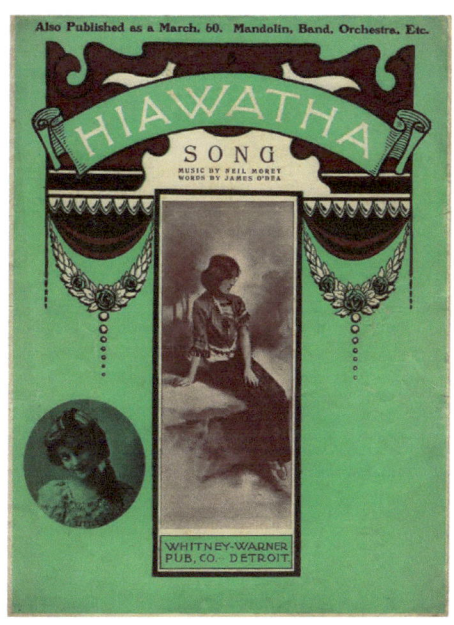  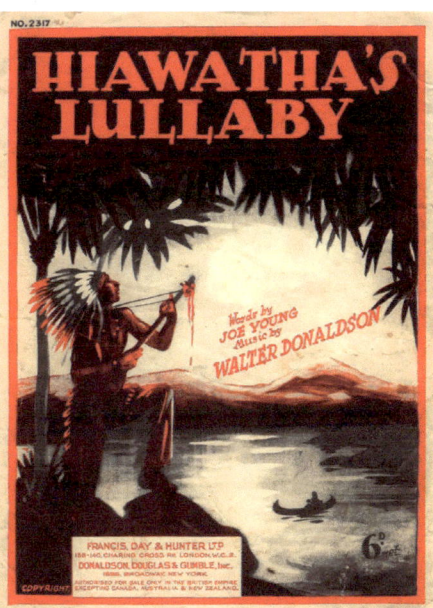 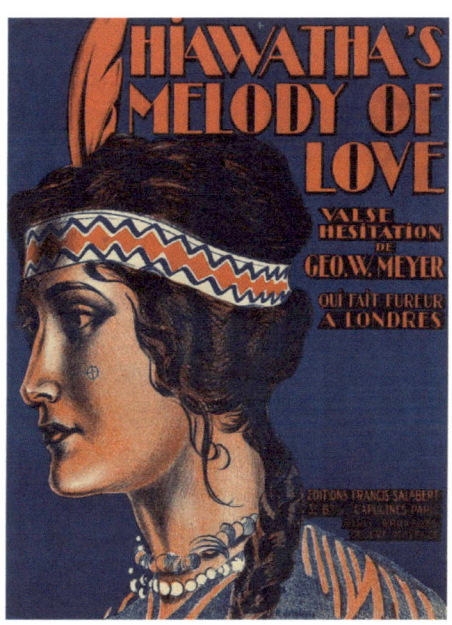

Hiawatha (song) – Neil Moret and James O'Dea 1903 [Tinari collection]

§

*Hiawatha [London] - Neil Moret, arranged by Fabian Scott 1901

The cover image is a charcol drawing of a seated American Indian chief.

Hiawatha Ballet Music (Suite of several pieces, 26 pp; African American composer) [UK] – Samuel Coleridge-Taylor 1919 ST [Tinari collection]

Hiawatha's Lullaby (illust Leff) [London] – Joe Young and Walter Donaldson 1933 [Tinari collection]

The cover depicts an American Indian man standing on the river bank and playing a stringed instrument for his beloved rowing toward him in her canoe.

Hiawatha's Melody of Love (Valse Hesitation) (illust de Valerio) [Paris] – George W. Meyer 1920 ST [Courtesy Sandy Marrone]

Hiawatha's Melody of Love (illust Manning) – Alfred Bryan, Artie Mehlinger and George W. Meyer 1920 ST [Tinari collection]

There is yet another song sheet of the same title with a Manning illustration featuring a lovely non-Indian woman. As such, it is not included in this book.

Hiawatha's Melody of Love (illust Starmer) – Alfred Bryan, Artie Mehlinger and George W. Meyer 1920 ST [Tinari collection]

Though a large photograph of the performers dominates the cover, illustrator Starmer decorated the borders and the top with American Indian insignia and a canoe.

I Didn't Raise My Boy to Be a Soldier (inset photo: Chief Tendehoa) – Al Piantadosi and Alfred Bryan 1915 [Tinari collection]

In a Dory from "Miss Pocahontas" (Barnet and Baker's Indian War Whoop) – Dan J. Sullivan, Harry H. Luther and Carl Wilmore 1906 [Tinari collection]

The comic opera is subtitled: An Indian War-Whoop in two Whoops. Book by R. A. Barnet and R. M. Baker. Other show songs include In a Jewelled Grotto; Whispering Shade; Mama, Do Not Leave Your Pappoose; Katie Carney.

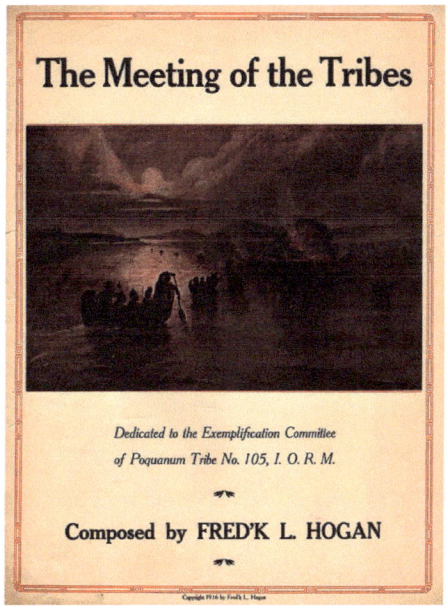

Land of My Prairie Dreams, The – Kutus Tecumseh 1926 ST [Tinari collection]

The photo description reads: successfully introduced by the composer and Indian tenor. It is not known if the composer was a descendent of Tecumseh of the Shawnees.

Meeting of the Tribes, The (Dedicated to the Exemplification Committee of Poquanum Tribe No. 105, I.O.R.M.) (self-pub) – Frederick L. Hogan 1916 [Tinari collection]

Minnehaha (Piano Composition) (illust Russell) – LeRoy Hartt 1903 [Tinari collection]

At the top of the music title page are ten lines from Longfellow's epic.

 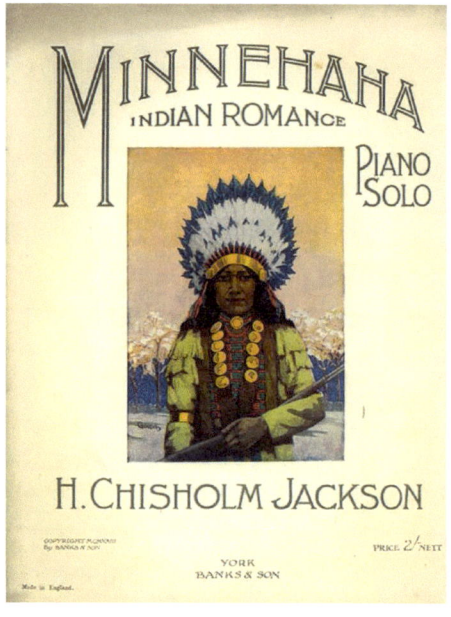  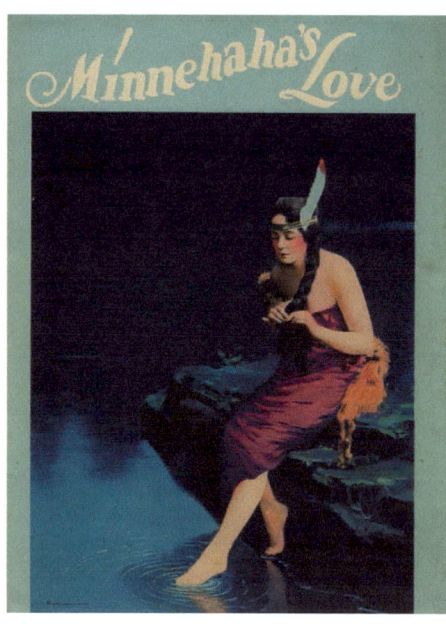

Minnehaha (Intermezzo and Two-Step) – Cora E. Dickerson 1912 [Courtesy Sandy Marrone]

§

*Minnehaha (Laughing Water) – F. H. Losey 1903

Minnehaha (Indian Romance) [England] – H. Chisholm Jackson 1923

Minnehaha's Answer – Philip L. Amon and E. F. Martin 1904 [Courtesy Sandy Marrone]

Martin's name is not shown on the cover.

Minnehaha's Love (While We Dream of) – Harley Rosso and Oscar Ericksen 1926 ST [Tinari collection]

The cover is unusual in that it does not list the composers. Nor does it give the full title of the song, though that is less unusual. The cover artist of the beautiful pastel-like painting is not given, but the source of Brown and Bigelow is printed in the lower left corner of the image.

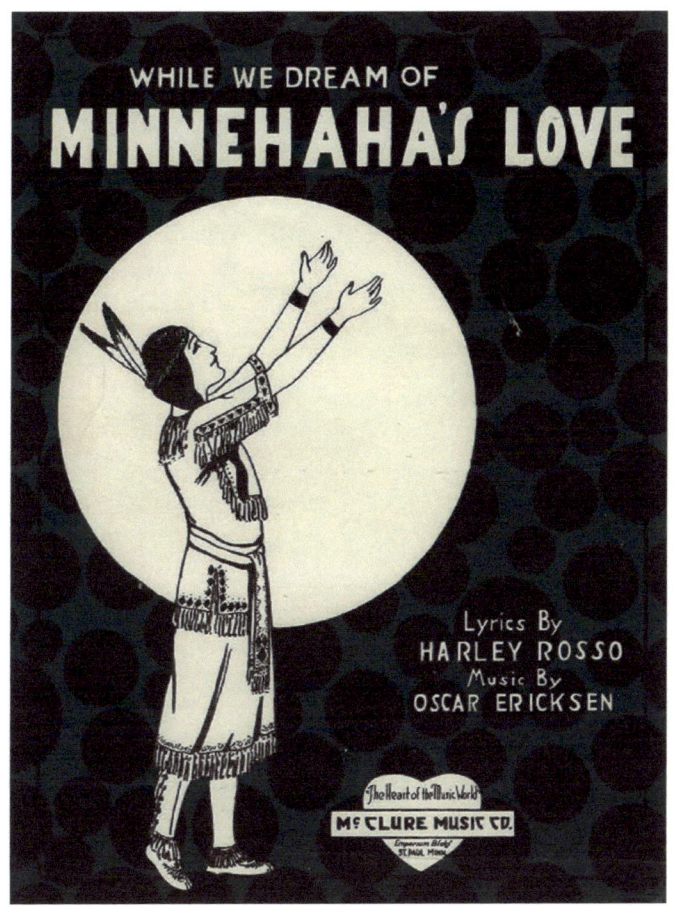

Minnehaha's Love (While We Dream of) – Harley Rosso and Oscar Ericksen 1926 [Tinari collection]

This cover of this version of the song shows an American Indian woman reaching up to the sky, with a large moon as her backdrop, all in black and white.

Mistletoe (illust Jenkins) – Edward Rose and Frederick W. Hager 1910 [Tinari collection]

The inset photo depicts Red Eagle, "America's Greatest Indian Vocalist"

§

*Miss Pocahontas (see In a Dory)

My Hiawatha – Edgar R. Carver 1927 ST [Courtesy Sandy Marrone]

See the notes under the song Hiawatha, previously.

Oleta (inset photo: American Indian woman, likely Miss Oleta Littleheart) – Carrie Morgan Ackerly 1910 [Tinari collection]

On the music title page, the composer's name is spelled Ackerley. The Author's Note states: "The following verses are inscribed to the beautiful talented young romance writer, Miss Oleta Littleheart, Daughter of a chief of the Chickasaws, Sulphur, Oklahoma."

Pocahontas (illust C. E.) – Vincent Bryan and Gus Edwards 1905 [Courtesy Sandy Marrone]

"Four verses tell the story of the Powhatan princess Pocahontas, her English husband John Smith, and her interfering father." (Short, *Covers of Gold*, p. 135) "Associated with the success of Jamestown—and a reminder of the deeply entangled history that Americans and American Indians share—Pocahontas has remained an indelible part of American national consciousness for more than four hundred years." (bookmark issued by the National Museum of the American Indian, www.AmericanIndian.si.edu)

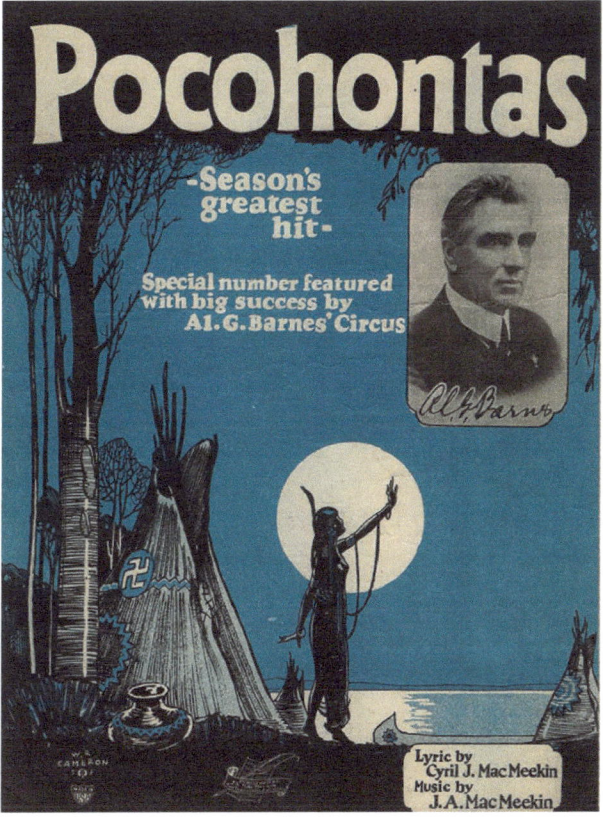

Pocahontas (A Song of Old Jamestown) (illust Barnes) (self-pub) – N. Brent Robertson 1907 [Courtesy Sandy Marrone]

Pocohontas (inset photo: Al. G. Barnes) (Special number featured with big success by Al. G. Barnes' Circus) – Cyril J. MacMeekin and J. A. MacMeekin 1920 ST [Courtesy Sandy Marrone]

Pocahontas (photo: Princess Watahwaso, the Indian Mezzo Soprano) – Cyril J. MacMeekin and J. A. MacMeekin 1920 ST [Tinari collection]

Born in 1882 to the Penobscot tribe, Lucy Nicola studied voice and music. She toured the Chautauqua circuit between 1913 and 1918, appearing with Leurance as Princess Watawaso. She later made the Indian-talk format her own, performing tribal melodies in buckskin as well as challenging operatic arias. (Deloria, pp. 206-7)

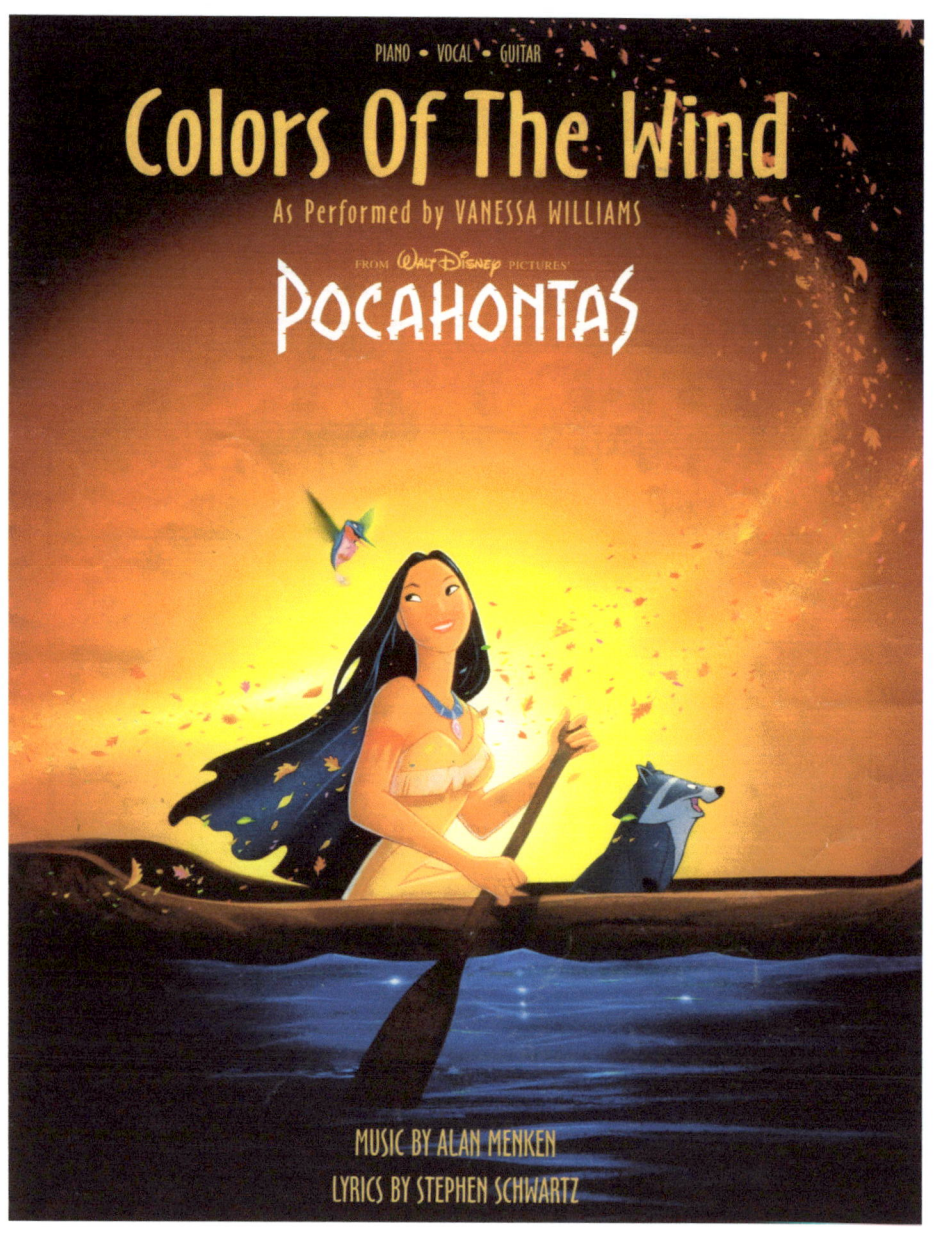
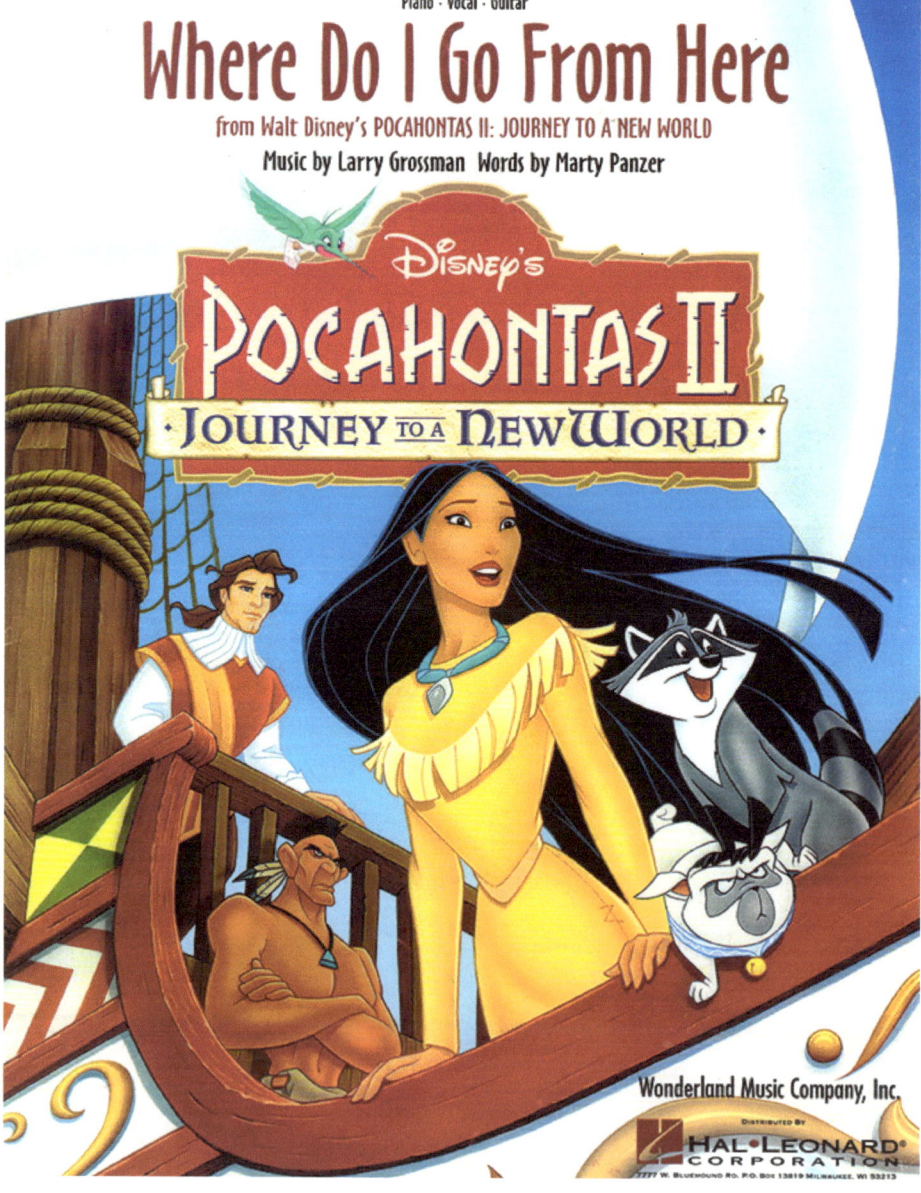

Pocahontas (animated film): Colors of the World – Alan Menken and Stephen Schwartz 1995 [Tinari collection]

Pocahontas II: Journey to a New World (animated film): Where Do I Go From Here –Larry Grossman and Marty Panzer 1998 [Tinari collection]

Pocahontas March and Two Step (color illustration: American Indian woman in traditional dress) – Theodore Manson 1903 [Tinari collection]

§

*Pocahontas Waltzes – Dora Hawthorne 1903

Princess Pocahontas March and Two-Step (inset photo: American Indian woman) ("Winner of the Prize Contest") – Al Trahern and Richmond F. Hoyt 1903 [Tinari collection]

There is another version with a cover illustration that depicts a scene of a long, winding river with an American Indian rowing in a canoe in the forefront. The author has never seen a copy of that sheet except as an advertised piece on the inside front cover of Hiji.

revival movement which spooked white officials at the Standing Rock Reservation. In 1890, Indian police stormed his cabin and he was killed in a bloody shootout. "For the 1905 version of *The Wizard of Oz*, costar Fred Stone, who played the Scarecrow, added *Sitting Bull* to 'The Dance of All Nations' number in which he sang the tune while dressed as an Indian chief surrounded 'by a chorus of girls dressed as Mexicans, cowgirls, and squaws.'" (Amundson, pp. 69-70)

Sitting Bull (illust Frew) (inset photo: Fred Stone) – Charles Zimmerman and Vincent Bryan 1905 [Courtesy Sandy Marrone]

Born Tatanka-lyotanka (c. 1831–1890), Sitting Bull was a stalwart defender of his people's lands and lifeways. U.S. actions provoked war in 1876 in which he and other leaders masterminded the defeat of U.S. troops at the Battle of the Little Bighorn. Later captured, he became a successful farmer and toured with Buffalo Bill's Wild West Show. He became an apostle of the Ghost Dance, an American Indian religious

Tecumseh (self-pub) – Charles A. Gouf 1906 [Tinari collection]

"Unquestionably, Tecumseh [Panther Springing across the Sky] was one of the most gifted and admirable of all Native American political and military leaders, but his career stands on its own merits. His biography should not be embellished with the romanticism of non-Indian historians." (R. David Edmunds in Hoxie, p. 621)

This is Our America (photo: Princess Pale Moon, singer) – Wil Rose 1976 ST [Tinari collection]

The back cover has an extensive explanation of the singer's background and views, presented by the National Heritage Foundation.

Trail to Long Ago, The (inset photo: Chief Shunstona, Director U.S. Indian Band) – F. Henri Klickmann, E. Clinton Keithley, William T. White and Clarence W. Erickson 1922 ST [Courtesy Sandy Marrone]

Uncas (The Last of the Mohicans) (illust Starmer) – Joseph J. Kaiser 1904 [Tinari collection]

"This song is a tribute to Chief Uncas of the powerful Mohican tribe in New England in the 1600s. He was pro-English and had their support in his campaign of conquest against other New England tribes including the Pequot and Narragansett." (Short, *Covers of Gold*, p. 133)

195

4
HUMOROUS AND WHIMSICAL TREATMENTS

The bright minds on Tin Pan Alley at the time were either working long overtime hours or simply applying comic or satirical themes, as they were doing for other types of musical genres, to the then-known American Indian stereotypes and phrases. "In 1905, Tammany became the first of the so-called comic songs about Indians…. Interestingly, the song was not about Native Americans but about whites who appropriated Indianness." (Amundson, p. 62) Thankfully, there are relatively few song sheets of this type as demonstrated by the number of pieces presented in this chapter.

Big Chief Battle-Axe (illust Starmer) (inset: Lew Dockstader, blackface) – Thos. S. Allen 1907 [Tinari collection]

Big Chief De Sota – Andy Razaf and Fernando Arbelo 1936 ST [Courtesy Sandy Marrone]

This piece served as an automobile promotion. American Indian names were and continue to be used liberally to name various automobile brands and models including Cadillac, Pontiac, Jeep Cherokee and Dodge Dakota.

Big Chief Dynamite – Jeffrey T. Branen and Al Piantadosi 1909 [Courtesy the Lester S. Levy Collection of Sheet Music, Sheridan Libraries, Johns Hopkins University]

Big Chief Hic-Cup – Walter Noona c. 1950s ST [Tinari collection]

Big Chief Killahun [or Kill-a-Hun] (illust Barbelle) – Maurice Abrahams, Alfred Bryan and Edgar Leslie 1918 [Courtesy Sandy Marrone]

The lyrics tell of the Big Chief going off to Berlin in WWI to "scalp the Kaiser." They "combine the racist stereotypes of the Indian comic songs with words like 'Big Chief,' 'war paint,' 'tomahawk,' and 'squaw'; the assimilation language of doing 'his share' because 'Uncle Sammy needs me'; and a complete denial of the relationship between Indians and the federal government with the suggestion that 'Uncle Sammy feeds me.'" (Amundson, p. 184)

Big Chief Wahoo – Allen Saunders and Arthur Charles 1940 ST

On the cover: "Inspired by the famous comic strip Chief Wahoo by Saunders & Woggon." The inside music title page includes a section of the comic strip.

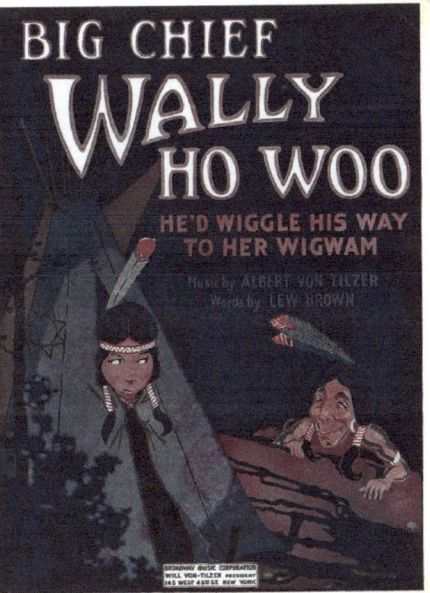

Big Chief Wally Ho Woo – Albert Von Tilzer and Lew Brown 1921 ST [Tinari collection]

The matchbook cover and advertisement shown here is a good example of how American Indian images were appropriated for commercial purposes.

199

   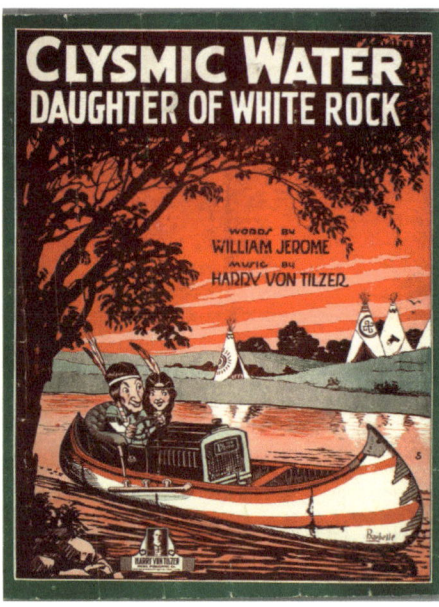

Big Indian Chief (illust Frew) – Cole & Johnson Bros. 1904 [Tinari collection]

African American composers Bob Cole and J. Rosamond Johnson wrote this for The Mask and Wig Club annual show at the University of Pennsylvania. (Short, *The Gold in Your Piano Bench*, p. 64) The cover is unusual, showing a black-skinned American Indian.

Chief Hokum – Harry Von Tilzer and George A. Kershaw 1923 ST [Courtesy Sandy Marrone]

Clicquot – Harry F. Reser 1926 ST [Tinari collection]

This sheet was published by the Clicquot Club Company. Its cover features a caricature of an Indian Eskimo holding a bottle of Clicquot Club, very likely a soda brand. The main illustration consists of the Clicquot Club Eskimos band "under the direction of Harry F. Reser." The back cover displays yet another company's promotion, this one for Wm. L. Lange's Paramount Banjos that were used by several players in the Clicquot band.

Clysmic Water, Daughter of White Rock (illust Barbelle) – William Jerome and Harry von Tilzer 1920 ST [Courtesy the Lester S. Levy Collection of Sheet Music, Sheridan Libraries, Johns Hopkins University]

The whimsical illustration shows an American Indian couple happily traveling in their canoe that is powered by a gasoline engine.

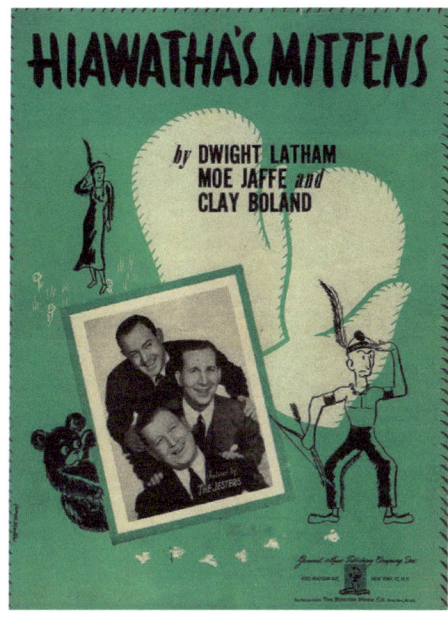

Great Big Chickapoo Chief, A (Burlesque Indian-Coon Song) – Edward Madden and Theodore Morse 1904 [Duke University Digital Collections]

Great Big Heap Much Bull – Albert Von Tilzer, Edward Laska and Neville Fleeson 1921 ST [Courtesy Sandy Marrone]

Hiawatha's Mittens (inset photo: The Jesters) – Dwight Latham, Moe Jaffe and Clay Boland 1948 ST [Courtesy Sandy Marrone]

The lyrics relay how Hiawatha went hunting with his lady for a bear from which mittens were made "with the fur inside."

Honest Injun (illust Pfeiffer) – Andrew Sterling, Ed Moran, Harry Von Tilzer 1915

One of the oddest cover illustrations, it depicts an American Indian man with a long hair braid holding a walking cane and dressed in a top hat and tuxedo, surrounded by head shot images of pretty women.

Minnehaha (She Gave Them All the Ha! Ha!) (illust Walton) – William J. Hart and Edward Nelson 1918 [Tinari collection]

Never Do a Tango with an Eskimo – Tommie Connor [London] 1971

No Squat-No Stoop-No Squint – Clarence Gaskill and Tom Hughes 1937 [Courtesy Sandy Marrone]

Oogie Oogie Wa Wa (Means "I Wanna Mama" to an Eskimo) (illust R.S.) – Grant Clarke, Edgar Leslie and Archie Gottler 1922 ST [Tinari collection]

The pictured "eskimo" woman is drawn to appear decidedly Caucasian. The inset photo is of Margaret Young. The French issue has a different cover illustration. See Amoureuse de Nanouck in Chapter 5.

Pow Wow March – Gerard L. H. Rugers 1913 [Courtesy Sandy Marrone]

Rain-in-the-Face (illust De Takacs) – Benjamin Hapgood Burt 1907 [Tinari collection]

Amundson (pp. 108-9) states the song has nothing to do with the actual Hunkpapa Lakota leader who was immortalized in Henry Wadsworth Longfellow's 1878 poem "The Revenge of Rain-in-the-Face." Rather, it ridicules the name in a stereotype that some scholars have come to call the "Ignoble Savage: The Drunk Injun." Composer Burt wrote many songs performed on Broadway. His 1933 comic song The Pig Got Up and Walked Away also lampooned alcohol in a story about a drunk.

Rosie the Redskin (illust Barbelle) (inset photo: Dalton Boys) – Al Stillman and Al Jacobs 1938 ST [Tinari collection]

She's Got the Wana Blues (illust Wright) [Engl.] – Edward E. Bryant and Hubert W. David 1923 ST [Tinari collection]

This is one of many songs issued by the prolific Lawrence Wright Music Company. The illustrator is thought to be Lawrence Wright because his name is penned on the cover next to the image of an American Indian chief.

Skookum (illust R.S.) (by permission of Skookum Apples) – Leo. Wood, John White and Martin Fried 1920 (war size) [Tinari collection]

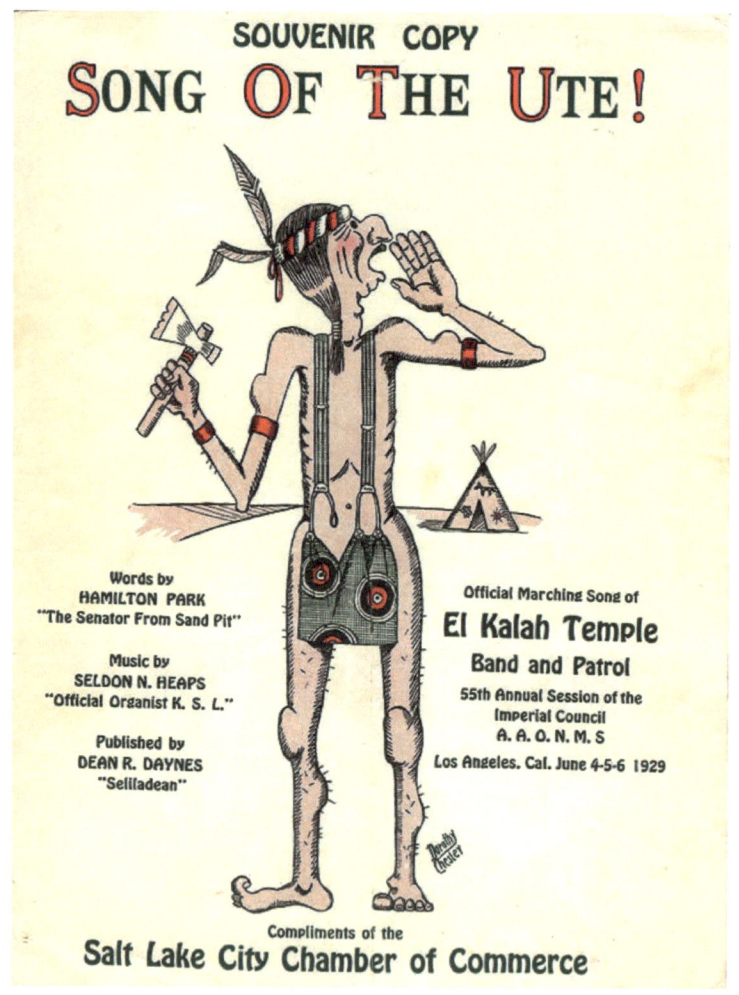

Song of the Ute! (Souvenir Copy) (illust Chesler) – Hamilton Park and Seldon N. Heaps 1929 [Tinari collection]

"Official Marching Song of El Kalah Temple," a Shriner's chapter. "Compliments of the Salt Lake City Chamber of Commerce." The inside front cover lists a series of "Interesting Facts" about Salt Lake City and Utah. The back cover has photos and an inviting description of Salt Lake City.

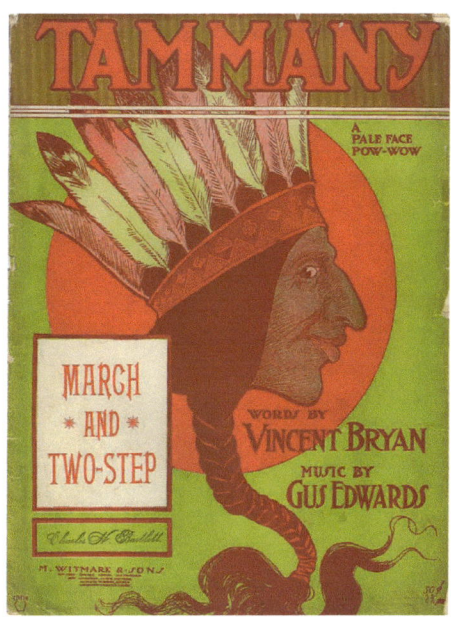

Tammany, a Pale Face Pow-Wow (illust C.K.) – Vincent Bryan and Gus Edwards 1905 [Tinari collection]

Founded in 1788, the political club took its name from a legendary Delaware Indian chief. Crew describes the cover illustration as a lithograph "of a stereotypic Indian in headdress. ... Different editions have different performers pictured on the cover." (*Suffragist*, p. 163) "Political corruption at the turn of the century did not go unnoticed. The bad reputation of Tammany Hall and the political 'bossism' of the Tweed Ring under infamous William Marcy 'Boss' Tweed of New York City in the late 1860s continued into the twentieth century. [The composers] wrote the song 'Tammany' described on the cover as 'a pale face pow-wow' for a gathering of the National Democratic Club of New York. The cover of a leering Indian in feathered headdress belies the actual lyrics of the song which are strongly political in nature. Eight verses good-humoredly poke fun at Tammany and its efforts to clean up its reputation." (Short, *More Gold in Your Piano Bench*, p. 168) It was reported that the song's composers "wrote the song as a spoof on popular Indian songs, with its references in the first line to *Hiawatha* and *Navajo* …." (Amundson, p. 63)

§

*Ten The Little Injuns, Comic Song, – 1868 (see listing in Chapter 1)

Tippecanoe (A Comic Indian Song) – Harry Williams and Egbert Van Alstyne 1904

The inset photo is of Billie Taylor, a popular performer around the turn of the century. The song also was issued featuring other performers such as William Gould.

Wana (When I Wana, You No Wana) (inset photo: "Green and Blyler featured in Eddie Cantor's Midnight Rounders") – Cliff Friend 1921 ST [Tinari collection]

When I Wanna—You No Wanna (illust Starmer) – Cliff Friend 1921 [Tinari collection]

The first line of the song is: "Way out West they tell a story of an Indian maid 'Wana' was her name."

§

*WirreisennachWildwest [We're Heading to the Wild West) (song) [Vienna] – Robert Huegel 1923

Although the main illustration is of an elegant couple, the bottom center illustration features, of all things, a young Indian cupid.

Wise Old Indian (illust Hirt) – Jack Mahoney and Theodore Morse 1909 [Tinari collection]

"Superficially touting Indian intelligence, this song … actually undercut the song's title by doing little more than poking fun at phrases that included the word Indian, thereby suggesting that Indians in fact were not wise. … Subtitled 'A Comical Conglomeration,' … to satirize American culture with references to war, politics, women's suffrage, and alcohol." (Amundson, p. 141)

5
SONG SHEETS FROM OTHER COUNTRIES

Though not common, song sheets with depictions of American Indians were issued in Europe and South America. While many issues displayed cover image reproductions of original U.S. issues, several colorful and artistic cover illustrations are among the pieces displayed here. Many of the images reproduced in this chapter were taken from the Belgian website, https://www.imagesmusicales.be that lists thousands of song sheets, most with cover images, and publishes articles about sheet music history and collecting.

Across the Prairies [Engl.] – Theodore Bonheur 1915 [Tinari collection]

Ah! Rose-Marie (illust Garmland) [Stockholm] – Rudolf Friml and S. S. Wilson 1924 [https://www.imagesmusicales.be/]

Amapu (illust de Valerio) [Paris] – Gideon Melville 1921 [https://www.imagesmusicales.be/]

§

*Arapahoe (piano solo) [Paris] – J. B. Lahaya 1920

§

*Black Hawk Waltz, The [UK] - listed in Chapter 3

Amoureuse de Nanouck (Oogie-Woogie-Wa-Wa) (illust Dulin) [Paris] – Archie Gottler, Leo Lelievre and Henri Varna 1919

The cover illustration depicts a flapper gal ogling a Native American Eskimo who is holding his hunting spear. See Oogie Woogie Wa Wa in Chapter 4 for the U.S. issue.

Cabeza de Indio [Argentina] – Armando La Valle c. 1920s [Tinari collection]

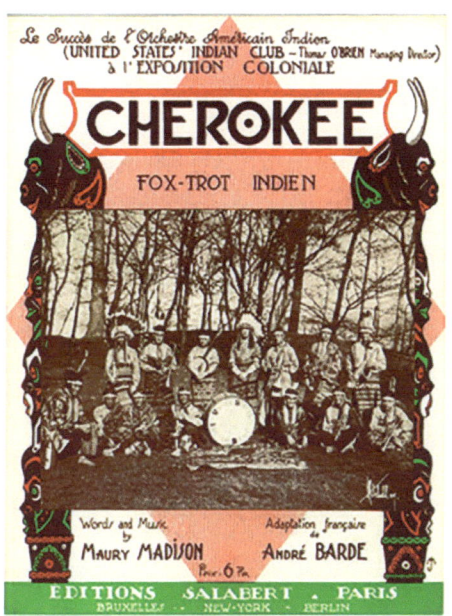

Cherokee (illust MJ) – Maury Madison and André Barde [Paris] 1931 [https://www.imagesmusicales.be/]

The top of the cover contains this description: The Success of the American Indian Orchestra (United States Indian Club, Thomas O'Brien, Managing Director) at the Colonial Exposition that was held in Paris.

§

*Cora (The Indians Maidens Song) [London] – shown in Chapter 1

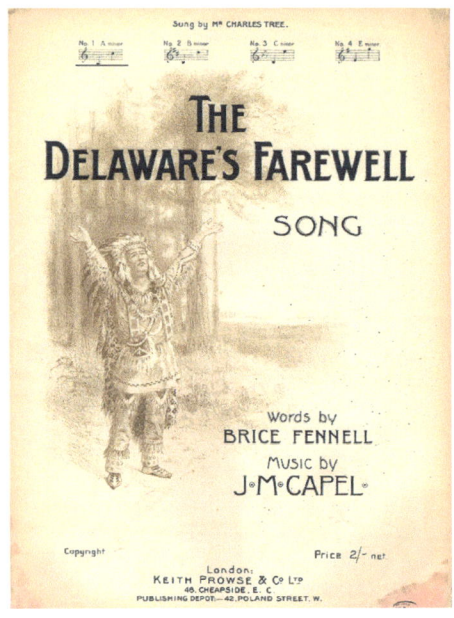   

Delaware's Farewell Song, The [London] – Brice Fennell and J. M. Capel 1904 [Tinari collection]

The cover image may give the impression that the Delaware tribe is leaving its homeland, but it is simply another song of lost love.

§

*Hiawatha's Melody of Love [Paris] – listed in Chapter 3

Fleetwing [Glasgow, Scotland] – S. Chandler c. 1920s ST [Courtesy Sandy Marrone]

§

*Hiawatha Ballet Music [UK] - listed in Chapter 3

§

*Hiawatha's Lullaby [London] – Joe Young and Walter Donaldson (displayed in Chapter 3)

Hobomoko (An Indian Romance) [Engl.] – Ernest Reeves 1907 [Courtesy Sandy Marrone]

§

*Hobomoko (illust George) (IndischeRomanze) [Germ.] – Ernest Reeves 1907

The cover illustration depicts a lone American Indian near some tepees viewing a vista of river, forest, and mountains.

Humoreskimo [Paris] – Pete Wendling, Henri Berchman and Alfred Bryan 1928 [https://www.imagesmusicales.be/]

Idylle a Colombo (Intermezzo) [South American] – Christine n.d. [Tinari collection]

Indian Hunter, The (Characteristic Rondo in F Major) [Eng] – Carl Hemann 1929 ST [Tinari collection]

§

*Indian Hunter's Bride, The [London] – see Chapter 1

Indian Maid [Canada] (self-pub) – C. L. Graves 1919

The cover's color illustration is a rightward-looking profile of an American Indian woman with feathers tucked into her head band. The tune is a typical love song of the era.

Indian Patrol (Patrouille Indienne) [Paris] – Marcel Learsi 1913 [https://www.imagesmusicales.be/]

Indian Ride, An [England] – Paul de Loetzc 1890

Indian Sérénade [Brussels] – Geo Arnold n.d. [https://www.imagesmusicales.be/]

Indian Shimmy [Berlin] – Billy Flower 1921 [https://www.imagesmusicales.be/]

§

*Indian Sun Dance, The [London] – listed in Chapter 1

Indiana [Paris] – G. Marcailhou n.d. [https://www.imagesmusicales.be/]

Indiandans (Dance of the Chippeway's) [Germany] – Charles Frey 1932 ST [https://www.imagesmusicales.be/]

Indianerständchen (Silver Heels) [Berlin] – Neil Moret 1919 [https://www.imagesmusicales.be/]

Readers will note that the same song, Silverheels, listed in Chapter 2, was published in America in 1905.

Indianetta [Paris] – Roger Dufas 1920 [https://www.imagesmusicales.be/]

Indianola [Spain] – S. R. Henry and D. Onivas n.d. [https://www.imagesmusicales.be/]

This edition and the next two have cover illustrations that are different than the American issue.

Indianola (illust de Valerio) [Paris] – S. R. Henry and D. Onivas 1918 [https://www.imagesmusicales.be/]

Indianola [Germany] – S. R. Henry and D. Onivas 1917

§

*Indianola [London] – S. R. Henry and D. Onivas 1917

The cover illustration is identical to the American version displayed in Chapter 2.

Indianskan [Stockholm] – Adolf Englund n.d. [https://www.imagesmusicales.be/]

La Indiada [Argentina] – Jose Martinez n.d [Tinari collection]

Mahtoree (Intermezzo) [Germ.] – Charles Rella 1913 [Tinari collection]

§

*Lily of the Prairie [UK] - Kerry Mills 1906

Unlike the USA isssue, presented in Chapter 2, the UK issue is printed in black and white.

 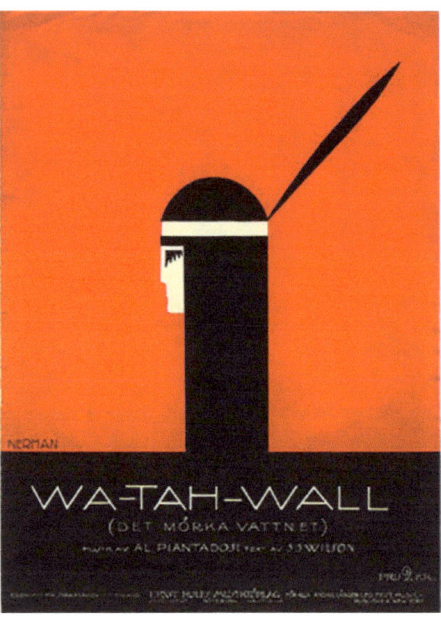  

Mama Ocllo (illustScudellari) – Armando Penagos [Peru] c. 1920s [Tinari collection]

Although this clearly portrays a South American Indian, likely an Incan woman, I include it here because it is so colorful.

Min lilla Wa-tah-wall (Det mörkavattnet-Indianskserenad) (illustNerman) [Stockholm] – Al. Piantadosi and S. S. Wilsons 1915 [https://www.imagesmusicales.be/]

§

*Minnehaha (Indian Romance) [England] – listed in Chapter 3

Moccassin Blues (illust Hal Kay) [London] – Ed. Stanelli 1920 [https://www.imagesmusicales.be/]

Mohawk, The (Indian Song) [Stockholm] – Gustaf Uppström n.d. [https://www.imagesmusicales.be/]

Mumblin' Mose [Peru] – T. W. Thurban 1913 [Tinari collection]

The cover image mimics the image on Navajo issued in 1903 in Stockholm.

Another version exists with an illustration of an African American man, which is more appropriate to the title than an American Indian.

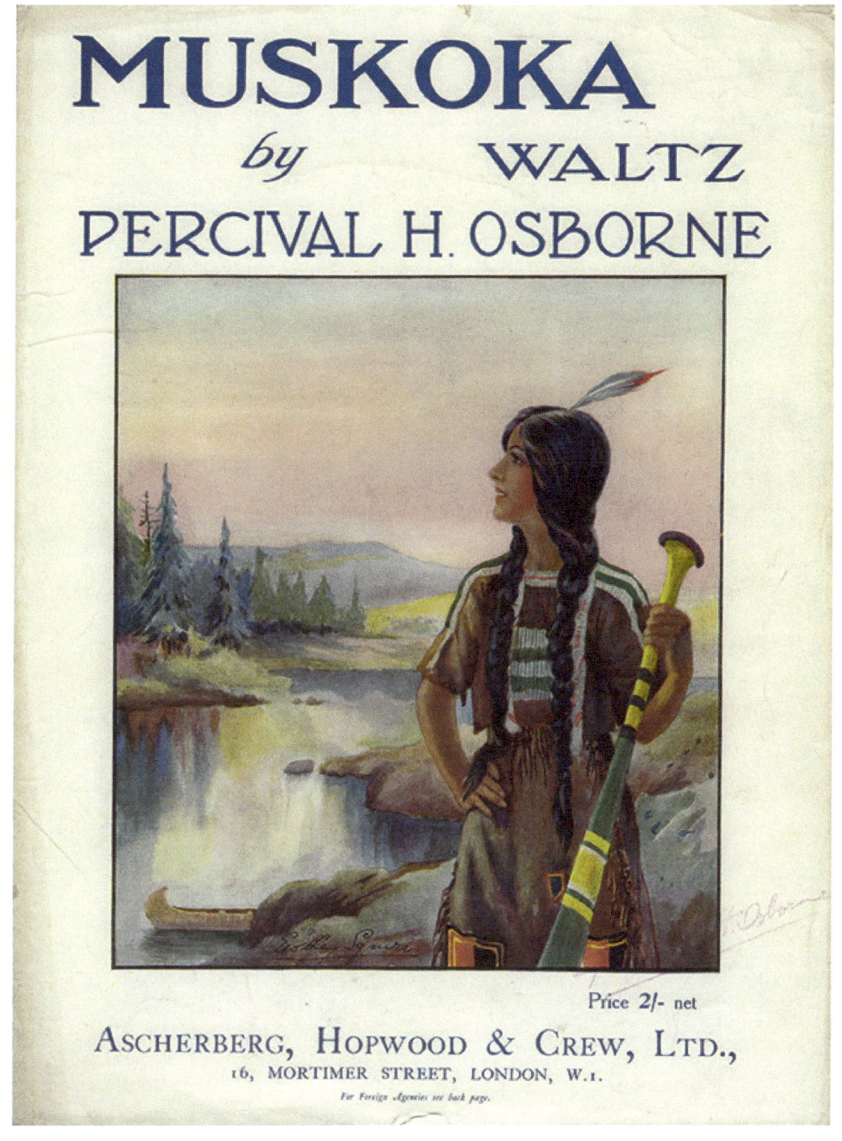

Muskoka Waltz [UK] – Percival H. Osborne 1921 [Tinari collection]

The music title page reads Muskoka ("Clear Sky") Waltz

My Wenonah [Toronto] – Sylvester Wittmark 1908 [Tinari collection]

Navajo [Paris] – Maurice Gracey 1903 [https://www.imagesmusicales.be/]

Navajo (IndianskMarsch) [Stockholm] – Egbert Van Alstyne 1903 [https://www.imagesmusicales.be/]

§

*Never Do a Tango with an Eskimo [London] – shown in Chapter 4

Nouhika – Wilfred Beaudry 1905 [Canada] [Tinari collection]

Also published as a song.

O-Hi-O (illust de Valerio) [Paris] – Abe Olman and Jack Yellen 1920 [https://www.imagesmusicales.be/]

§

*Ofrenda de la Elegida (piano solo) (illust Baratta) [El Salvador] – Maria M. de Baratta 1930

The colorful illustration depicts a worshipping Indian, perhaps Aztec or Inca, flanked by many pictographs and symbols.

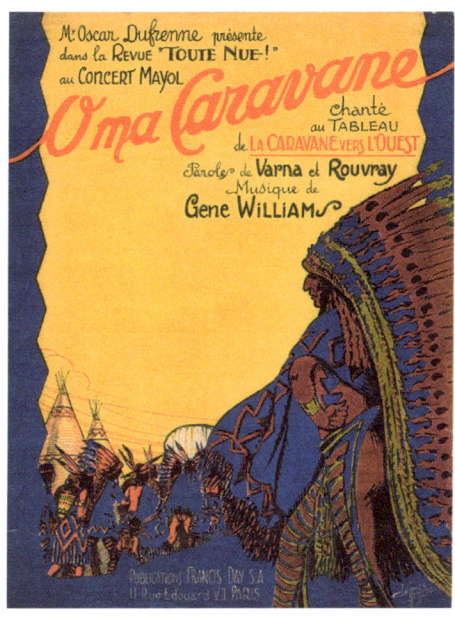   

O Ma Caravane (song) (illust Fere) [Paris] – Gene Williams, Henri Varna and Fernand Rouvray 1924 [Tinari collection]

This song was featured as part of a revue called La Caravane vers L'ouest (Caravan to the West).

Oh, By Jingo! (Vocal One-Step) [UK] – Lew Brown and Albert Von Tilzer 1919 [Tinari collection]

The music title page gives an extended title as follows: (Oh! by Gee! by Gosh! By Gum! By Juv!) Oh By Jingo! Oh By Gee! (You're the Only Girl for Me)

On The Rainbow Trail (illust Cliff Miska) [London] – Coleman Goetz, May Singhi Breen and Peter de Rose 1930 ST [https://www.imagesmusicales.be/]

The image is identical to the U.S. issue, shown in Chapter 2.

On the War-Path (illust Gilson) [UK] – E. Falknor 1914 [Courtesy Sandy Marrone]

Rainbow (Regenbogen) [Berlin] – Percy Wenrich 1909 [https://www.imagesmusicales.be/]

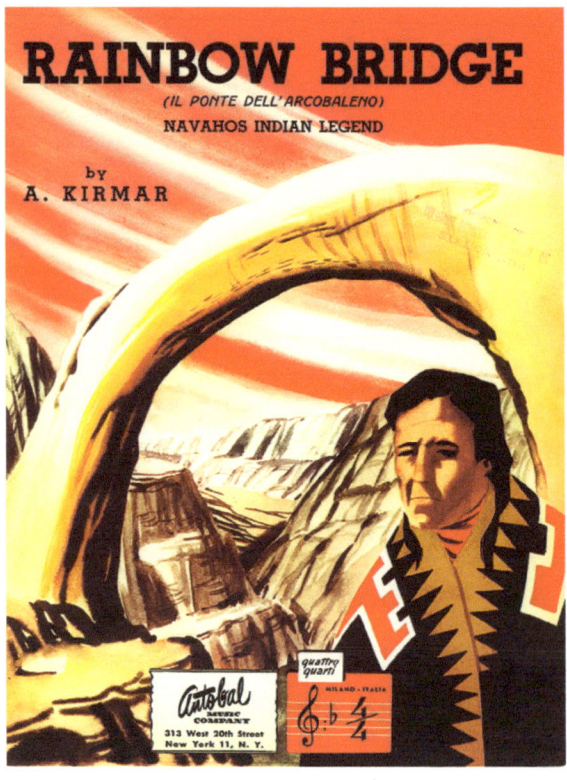

Rainbow Bridge (Navahos Indian Legend) [Italy] – A. Kirmar 1955 [Tinari collection]

Prairie Lilie (Lily of the Prairie) [Berlin] – Kerry Mills 1910 [https://www.imagesmusicales.be/]

This is the German version of Lily of the Prairie, displayed in Chapter 2.

220

Red Bead (La Perla Roja) (illust Corine) [Argentina] – Henry Laurenz 1916 [Tinari collection]

This is the original multi-colored issue with detailed information about the edition printed at the bottom of the cover, with further musical instruction and notation on the back cover.

Red Bead (La Perla Roja) [Uruguay] – Henry Laurenz c. 1920 [Tinari collection]

This version is likely an unauthorized copy, using only red and blue, and displaying a much simpler, unsigned illustration. Its back cover is blank.

§

*Redskin (from *Redskin* film) [Eng] – see Chapter 2

Red Wing (Rotfeder) [Berlin] – Kerry Mills 1907 [https://www.imagesmusicales.be/]

Although this is a near exact copy of the American issue illustrated by Hirt (see Chapter 2), his name is absent from the image.

Redwing (illust Artemio) [unknown South American country] – Kerry Mills 1907 [Tinari collection]

Red Wing (Intermezzo Indiano) [Argentina] - Kerry Mills 1912

221

*Seminola [London] – Robert King and Harry Warren 1925

Like the preceding song sheet, the cover illustration, in black pen on a white background, depicts a group of tepees and an American Indian gliding along in his canoe. But instead of featuring a photo of Stanley, as previously, there is a photo of the actress called Little Emmie. On the cover we read: "Featured by Little Emmie in Madame Pauline Rivers 1925 Production 'Pansies'." The small close-up photo of a woman dressed in a fashionable hat is likely Rivers.

§

*Seminola (inset photo: Bernard Manning) [Engl.] – Robert King and Harry Warren 1925

The cover illustration is a near duplicate of the U.S. issue. At the top we read: "Specially featured by Bernard Manning in J. C. Willamson's Gorgeous Christmas Pantomime 'Aladdin'"

Ruses d'Indiens (illust Valéry) [Brussels] – Hippolyte Ackermansand Alberta Nichols n.d. [https://www.imagesmusicales.be/]

Seminola (An Indian Love Song) (photo: Gwladys Stanley) [London] – Robert King and HarryWarren 1925 [Courtesy Sandy Marrone]

Another version features a photograph of performer Miss Dorothy Ward.

Seminola (An Indian Love Song) (illust Rohman) [Stockholm] – Robert King, Harry Warren and S. Wilson 1925 [https://www.imagesmusicales.be/]

§

*She's Got the Wana Blues [Engl.] – listed in Chapter 4

222

Silver-Cloud (An Indian Maiden's Song) (illust Aveline) [Engl.] – Albert W. Ketèlbey 1915 [Tinari collection]

Silverheels [Engl.] – Neil Moret 1905 [sheetmusicwarehouse.co.uk]

The image is nearly a duplicate of the U.S. issue illustrated by Bertha Young, except the dancer's face is drawn with a different expression and the entire image is in black and white.

Siwaja – Charles Rella 1913 [Germany] [Tinari collection]

The illustrator of the beautiful American Indian woman is uncredited.

Skookum (illust de Valerio) [Paris] – John White and Martin Fried 1920 [https://www.imagesmusicales.be/]

Song of India (composer's melodies arr. by Massanet Goula) [Uruguay] – Rimsky Korsakoff c. 1910 [Tinari collection]

South Sea Moon (illust de Valerio) [Paris] – Louis A. Hirsch, Gene Buck and Dave Stamper 1922 [https://www.imagesmusicales.be/]

Squaw's Lament, The (illust George) (Valse Indienne) [London] – Ivan C. Maclean 1912 [Courtesy Sandy Marrone]

The cover of this issue contains an exact duplicate of the title and side decorations of the U.S. issue but renders a different American Indian face. It also eliminates any mention of the apple producer who sponsored the original U.S. version.

Ten Little Indians [Denmark] – Bill Haley 1953 [Tinari collection]

This song sheet was issued both with a photo of musicians set within the half-moon of the cover illustration, and without any photo in the half-moon, as displayed here. The song sheet in the Tinari collection contains the photo that has printed below it "Featured and Broadcast by a trio called The Londonaires."

Tomahawk Blues (Fox Trot Song) (illust Dee) [London] – Cal De Voll and Merle Yagle 1923 [Tinari collection]

The U.S. issue features an American Indian man doing a dance near a boiling kettle on a fire outside his tepee.

Wana (When I wanna you no wanna) [London] – Cliff Friend 1922 [https://www.imagesmusicales.be/]

Wana (illustDulin) – Cliff Friend, Nazelles and Lemarchand [Paris] 1921 [Tinari collection]

The cover states that the song was a great success in the Follies-Bergere's "Follies sur Follies." See the U.S. issues in Chapter 4.

Wayawais [Spain] – W. Keppler-Lais 1922 [Tinari collection]

The lyrics are by R. Berraondo whose name is not listed on the cover.

Whoopee, My Baby Just Cares for Me – Walter Donaldson and Gus Kahn 1930

The cover depicts a horse rearing up with a woman rider. Printed across the top is "Talking Film Edition." After closing a successful 1928-29 run on Broadway, *Whoopee!* was filmed in 1930 as an American musical comedy. This song was not in the original Broadway production. This illustration of the fully clothed woman rider is more modest than the U.S. issue (see Chapter 6) that displays her nude.

Winnetou (Amerikanisches Intermezzo) [Germany] – H. Oldhouse 1913 [https://www.imagesmusicales.be/]

Winnetou (Rumba) (illust Aigner) [Vienna] – Friedrich Maschner and Hans Werner 1947 [https://www.imagesmusicales.be/]

Winona (illust Bombach) [Berlin] – S. J. Floyd 1903 [https://www.imagesmusicales.be/]

Yucatan (illust Desains) [Paris] – J. B. Ropp 1922 [https://www.imagesmusicales.be/]

Zohima (illust Prevel) [Paris] – Bob Rice 1919 [https://www.imagesmusicales.be/]

§

*WirreisennachWildwest [We're Heading to the Wild West) [Vienna] – listed in Chapter 4

6
POST-1930 SONG SHEETS: NOSTALGIA MEETS STEREOTYPE

By the 1930s, most song sheets were being issued in standard size format, so the ST abbreviation used in previous sections of this book would be redundant here. All song sheets in this part are standard size unless noted otherwise. For some song sheets that already have been listed in previous chapters, a note referencing the earlier chapter is given. Most of the cover illustrations are relatively basic in design, not nearly approaching the artistry of illustrators exhibited on covers in the early part of the twentieth century. As such, very few signed illustrations are found among them. Many of these pieces use simple depictions of stereotypical scenes, views of American Indian cultures such as war dances, tom-toms, untamed nature, tepees and the like. But all are included here to be as comprehensive as possible.

Many song sheets issued after 1930 are noted herein as EPP for "educational piano piece," indicating that they were and are used as part of the repertoire of tunes that teachers ask their piano students to learn. As Deloria states: "Generations of children at piano practice have almost always found an Indian-sound piece in their first lesson book." (p. 183)

Apache Braves – Dennis Alexander 2001 EPP [Tinari collection]

Apache Drums – Carolyn C. Setliff 2003 EPP [Tinari collection]

§

*Big Chief De Sota – see listing in Chapter 4

Apache Indian Dance – John W. Schaum 1955 EPP [Tinari collection]

The cover illustration is labelled "Apache Devil Dancer."

§

*Big Chief Hiccup – see listing in Chapter 4

Big Chief Thundercloud – Mark Nevin 1950 [Tinari collection]

The cover illustration is more abstract than most, communicating an ephemeral yet respectful feeling.

§

*Big Chief Wahoo – see listing in Chapter 4

Big Injun Chief, The – Marie F. Hall 1941 EPP [Courtesy Sandy Marrone]

Brave Warrior – Kim Williams 2000 EPP [Tinari collection]

§

*Cherokee Blues (see Yaw La Boo La Hoola)

Cherokee Love Theme – Lemuel Childers 1929 [Tinari collection]

Though this predates by a year the song sheets in this chapter, its design makes it appropriate for placing it here.

Cherokee (Indian Love Song) – Ray Noble 1972 arrangement EPP [Tinari collection]

§

*Chief Joseph of the Nez Perce Indians – see listing in Chapter 3

Chief Red Feather (Indian War Dance) – Katherine Allan Lively 1944 EPP [Tinari collection]

Choctaw Indian Dance – Hazel Volkart 1946 EPP [Courtesy Sandy Marrone]

Comanche (illust MPS) – Everett Stevens 1945 [Tinari collection]

Dance of the Braves – Charles Beaton 1932 EPP [Courtesy Sandy Marrone]

§

*Cowboys and Injuns (a piano solo) (illust Gardner) - Olive Smith 1939 EPP

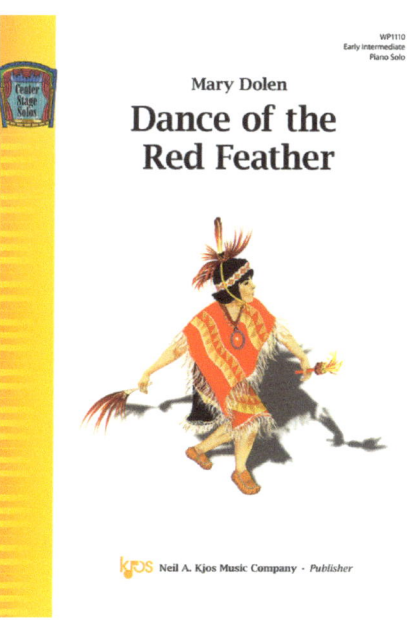

television versions, and several songs became American standards. Identical cover illustrations were used for other songs from the show.
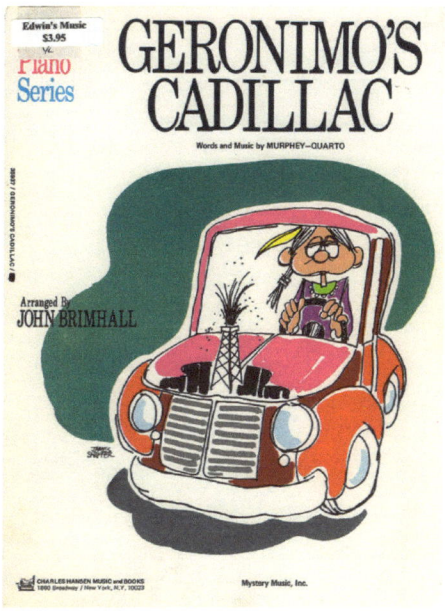

Dance of the Red Feather – Mary Dolen 2005 EPP [Tinari collection]

Doin' What Comes Natur'lly from *Annie Get Your Gun* – Irving Berlin 1946

The busy cover illustration includes a stylized face of an American Indian in feathered headdress, apparently blowing on a thin trumpet. In the plot, Chief Sitting Bull adopts Annie into the Sioux tribe. The Broadway musical is a fictionalized version of the life of Annie Oakley (1860–1926), a sharpshooter who starred in Buffalo Bill's Wild West, and her romance with sharpshooter Frank E. Butler. The successful show spawned film and

Geronimo's Cadillac – Murphey-Quarto 1972 EPP [Tinari collection]

The lyrics tell of the white man stealing Geronimo's land and sending him a Cadillac.

Go My Son – Carnes Burson and Arlene Nofchissey Williams 1971

The song was performed by a Mormon group called the Lamanite Generation, founded in 1971, that consisted of young American Indians, Latin Americans, and Polynesians who perform traditional and modern arrangements of music and dance native to their cultures. The Lamanites are one of the four ancient peoples described in the Book of Mormon as having settled in the ancient Americas. From its base at Brigham Young University, the group performed extensively throughout North America and around the world.

Gospel Set to Grand Opera, The – As Sung by Chief White Feather, Teyet Ramar Sitting Bull 1947

Great Spirit, The (An Indian Legend) – George F. Hamer 1935 EPP [Tinari collection]

The cover photograph is of a sculpture of an American Indian seated on his horse and praying. Although taken at a different angle, it is the same sculpture by Dallin placed on the cover of America's "Appeal to the Great Spirit" shown in Chapter 2.

 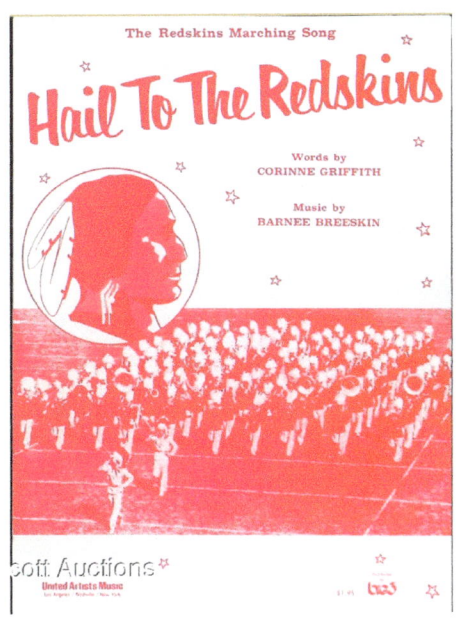  

Hail to the Redskins (Rally Song of the Washington Redskins) – Corinne Griffith and Barnee Breeskin 1938 [Courtesy the Lester S. Levy Collection of Sheet Music, Sheridan Libraries, Johns Hopkins University]

The cover drawing shows an American Indian football player ready to kick the ball.

Hail to the Redskins (The Redskins Marching Song) – Corinne Griffith and Barnee Breeskin 1938

This version features a photograph of a marching band and contains an inset drawing of the bust of an American Indian. The original was issued with a tan/golden background and lettering, drawing and photograph in a maroon color. The version displayed here was printed with a white background and everything else in a pinkish red color.

Half-Breed (photo of Cher on a horse) – Mary Dean and Al Capps 1973 [Tinari collection]

Half-Breed – Mary Dean and Al Capps 1973 [Tinari collection]

The cover contains a full-body photo of Cher in what might be called contemporary Indian-like dress. The lyrics tell of a woman who is half-breed and not accepted by either Native Americans or whites, causing her lifelong grief. Although Cher's mother claimed partial Cherokee ancestry, this song can hardly be said to be biographic. Cher loved to wear elegant and striking outfits in her performances. Like many contemporary song sheets, this one is slightly smaller than standard size, measuring 8.5" by 11."

Heap Big Injun – Walter Rolfe 1935 EPP [Courtesy Sandy Marrone]

§

*Heap Big Injun Chief – Virginia Obenchain 1959 EPP

I'm an Indian – Mary Elizabeth Clark 1969 EPP [Tinari collection]

§

*Hiawatha's Mittens – see listing in Chapter 4

§

*Hiawatha's Lullaby [Eng.] – shown in Chapter 3

In the Hills of Cherokee – Don MacPherson and O. V. Parker 1939 [Courtesy Sandy Marrone]

The back cover of this song sheet, displayed here, contains numerous small photos of American Indians.

§

*I'll Still Belong to You – see *Whoopee* listing below

236

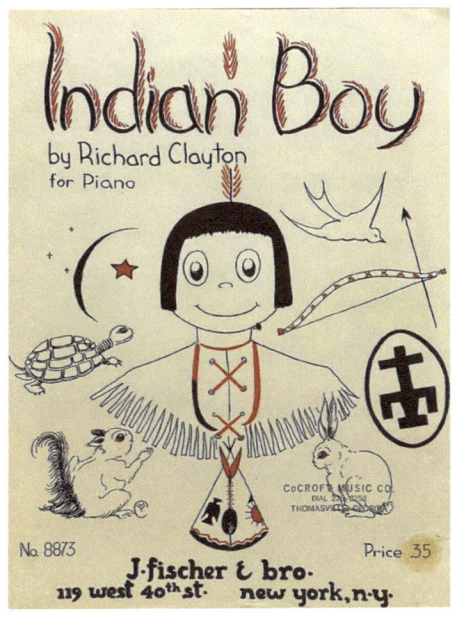

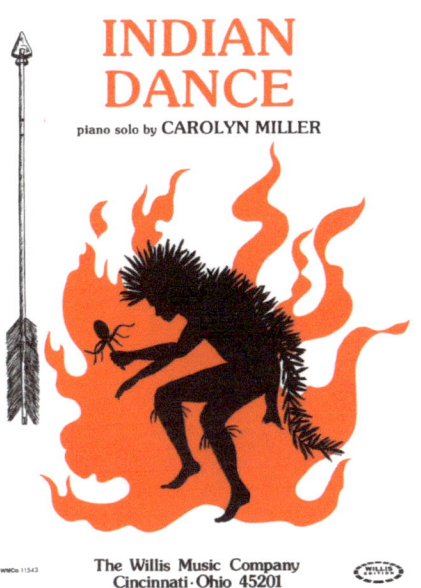

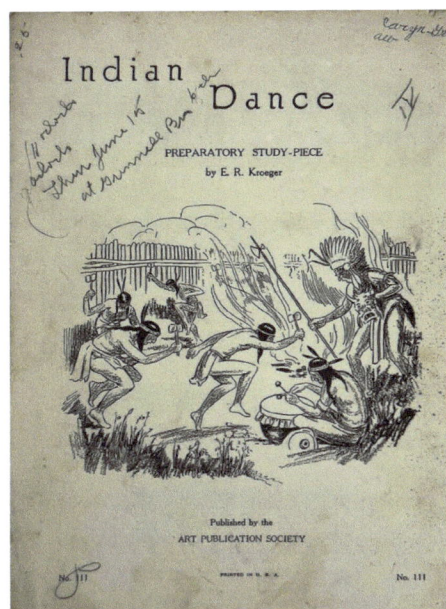

Indian Boy – Richard Clayton 1955 EPP

§

*Indian Ceremonial Dance – Edward Turechek 1955 EPP

The cover states: "An original piano duet." Issued by the Art Publication Society.

Indian Dance – Carolyn Miller 1991 EPP [Tinari collection]

Indian Dance – E. R. Kroeger 1942 EPP

Issued by the Art Publication Society. Originally copyrighted in 1914.

Indian Dance of Welcome (Danced by Princess of Tula'lip Tribe) – Verna Wells 1938 EPP [Courtesy Sandy Marrone]

Indian Drum – Katherine K. Davis 1932 [Tinari collection]

§

*Indian Drumbeats (The Alfred Signature Series) – Margaret Goldston c. 1990 EPP

§

*Indian Echoes – Penny Simpson 1968 EPP

The cover illustrates an American Indian standing in front of his campfire and speaking or singing as he looks upward toward the distant mountain.

§

*Indian Feather Dance (The Alfred Signature Series) – Margaret Goldston c. 1990 EPP

§

*Indian Festival – Bjarne Rolseth 1934 EPP

The cover drawing depicts a seated American Indian holding a decorated spear in his right hand with a long pipe in his left.

§

*Indian Fun (David Carr Glover Program Solo Series) – Bret Adams 1969 EPP

Indian Hunters of the Plains (illust Hering) – Indian Melody by June Weybright 1952 EPP [Tinari collection]

The back page indicates that this is one of many "Original Compositions and Arrangements for piano by June Weybright" published by Belwin, Inc. This piece appears to be their only contemporary piece related to American Indians.

Indian Lament – Edward Schroeder Jr. 1931 [Tinari collection]

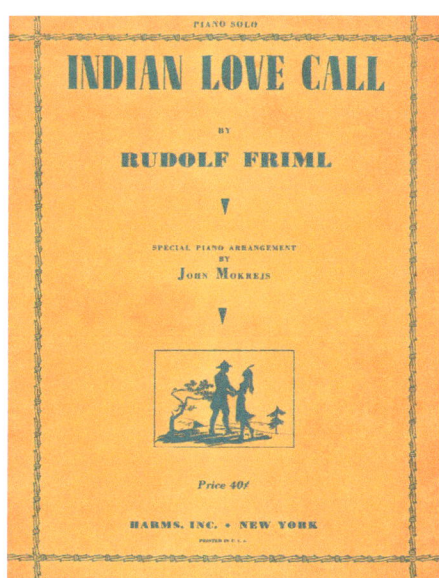

Indian Love Call – Rudolf Friml 1939

Indian Medicine Man (illust Cooke) – Ada Richter 1934 EPP [Courtesy Sandy Marrone]

The inside cover page describes this instrumental piece: "The composer received his inspiration from a visit to the grave of Julien Dubuque, Dubuque, Iowa. Tradition has it that the love and respect of the Indians for Dubuque was such as to cause them to burn a lamp over his grave for many years after his death. The picture on the front page portrays an Indian lamenting the passing of the best white friend he ever had. It is this lament, this song of sorrow made strangely tender and human with the flowing of the years, that the composition embodies."

§

*Indian Legend – Edna Baylor Shaw EPP

The cover depicts a tepee at the edge of a river.

Indian Pony Race – David Carr Glover Jr. 1953 EPP

Indian Pow-Wow – Louise Garrow 1951 EPP [Tinari collection]

The cover depicts three seated American Indian men having a discussion.

Indian Prayer – Zez Confrey 1932 [Tinari collection]

Indian Rain Dance (Bernard Wagness Piano Series) – John Stockbridge 1938 [Tinari collection]

Indian Rain Dance (illust Hauman) (John Thompson's Student Series) – George Western 1951 EPP [Tinari collection]

Indian Serenade (The Alfred Signature Series) – Martha Mier 1990 EPP [Tinari collection]

§

*Indian Slumber Song – Joseph Mendelson and F. Francis Hayden 1937

Indian Smoke Signal (illust Redko) – John W. Schaum 1952 EPP [Tinari collection]

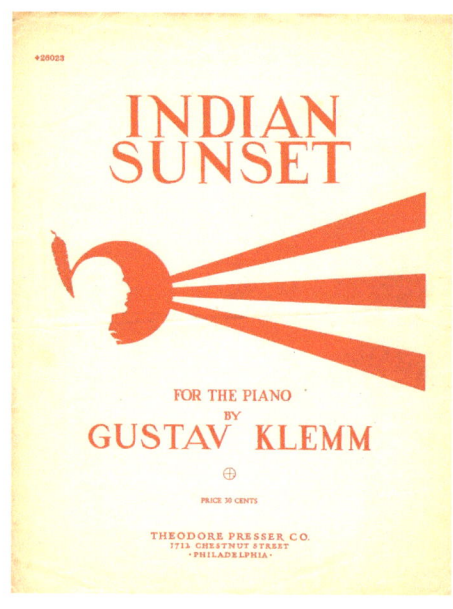   

Indian Sunset – Gistav Klem 1941 EPP

Indian Tale – Jean Williams 1943 EPP [Courtesy Sandy Marrone]

Indian War Call – Alfred Marlhom 1934 EPP [Courtesy Sandy Marrone]

Indian War Call (for Piano) – Margaret Wright 1939 EPP [Tinari collection]

§

*Indian Warrior (piano solo) - Frances Austin 1964 EPP

§

*Indian Warriors' Song (illust Starmer) - Lawrence J. Munson 1950 EPP

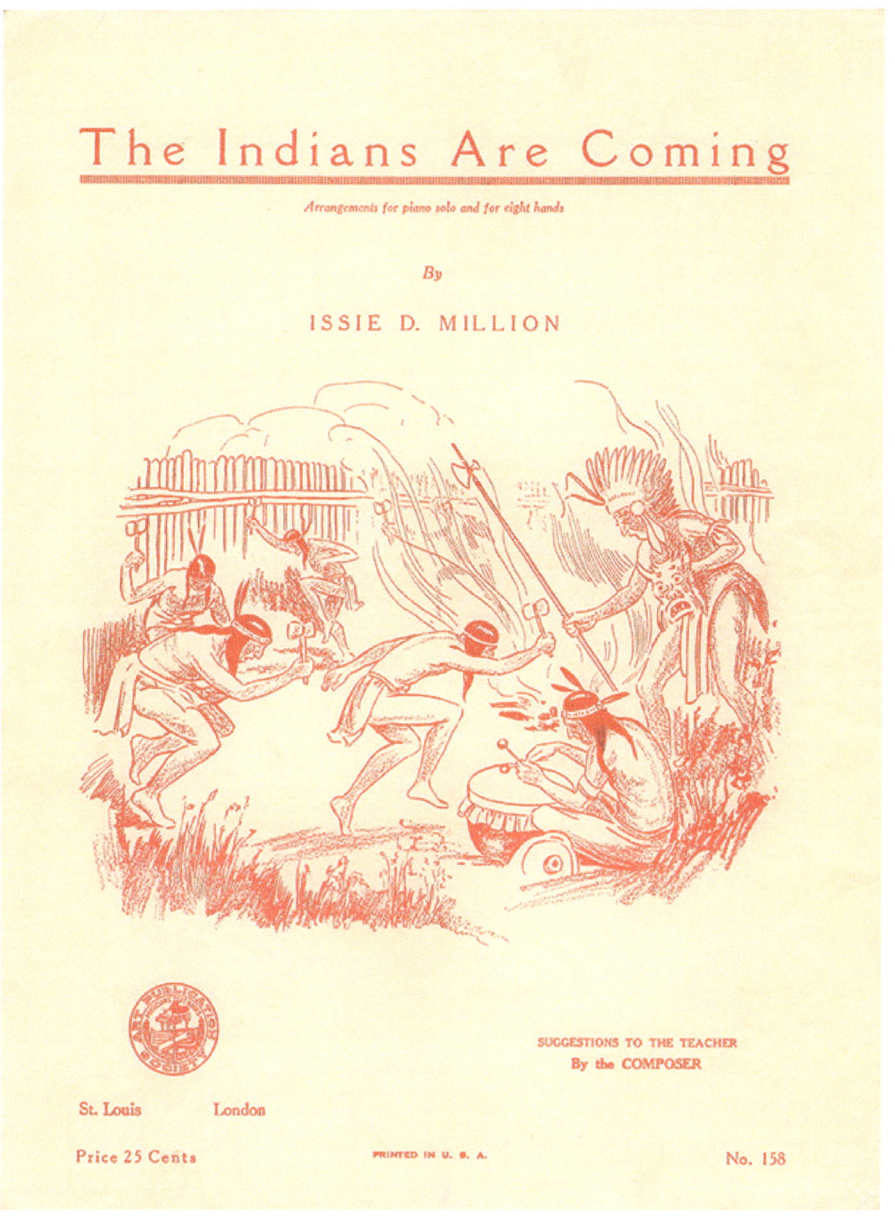

Indians and Trees – George M. Cohan 1933 [Courtesy Sandy Marrone]

Indians are Coming, The – Issie D. Million 1935 EPP [Courtesy Sandy Marrone]

The cover image is identical to that of Indian Dance by Kroeger.

Isle of Que Waltz (Official Selinsgrove Centennial Song) – J. Howard Burns and Kathryn Mull 1953 [Tinari collection]

§

*Juanita (Wa-Nee-Ta) – M. Klauber and Bill Munro 1931

Janey (from *The Far Horizon*) – Wilson Stone and Hans Salter 1955 [Tinari collection]

"*The Far Horizon* was Hollywood's version of the Lewis and Clark expedition to the Pacific Northwest in 1804–1806. Charlton Heston played William Clark, and Donna Reed was the Indian guide Sacajawea." (Short, *Hollywood Movie Songs*, p. 60)

Kille Kille (Indian Love Talk) – Vic Mizzy and Irving Taylor 1942 [Tinari collection]

Legend of Tiabi, The (illust Barbelle) – Kay Twomey, Fred Wise and Al Frisch 1948 [Courtesy Sandy Marrone]

Little Indian Brave – Mary Ann Mitchell 1969 EPP [Tinari collection]

§

*Land of a Thousand Dances – Chris Kenner and Antoine Fats Domino 1969

The cover illustration presents a somewhat abstract face profile of an American Indian wearing a headband. The song has been recorded by numerous people. This version is by a group called The Electric Indian.

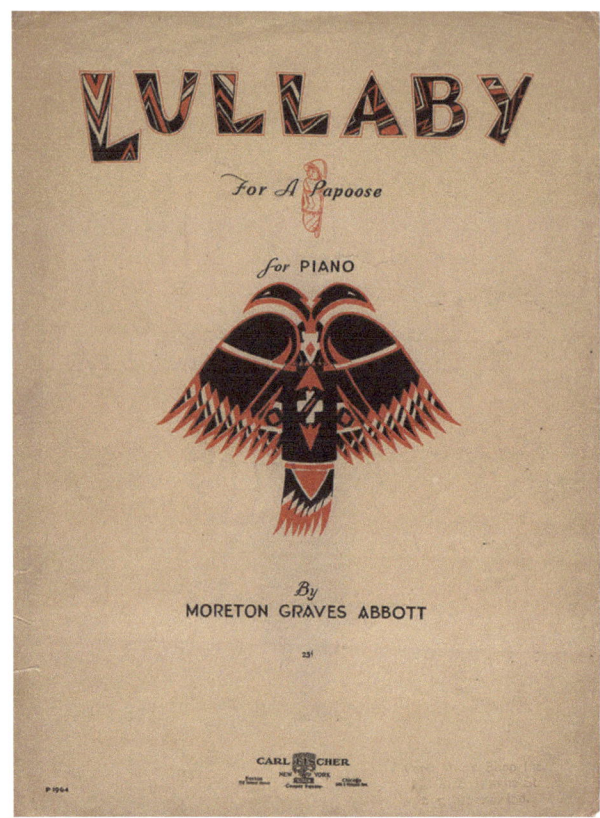
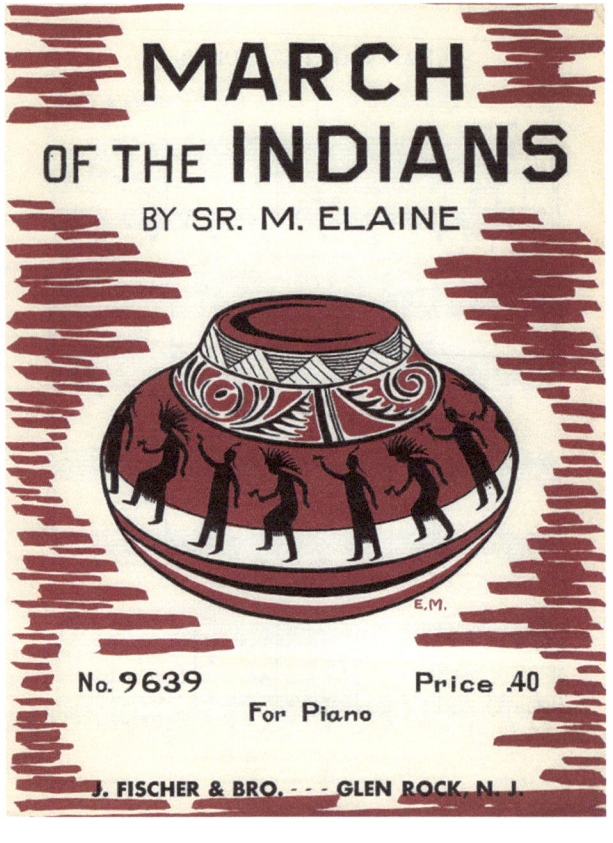

Little Navajo, The – Maxim Littoff 1929 EPP

This was issued in blue as well as in red.

Lullaby (for a Papoose) – Moreton Graves Abbott 1933 EPP [Courtesy Sandy Marrone]

March of the Indians (illust E. M.) – Sister M. Elaine 1966 EPP [Courtesy Sandy Marrone]

Marr Kee, I'm Calling for Thee (illust Wolff) – M. Louisa Irwin 1932 [Courtesy Sandy Marrone]

The inset photograph is of Princess Red Feather. See the note regarding Red Feather under Mulberry Moon, listed in Chapter 2.

Moccasin Dance (John Thompson's Student Series) – Lois Long 1936 EPP [Tinari collection]

§

*My Baby Just Cares for Me (see *Whoopee* listing later in this chapter)

Navajo Love Song (self-pub) – William P. Voita 1934 [Tinari collection]

§

*Never Do a Tango with an Eskimo – listed in Chapter 4

New Orleans - Natalicio M. Lima 1964 [Tinari collection]

Los Indios Tabajaras (The Tabajara Indians) was a guitar duo of two brothers, Antenor Lima and Natalicio (Nato) Lima, from Brazil. They recorded an instrumental album in 1964 with American guitarist Chet Atkins and pianist Floyd Cramer that includes this tune. Their breakthrough tune was "Marie Elena" in 1963. The group name refers to the indigenous people who lived on coast of northeast Brazil in the period before and during Portuguese colonization in the 16th century.

§

No Squat – No Stoop – No Squint – listed in Chapter 4

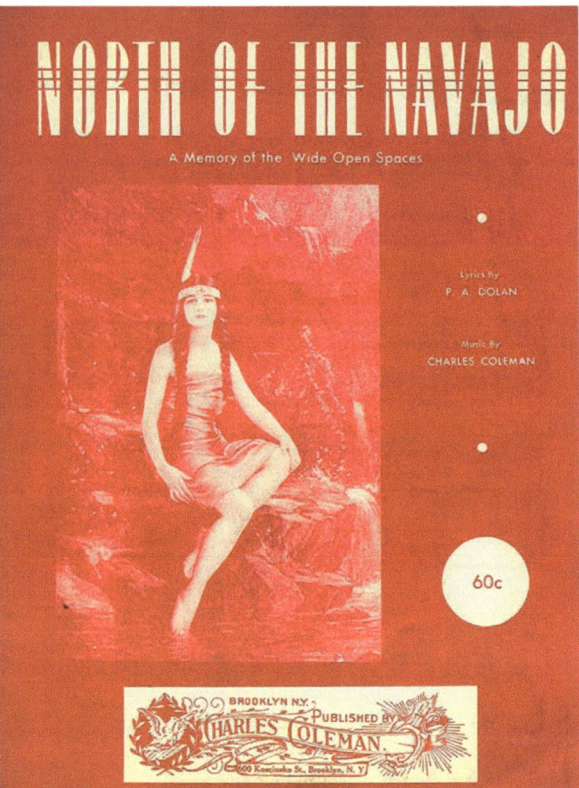

North of the Navajo – Dolan and B. [or D.] Coleman 1941 ST [Tinari collection]

Occoneechee (illust Sisson) – Robert Frank Jarrett and Sadie T. Hutchinson 1936 [Courtesy Sandy Marrone]

The inside front cover relates the scene of the myth upon which the story of this song is based: "Westward from the headwaters of Oconalufree river, in the wildest depths of the Great Smoky Mountains, which form the line between North Carolina and Tennessee, is the enchanted lake of Atagahi, 'Gall place.'"

Old Chief Powhatan – Martha Beck 1951 EPP [Courtesy Sandy Marrone]

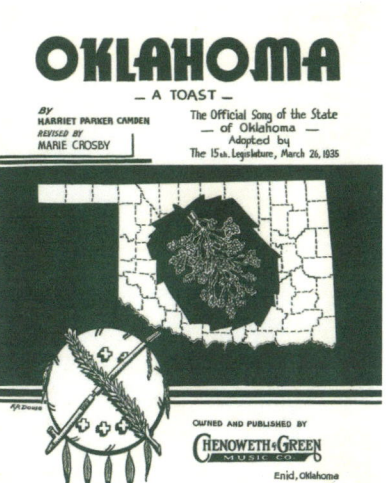

Oklahoma (A Toast) (illust Douse) – Harriet Parker Camden; revised by Marie Crosby 1939 [Tinari collection]

The cover contains the following: The Official Song of the State of Oklahoma, adopted by the 15th Legislature, March 26, 1935.

§

*Oklahoma I Love You (illust Blue Eagle) (composer sign.) – Opal Harrison Williford 1938

On the Painted Desert (An Indian Legend) – Jimmy Kennedy and Nat Simon 1948 [Tinari collection]

The inset photo features Vic Damone. The song sheet was also issued featuring other performers, both in the USA and UK.

"Theme song used in dedication pageant Will Rogers memorial." The cover illustration depicts everything in black silhouette against a tan background, including a cowboy on his horse, with a large moon as his backdrop, and an American Indian standing on the left. Both are presumably looking out at the land which comprises Oklahoma.

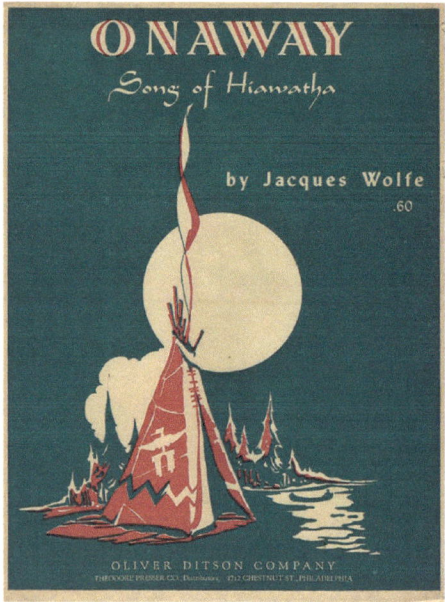   

Onaway (Song of Hiawatha) – Jacques Wolfe 1945 [Courtesy Sandy Marrone]

Oshkosh – Walter J. Crawford 1950 [Tinari collection]

The photo is of a statue of an American Indian warrior labeled Oshkosh. "Song and Indian Dance as introduced in Elks Jollies of 1950 by Oshkosh Lodge, No. 292, B. P. O. Elks" A black and white photo of this song sheet is reproduced in Corenthal, p. 340, as an example of the popularity of music from Wisconsin.

Pale Moon (concert edition) (illust Morgan) – Jesse G. M. Glick and Frederic Knight Logan 1945 [Tinari collection]

Pale Moon (popular edition) (illust Morgan) – Jesse G. M. Glick and Frederic Knight Logan 1945 [Tinari collection]

This sheet was also issued in different versions such as a vocal edition. The song was originally copyrighted in 1920.

Papoose Dreams – Elaine Genteman 1961 EPP [Courtesy Sandy Marrone]

Pretty LittleYoKaYo – Georgie M. Stern 1939 [Tinari collection]

Rain Dance – Scott Watson 1958 EPP [Tinari collection]

Red Feather – W. W. Robinson 1959 EPP [Tinari collection]

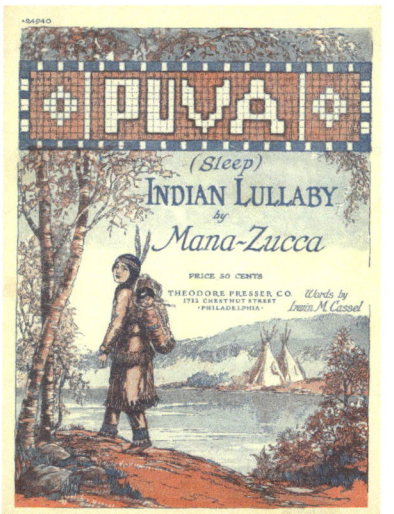

Puva (sleep) - Mana-Zucca and Irwin M. Cassel 1930 [Tinari collection]

The cover depicts an American Indian woman with a baby strapped to her back. Tepees are nestled at water's edge on the opposite shore.

The cover includes what are termed "Indian Signs" referring to musical expressions such as loud and soft.

The inside back cover has pen and ink drawings of five scenes of American Indian life. See the note regarding Red Feather under Mulberry Moon, displayed in Chapter 2.

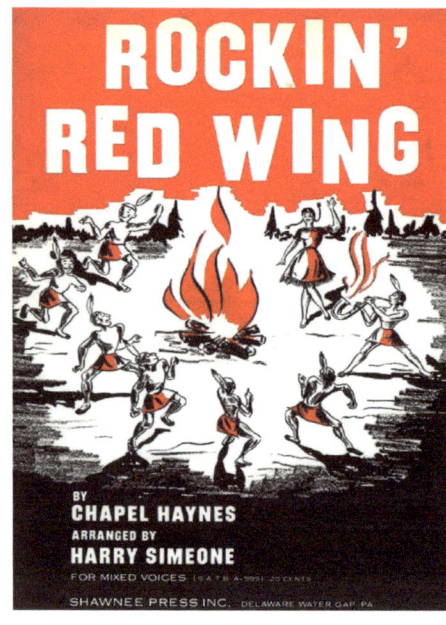   

Rockin' Red Wing – Chapel Haynes arranged by Harry Simeone 1961 war size [Tinari collection]

§

*Rosie the Redskin – see listing in Chapter 4

Seminole Lullaby – Vivian Yeiser Laramore and Olive Dungan 1948 [Tinari collection]

§

*Silver Star (An Indian Serenade) – Harold Levey and John W. Bratton 1940

Snoqualimie Jo Jo – Joe Greene 1944 [Tinari collection]

Squaws Along the Yukon, The – Cam Smith 1936 [Tinari collection]

The back cover gives five "Indian" words and their meaning. For example, "Mush" is trek or walk.

Sun Dance – Leo Friedman 1958 EPP

This is a simpler arrangement by the Schaum group of the original 1901 piece.

§

*Tale of the American Indian Drum, The – Dorothy Jenkins 1959 EPP

§

*Tepee for Two, A (self-pub) – W.N. LaMance 1937

That's Why Redskins are Blue – Jack Scholl and Max Rich 1936 [Tinari collection]

This cover is identical to that on Navajo Love Song issued two years earlier.

§

*This is Our America – see listing in Chapter 3

Tomahawk Dance – Cora Sadler Payne 1977 EPP [Tinari collection]

Tomahawk Trail – Hubert Tillery (piano solo) 1949 EPP [Tinari collection]

'

   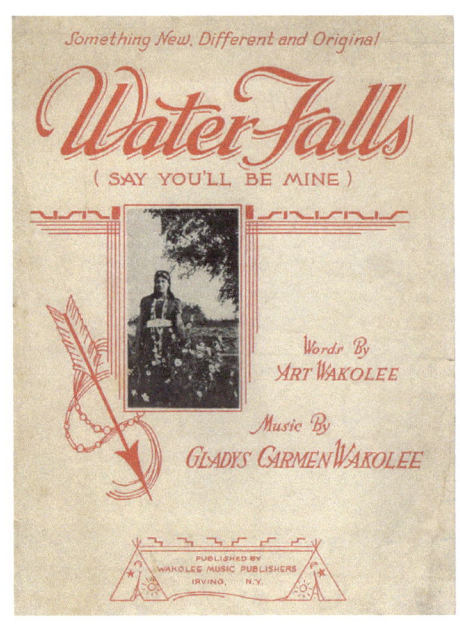

Twas in the Moon of Winter-Time (The Christmas Carol of the Indians) (arr. by Pietro Yon) – St. Jean de Brebeuf 1936 [Tinari collection]

War Paint – Louise Garrow 1959 [Courtesy Sandy Marrone]

Warriors March, The – Arthur A. Rock 1948 [Tinari collection]

Water Falls (Say You'll Be Mine) (self-published by American Indian composers) – Gladys Carmen Wakolee and Art Wakolee 1932 [Courtesy Sandy Marrone]

When Our Country Was Born – Gloria Parker and Barney Young 1949 [Tinari collection]

When the Moon is a Silver Canoe – Capt. Don Saunders and Frank L. Carr 1950 [Tinari collection]

The description and photograph on the back cover describe some American Indian legends connected to the waters of Chapel George, Wisconsin.

Where the Oregon Rolls – Lewis Yeager and J. Charles McNeil 1944 [Tinari collection]

The cover image is identical to the image used eight years earlier on the cover of That's Why Redskins are Blue, displayed earlier in this book.

Whoopee – My Baby Just Cares for Me (illust Manning) – Walter Donaldson and Gus Kahn 1930 [Tinari collection]

The cover depicts a horse rearing up with a woman rider who is nude except for her full Indian headdress. After closing a successful 1928-29 run on Broadway, *Whoopee!* was filmed in 1930 as a musical comedy. The plot followed the stage version closely about Sally who loves Wanenis, an American Indian man, and whose father forbids a marriage, but much of the music was changed. This song was not in the original Broadway production. The illustrator is likely reflecting Florenz Ziegfeld's penchant for showcasing nude or nearly nude women in his shows. For a tamer illustration, see Chapter 5 for the cover image of the same song issued in London.

256

Whoopee – I'll Still Belong to You–Nacio Herb Brown and Edward Eliscu 1930

The uncredited cover illustration is different from the preceding Manning illustration.

§

*Whoop-Up - Sorry for Myself - Norman Gimbal and Moose Charlap 1958

The cover image is the show title designed as a feathery headress. This is one of six song sheets from the musical.

§

*Wigwam Melody – Elizabeth Hopson 1938 EPP

§

*Witch Queen of New Orleans [Eng.] - P. Vegas and L. Vegas 1971

The song is based on a 19th century legend and was performed by Redbone. The cover depicts American Indian men smoking a peace pipe.

Yaw La Boo La Hoola – Curtis Williams 1941 [Courtesy Frances G. Spencer Collection of American Popular Sheet Music. Arts and Special Collections Research Center, Baylor University, Waco, Texas]

An alternate title is Cherokee Blues. The inset photo presents an unidentified man in full American Indian headdress.

AMERICAN INDIAN SONG SHEET ILLUSTRATORS

There are 116 illustrators listed here, responsible for more than 230 song sheet cover images presented in this book. The Starmer Brothers dominate the list with 43 images to their credit.

Aigner
    Winnetou

C. Artemio
    Redwing

Frank Aveline
    Silver-Cloud

A. Baratta
    Ofrenda de la Elegida

Albert Barbelle
    Big Chief Killahun (or Kill-a-Hun)
    Black Hawk Waltz
    Clysmic Water, Daughter of White Rock
    Good Bye, Red Man, Good Bye
    Indian Butterfly NAOMI
    Indi-Ana (Intermezzo)
    Laughing Water, Stop Your Crying
    The Legend of Tiabi
    Red Wing
    Rosie the Redskin
    Silver Water
    White Dove

W. Barnes
    Pocahontas

J. Bazant
    Ooh La La

Anthony Beck
    Wanita

Bodine
    That Tomahawk Rag

Bombach
    Winona [Germany]

Brandard
    Cora

A. J. Brewster
    Na-Gar-Ah

A. D. Brown
    Di-Wen-Da

Bryant
    Red Cloud

Gene Buck
    Seminole
    Wenonah

Buck & Lowney Art Dept
    Snowbird

C. E
    Pocahontas

C.K.
    Tammany

Caagat or Chagat
    Smiling Eyes

W. R. Cameron
    Moon Deer

Carter
    Feather-Queen
    Flying Arrow

H. Carter
    Indian Sun Dance

Dorothy Chesler
    Song of the Ute!

H. G. Chilberg
    Silver Star

W. W. Clarke
    A Real, Live, Regular Town

Bert Cobb
    Arizona

Cooke
    Indian Medicine Man

R. Cooke
    Shawmut Quick Step

Corine
    Red Bead

Dean Cornwell
    Tonawanda

S.F. Crews
    Osceola

Dee
    Tomahawk Blues

Andre De Takacs
    Arrah Wanna
    Arrah' Wanna
    Blue Feather
    Forest Queen
    Iola (Song)
    Mulberry Moon
    Opechee (Robin)
    Ottawah
    Owatonna
    Rain-in-the-Face
    Rainbow
    Topeka
    Valley Flower

Roger de Valerio
    Amapu
    Hiawatha's Melody of Love
    Indianola [Paris]
    O-Hi-O
    Skookum
    South Sea Moon

George Desains
    Yucatan

Dittmar & Furman
    The Lost Phase

F. P. Douse
    Oklahoma (A Toast)

Dorothy Dulin
    Amouresse de Nanouck
    Wana [France]

J. B. Eddy
    My Indian Maiden

A. J. Elder
    Song of Mo-ha-ve
    Up on the Top of the Hill

E.M.
    March of the Indians

Emerson
    Anowon

E. P. C.
    Minnie-Ha-Ha Donohue
    My Prairie Song Bird

Etherington
    My Morning Rose
    Scouting on the New Warpath

Clerice Fere
    O Ma Caravane

E. S. Fisher
    Feathers
    My Pretty Indian Maid
    Onawa
    Pearl Eyes
    Samos
    Wah-Na-Loo
    Wahneka

John Frew
    Big Indian Chief
    Black Hawk Waltz
    Black Hawk Waltzes
    Nat-U-Ritch
    Ogalalla
    Oraibi
    Sitting Bull

Ted Fullam
    Red Fern

Paul Fung (a cartoonist)
    Oriole

Garmland
    Ah! Rose-Marie

W. George
    Hobomoko [Germany]
    The Squaw's Lament

Gilliam
    Geronimo

T. Gilson
    On the War-Path

George Hauman
    Swaying Willow

H. & G. Hauman
    Indian Rain Dance

Havelka
    The Sun Dance

Hayward
    Ola

Henrich
    Fawn-Eyes
    Indi-Ana
    Reindeer
    Topeka

Hering
    Indian Hunters of the Plains

Herse
    Tishomingo

Joseph Hirt
    Lily of the Prairie
    My Kickapoo
    My Pretty Little Kick-Apoo
    Red Wing
    Smiling Star

    Sun Bird
    Wise Old Indian

Hoen
    Arizona

IM-HO
    Cherokee

Jenkins
    Sunshine

Austin Jewell
    Red Feather

Hal Kay
    Moccassin Blues

Keller
    Wigwam Dance (A Reservation Innovation)

Conway Kiewitz
    Anawanda March

T. W. Lee
    The Indian Hunter's Bride

Leff
    Hiawatha's Lullaby

Charles Lussier
    What Cheer

Wilson MacDonald
    Old Loves Are Best

Frederick S. Manning
    Cherokee (Song)
    Hiawatha's Melody of Love
    I Left Her on the Shores of Minnetonka
    Indian Love Moon
    My Baby Just Cares for Me

Paul C. Marashiel
    Nokomis

Merrian
    Iola

Meserow
    Lovelight

L. C. Miller
    Pawnee Queen

Cliff Miska
    On the Rainbow Trail

Mitchel R.
    Squaw Man

MJ
    Cherokee [Paris]

Van Doorn Morgan
    Fallen Leaf
    Pale Moon

MPS
    Comanche

M. C. Myers
    Singing Bird

Nerman
    Min lilla Wa-tah-wall

William S. Nortenheim
    By the Waters of Minnetonka

Josef Pierre Nuyttens
    Lawana

Perret
    Oklahoma Indian Jazz

E. H. Pfeiffer
    Dancing Starlight
    Honest Injun
    Iroquois Fox Trot
    The Pipe of Peace
    Sagamore
    There's a Land Beyond the Rainbow
    Wandalola
    Whippoorwill
    White Bird
    Winona

Vincent C. Plunkett
    Pretty Little Rainbow

L. Prevel
    Zohima

Redko
    Indian Smoke Signal

Redmond
    The Genius of Ka-Noo-No

Rickert
    Natoma

E. Robyn
    Sioux March and Waltz

Rohman
    Seminola [Stockholm]

Rose
    The Mohawk Trail
    My Pretty Firefly

A. Russell
    Minnehaha

R. S.
    Oogie Oogie Wa Wa
    Skookum

Scudellari
    Mama Ocllo

Carlos M. Sisson
    Occoneechee

H. R. Smith
    La Owna

Starmer
    The English-born brothers William Austin Starmer (1872–1955) and Frederick Waite Starmer (1878–1962) came to New York in 1898. William billed himself as a "commercial artist" while Fred billed himself as an "illustrating artist." In sheet music, they worked primarily for Jerome Remick. "Because each [Starmer] brother signed only his last name, it is impossible today to determine which created which covers. That said, scholars of their work suggest that the two created about one-fourth of all sheet music artwork in the ragtime era. Their images usually include realistic looking people rather than caricatures …." (Amundson, p. 168)

    Big Chief Battle-Axe
    Cloud-Chief
    Custer's Last Charge
    Down on the Lakes of Manitoba
    Falling Star
    Feather Foot
    Gleaming Star
    Golden Arrow
    Golden Deer
    Heap Big Injun
    Hiawatha's Melody of Love
    Huckleberry Indians or It's Up to You
    Indian Blues
    Indian Sagwa
    Indian Warriors' Song
    Indianola
    The Irish Indian
    Katunka
    Ki-Yo
    Laughing Water
    Montauk Waltzes
    Moonlight Dear
    My Fair Red Feather
    My Forest Flower Red Skin Rose

My Ramapoo
Navajo
Oh That Navajo Rag
Papoose
Pawnee
Piney Come Out in the Moonlight
Pretty Little Maid of Cherokee
The Red Moon
Silver Star
Snow Deer
Sparkling Eyes
Sweet Little Caraboo
That Kickapoo Indian Man
Tonkawa
Uncas
Wan-a-tea
Waters of the Perkiomen
When I Wanna—You No Wanna
While the Tom-Tom Plays
Wildflower

William Staubach
   The Round Up

J. Stillmunk
   My Irish Prairie Queen

E. B. Stone
   The Wooing of Sha-Wah-Wah

R. B. Thompson
   Waupanseh

Travis
   Indian Blues

V. Valery
   Ruses d'Indiens

C. R. Vance
   Pawnee Dear

Edward F. Walton
   Minnehaha (She Gave Them All the Ha! Ha!)
   Oklahom

Werner
   Winona

Wohlman Studios
   Snow Bird

J. Wolff
   MarrKee, I'm Calling for Thee

Lawrence Wright
   She's Got the Wana Blues

Bertha Young
   Moon-Bird
   Morning Star
   Silverheels
   Wild Rose

ZUS
   Laughing Waters

SONG TITLE INDEX

Listed here alphabetically are the song sheet titles from all chapters. Each entry is followed by the chapter number or numbers in which the song sheet may be found.

A

A-m-e-r-i-c-a, 2
Across The Prairies, 5
Ah! Rose-Marie, 5
Ah-Wa-Ne-Da, 2
Aisha, 2
Alameda Waltzes, 2
Algonquin, 2
Amapu, 5
America, I Love You, 2
America's Appeal to the Great Spirit, 2
American Indian Rhapsody, 2
Americana, 2
Amerinda, 2
Amora, 2
Amoureuse de Nanouck, 5
Anawanda, 1, 2
Anawanda March, 2
Anona, 2
Anowon, 2
Apache Braves, 6
Apache Drums, 6
Apache Indian Dance, 6
Arapahoe, 5
Arizona, 2
Arizona (Indian Romance), 2
ArrahWanna, 2
Arrah' Wanna, 2
At the Indian Cabaret, 2
At The End of The Sunset Trail, 3

B

Be the Sunlight of My Heart, 2
Big Chief Battle-Axe, 4
Big Chief De Sota, 4
Big Chief Dynamite, 4
Big Chief Hic-Cup, 4
Big Chief Killahun, 4
Big Chief Penobscot, 2
Big Chief Thundercloud, 6
Big Chief Wahoo, 4
Big Chief Wally Ho Woo, 4
Big Foot, 2
Big Indian Chief, 4
Big Injun Chief, The, 6
Big Pow Wow, 2
Black Bead, 2
Black Eyes, 2
Black Hawk Quick Step, 1
Black Hawk Waltz, 1, 3
Black Hawk Waltz, The, 3
Black Hawk Waltzes, 3
Blue Beads, 2
Blue Eyes, 2
Blue Feather, 2
Blue Indian, 2
Blue Juniata, The, 1
Bow & Arrow, 2
Brave Warrior, 6
Buffalo Means Business, 2
Buffalo City Guards, 1
Burial of De Soto, The, 1
By the Listening Willows I Wait, 2
By the Waters of Minnetonka, 2

C

Cabeza de Indio, 5
Call of The First American, 3
Canoe Song of Hiawatha, 2
Cherokee, 2, 5, 6
Cherokee Blues, 6
Cherokee Love Theme, 6

Cherokee Rose, 2
Cherry Cherokee, 2
Chief Hokum, 4
Chief Joseph of The Nez Perce Indians, 3
Chief Paxinosa Waltzes, 1
Chief Red Feather, 6
Chief's Grand March, 1
Chieftain's Daughter, The, 1
Chilkoot March, The, 1
Chippewa, 2
Chippewa Rag, 2
Choctaw Indian Dance, 6
Clear The Way, Song of The Wagon Road, 1
Clicquot, 4
Cloud-Chief, 2
Clysmic Water, Daughter of White Rock, 4
Col. J. S. Amory's Quick Step, 1
Comanche, 6
Cora, 1
Cora, The Indian Maiden's Song, 1
Cowboys and Injuns, 6
Crazy Snake, 2
Crimson Arrow, 2
Custer's Last Charge, 2

D
Dacota Waltz, 1
Dance of the Braves, 6
Dance of the Red Feather, 6
Dancing Starlight, 2
Dancing Sunshine, 2
Dawn, 2
Death of Minnehaha, The, 1
Deh-ge-wa-nus, 2
Delaware's Farewell Song, The, 5
Di-Wen-Da, 2

Doin' What Comes Natur'lly, 6
Down on the Lakes of Manitoba, 2

E
Eulah! Eulah! 2

F
Fallen Leaf, 2
Falling Star, 2
Fawn-Eyes, 2
Feather Foot, 2
Feather Queen, 2
Feather-Queen, 2
Feathers, 2
Firefly, 2
First American, The, 3
Fleetfoot, 2
Fleetwing, 5
Flying Arrow, 2
Flying Bird, 2
Folk-Music of The Omaha Indians for Young Pianists, 1
Forest Queen, 3
Forester's Bride, The, 1
Fort Harrison March, 1
Fun with the Boys, 1

G
General Custer's Last March, 1
Genius of Ka-Noo-No, The, 2
Geronimo, 3
Geronimo's Cadillac, 6
Geronimo's Own Medicine Song, 3
Get the Safety Habit, 2
Gleaming Star, 2
Glory of Jamestown, 2
Go-Wan-Go-Mohawk, 2

Golden Arrow, 2
Golden Deer, 2
Golden Feather, 2
Golden Potlatch, 2
Good Bye, Red Man, Good Bye, 2
Gospel Set to Grand Opera, The, 6
Grand Bi-Centennial March, 1
Grand Western Pageant, 2
Great Big Chickapoo Chief, A, 4
Great Big Heap Much Bull, 4
Great Spirit, The, 6
Great Wahoo Polka, The, 1

H
Hail Milwaukee, 2
Hail to the Blackhawk, 2
Hail to the Redskins, 6
Half-Breed, 6
Happy Hunting Grounds, 2
Harrison Song, The, 1
Heap Big Injun, 2, 6
Heap Big Injun Chief, 6
Heart of Wetona, 2
Hee-Lah-Dee, 1
Hello Miss Spokane, 2
Her Shadow, 2
Here Come the Tribes, 2
Hiawatha, 3
Hiawatha Ballet Music, 3
Hiawatha's Lullaby, 3
Hiawatha's Melody of Love, 3
Hiawatha's Mittens, 4
Hiji, 2
Ho! For The Kansas Plains, 1
Hobomoko, 5
Hollywood, 2

Honest Injun, 4
Hotfoot, 2
How I Love That Man, 2
Huckleberry Indians or It's Up to You, 2
Hudson-Fulton March, 2
Humming Bird, 2
Humoreskimo, 2, 5
Hundred Years Hence, A, 1

I
I Didn't Raise My Boy to Be a Soldier, 3
I Left Her on the Shores of Minnetonka, 2
I'll Still Belong to You, 6
I'm an Indian, 6
Idaho, 2
Idol Star, 2
Idylle a Colombo, 5
If You Are True to Me, 2
Igloo Eyes, 2
In a Dory, 3
In a Little Wigwam Built for Two, 2
In Tepee Land, 2
In the Hills of Cherokee, 6
In the Hills of Spavinaw, 2
Indi-Ana, 2
Indian and His Bride, The, 1
Indian Blues, 2
Indian Boy, 6
Indian Bride Song, The, 2
Indian Butterfly NAOMI, 2
Indian Ceremonial Dance, 6
Indian Cradle Song, 2
Indian Dance, 2, 6
Indian Dance of Welcome, 6
Indian Dawn, 2
Indian Drum, 6

Indian Drumbeats, 6
Indian Echoes, 6
Indian Faith, 2
Indian Feather Dance, 6
Indian Festival, 6
Indian Fun, 6
Indian Girl, 2
Indian Girl's Lament on The Banks of The Kennebec, The, 1
Indian Hunter, The, 1, 5
Indian Hunter Quick Step, 1
Indian Hunters of the Plains, 6
Indian Hunter's Bride, The, 1
Indian Lament, 2, 6
Indian Legend, 6
Indian Love Call, 6
Indian Love Moon, 2
Indian Love Song, 2
Indian Love Song, An, 2
Indian Lover's Serenade, 2
Indian Lullaby, 2
Indian Maid, 5
Indian Medicine Man, 6
Indian Patrol, 2, 5
Indian Pony Race, 6
Indian Pow-Wow, 6
Indian Prayer, 6
Indian Rag, 2
Indian Rain Dance, 6
Indian Reverie, 2
Indian Ride, 5
Indian River Dance , 2
Indian Runner, The, 2
Indian Sagwa, 2
Indian Serenade, 5, 6
Indian Shimmy, 5
Indian Slumber Song, 6

Indian Smoke Dance, 2
Indian Smoke Signal, 6
Indian Snake Dance, 2
Indian Soldier's Request, An, 2
Indian Spring Bird, 2
Indian Sun Dance, The, 1
Indian Sunset, 6
Indian Tale, 6
Indian Two Step, The, 2
Indian War Call, 6
Indian Warrior, 6
Indian Warriors' Song, 6
Indian's Serenade, An, 2
Indiana, 5
Indiandans, 5
Indianerständchen, 5
Indianetta, 5
Indianola, 2, 5
Indians and Trees, 6
Indians are Coming, The, 6
Indianskan, 5
Injun Gal, 2
Iola, 2
Iolanthe, 2
Irish Indian, The, 2
Iroquois, 2
Iroquois Fox Trot, 2
Isle of Que Waltz, 6
It's a Pontiac, 2

J
Janey, 6
John Ross, 1
Juanita (Wa-Nee-Ta), 6
Juanita, 1

K

Ka-Noo-No Maid, 2
Kachina-Hopi Girl's Dance, 2
Kalooka, 2
Kansas Pacific R. W. Grand March, 1
Katunka, 2
Keokuck Quick Step, 1
Ki-Yo, 2
KilleKille, 6
King Philip's Quick Step, 1
Kiowana, 2
Kiss-I-Mee, 2
Kissamee, 2
Kissing Song, 1

L

La Belle Indienne, 1
La Crosse Galup, 1
La Indiada, 5
La Owna, 2
La Santa Fe, 2
Lackawanna, 2
Land of a Thousand Dances, 6
Land of My Prairie Dreams, The, 3
Land of Washington, 1
Laughing Eyes, 2
Laughing Water, 2
Laughing Water! Ha, Ha, Ha, 2
Laughing Water, or The Enchanted Dell of Minnie-Ha-Ha, 1
Laughing Water, Stop Your Crying, 2
Laughing Waters, 2
Lawana, 2
Legend of Tiabi, The, 6
Lenore Song, 2
Lily of the Prairie, 2, 5
Linganore, 2

Little Bright Eye, 1
Little Indian, 2
Little Indian, A, 2
Little Indian Brave, 6
Little Indian Chief, 2
Little Indian Maid, 2
Little Min-Ne-Ha Ha, 2
Little Navajo, The, 6
Little White Rose, 2
Lo-Nah, 2
Lost Arrow, 2
Lost Phase, The, 2
Love Bird, 2
Love Song, 2
Lovelight, 2
Lover's Wooing, 2
Lullaby (for a Papoose), 6

M

Mahtoree, 5
Maid of the Midnight Moon, 2
Maiden America, 2
Mama Ocllo, 5
Manisot, 2
Mar-An-Da, 2
March of the Black Hawks, 2
March of the Indian Phantoms, 2
March of the Indians, 6
March of the Red Man, 2
March of the Redmen, 2
March of the Santa Fe Trail, 2
Marr Kee, I'm Calling for Thee, 6
Meadow Lark, 2
Meet Me on the Warpath at the Jamestown Fair, 2
Meeting of The Tribes, The, 3
Metacom's Grand March, 1

Min lilla Wa-tah-wall, 5
Minnehaha, 2, 3, 5
Minnehaha or Laughing Water Polka, 1
Minnehaha Schottisch, 1
Minnehaha (She Gave Them All the Ha! Ha!), 4
Minnehaha's Answer, 3
Minnehaha's Love, 3
Minnetonka, 2
Minnie-Ha-Ha Donohue, 2
Minnie Ha Ha Ha, The, 2
Minnie-Waha, 2
Miss Pocahontas, 3
Missoula, 2
Mistletoe, 3
Moccasin Blues, 2
Moccasin Dance, 6
Moccasin Maiden, 2
Moccasin Rag, 2
Moccassin Blues, 5
Mohawk, The, 5
Mohawk Trail, The, 2
Moki Maid, The, 2
Montauk Waltzes, 2
Moon-Bird, 2
Moon Deer, 2
Moonbeam, 2
Moonlight Dear, 2
Moonlight Waltz, 2
Morning Star, 2
Mulberry Moon, 2
Multnomah, 2
Mumblin' Mose, 5
Muskoka Waltz, 5
My Baby Just Cares for Me, 6
My Black Papoose, 2
My Cherokee, 2

My Chippewa, 2
My Copper Colored Squaw, 2
My Fair Red Feather, 2
My Forest Flower Red Skin Rose, 2
My Hiawatha, 3
My Indian Maid, 2
My Indian Maiden, 2
My Indian Queen (Sacajawea), 2
My Irish Indian, 2
My Irish Prairie Queen, 2
My Kickapoo, 2
My Little Indian Maid, 2
My Little Pappoose, 2
My Love, My Lark, 2
My Moonbeam, 2
My Morning Rose, 2
My New England Home, 1
My Prairie Maid, 2
My Prairie Queen, 2
My Prairie Song Bird, 2
My Pretty Firefly, 2
My Pretty Indian Maid, 2
My Pretty Little Indian Maid, 2
My Pretty Little Kick-Apoo, 2
My Ramapoo, 2
My Silver-Throated Fawn, 2
My Sweet Dakotah Maid, 2
My Sweet Love Call, 2
My Tom Tom Man, 2
My Wenonah, 5
My Wigwam Queen, 2
My Wild Deer, 2

N
Na-Gar-Ah, 2

Na-Jo, 2
Nahmeokee Waltz, 1
Naoma, 2
Napanee, 2
Nat-U-Ritch, 2
National Lancers Grand Parade, 1
Natoma, 2
Navajo, 2, 5
Navajo Love Song, 6
Never Do a Tango with an Eskimo, 4
New Mexico March, 2
New Orleans, 6
Nippinittic, 2
Nississhin, 2
No Squat-No Stoop-No Squint, 4
Nokomis, 2
North of the Navajo, 6
North American, The, 2
Nouhika, 5

O
O Ma Caravane, 5
O'Wahneta, 2
O-Gal-La-La, 2
O-Hi-O, 5
O-Wah-Hoo!!, 2
Obeja, 2
Occoneechee, 6
Oclemena, 1
Ofrenda de la Elegida, 5
Ogalalla, 2
Ogarita, 2
Oh, By Jingo!, 5
Oh That Navajo Rag, 2
Ohio My Ohio, 2
Ojibways' Canoe Song, 2

Oklahom, 2
Oklahoma (A Toast), 6
Oklahoma I Love You, 6
Oklahoma Indian Jazz, 2
Ola, 2
Old Betz, 1
Old Chief Powhatan, 6
Old Loves Are Best, 2
Old Tippecanoe, 1
Oleta, 3
On a Cloud I Will Ride, 2
On the Painted Desert, 6
On the Rainbow Trail, 2, 5
On the Road Called Santa Fe, 2
On The War-Path, 5
On the Warpath, 2
On-ka-hye Waltz, 1
Onawa, 2
Onawanda, 2
Onaway, 6
Oneonta, 2
Onondaga Polka, The, 1
Ontario, 2
Oogie Oogie Wa Wa, 4
Ooh La La, 2
Opechee, 2
Oraibi, 2
Origin of the Rainbow, The, 2
Oriole, 2
Os-ka-loo-sa-loo, 2
Osceola, 2
Osceola Quick Step, 1
Oshkosh, 6
Ottawah, 2
Over the Mohawk Trail, 2
Owatanna, 2
Owatonna, 2

P
Pale Moon, 2, 6
Paleface, 2
Papoose, 2
Papoose Dance, 2
Papoose Dreams, 6
Passing of the Dakotahs, The, 2
Passing of the Red Man, 2
Pawnee, 2
Pawnee Dear, 2
Pawnee Queen, 2
Paxinosa, 2
Pearl Eyes, 2
Pilgrim's Legacy, The, 1
Pipe of Peace, The, 2
Pliney Come Out in the Moonlight, 2
Pocahontas, 3
Pocahontas, 3
Pocahontas II: Journey to a New World, 3
Pocahontas March and Two Step, 3
Poverty Ballad, 1
Pow Wow March, 4
Powhatan's Daughter March, 2
Prairie Echoes, 2
Prairie Flower, 1
Prairie Lilie, 5
Prairie Rose, 2
Pretty Little Maid of Cherokee, 2
Pretty Little Rainbow, 2
Pretty Little YoKaYo, 6
Princess Pocahontas March and Two-Step, 3
Prize Banner Quick Step, The, 1
Puritans' Mistake, The, 1
Puva, 6

Q
Queen of the Cherokees, 2
Queen of the Everglades, 2

R
Rain Dance, 6
Rain-Flower, 2
Rain-in-the-Face, 4
Rainbow, 2
Rainbow Bridge, 5
Rainbow (Regenbogen), 5
Rally Round the Safety Habit, 2
Ramona, 2
Ramona's Dream, 2
Reading Sesqui-Centennial March, The, 1
Real, Live, Regular Town, A, 2
Recollections of Buffalo, 1
Red Bead, 5
Red Cloud, 2
Red Deer, 2
Red Feather, 2, 6
Red Fern, 2
Red Man, The, 2
Red Moon, 2
Red Moon, The, 2
Red Skin, The, 2
Red Wing, 2, 5
Red-Man, 2
Redskin, 2
Redwing, 2, 5
Reed Bird, 2
Reindeer, 2
Roarers, The, 1
Rockin' Red Wing, 6
Rosie the Redskin, 4

Round Up, The, 2
Rowena, 2
Ruses d'Indiens, 5

S
Sacajawea Lullaby, 2
Sachem's Daughter, 1
Sagamore, 2
Sagawana, 2
Samos, 2
Scouting on The New Warpath, 2
Screeching Eagle, 2
Seattle, 2
Seek the Lodge Where the Red Men Live, 1
Seenah, 2
Seminola, 2, 5
Seminole, 2
Seminole Lullaby, 6
Shanewis, 2
Shawmut Quick Step, 1
Shawondasee Waltz, 2
She's Got the Wana Blues, 4, 5
She-Boy-Gan, 2
Shining Star, 2
Silent Enemy, The, 2
Silver Bell, 2
Silver Cloud, 2
Silver Heels, 2
Silver Star, 2, 6
Silver Water, 2
Silver-Cloud, 5
Silverheels, 2, 5
Since ArrahWanna Married Barney Carney, 2
Singing Bird, 2
Singing Water, 2
Sioux March and Waltz, 1
Sioux Song, 2
Sitka, 2
Sitting Bull, 3
Siwaja, 5
Skookum, 4, 5
Skowhegan, 2
Sleepy Eye, 2
Smiling Eyes, 2
Smiling Star, 2
Snoqualimie Jo Jo, 6
Snow Bird, 2
Snow Deer, 2
Snowbird, 2
Soldier and His Bride, The, 1
Song Bird, 2
Song for New England, A, 1
Song of India, 5
Song of Mo-ha-ve, 2
Song of The Red Man, The, 1
Song of the Ute!, 4
Song of the Waters, 2
Songs of Song-ah-tah, 2
South Sea Moon, 5
Sowania, 2
Sparkling Eyes, 2
Spotted Fawn, The, 1
Spring Song of the Robin Woman, 2
Squaw Man, 2
Squaw Man, The, 2
Squaw's Lament, The, 5
Squaws Along the Yukon, The, 6
St. Lawrence Quadrilles, The, 1
Star and the Flower, The, 2
Starlight Sioux, 2
Stomp Dance, 2
Storm Cloud, 2

Strongheart, 2
Sun Bird, 2
Sun Dance, 6
Sun Dance, The, 2
Sunbeam, 2
Sunlight, 2
Sunray
Sunset Dreams, 2
Sunset Song, 2
Sunset Trail, The, 2
Sunshine, 2
Sure Fire Rag, 2
Swaying Willow, 2
Sweet Little Caraboo, 2

T
Tale of the American Indian Drum, The, 6
Talking to the Moon, 2
Tammany, a Pale Face Pow-Wow, 4
Tecumseh, 3
Ten Little Indians, 5
Ten Little Injuns, 1
Tepee for Two, A, 2, 6
Tepee Just for Two, A, 2
That Indian Rag, 2
That Kickapoo Indian Man, 2
That Tom Tom Tag, 2
That Tomahawk Rag, 2
That's Why Redskins are Blue, 6
There's a Land Beyond the Rainbow, 2
This is Our America, 3
Thunder Cloud, 2
Tip-Tip-Tippy Canoe, 2
Tippecanoe, 4
Tippecanoe March, 1
Tippecanoe Quick Step, The, 1

Tippecanoe Slow Grand March, 1
Tishomingo, 2
Tomahawk Blues, 5
Tomahawk Dance, 6
Tomahawk Trail, 6
Tonawanda, 2
Tonkawa, 2
Topeka, 2
Trail to Long Ago, The, 3
Trailing the Trail, 2
Twas in the Moon of Winter-Time, 6

U
Uncas, 3
Uncle Sam's Chief, 2
Underneath the Harvest Moon, 2
Up on the Top of the Hill, 2

V
Valley Flower, 2

W
Wa-Ne-Ta, 2
Wa-nee-ta, 2
Wa-Pa-Tee-Tah, 2
Wah-Na-Loo, 2
Wahneka, 2
Wait No More for Me, 2
Walla Ki-Ki, 2
Wan-a-tea, 2
Wana, 5
Wana (When I Wana, You No Wana), 4, 5
Wanda Waltzes, 2
Wandalola, 2
Wanita, 2
War Paint, 6

Warriors March, The, 6
Water Falls (Say You'll Be Mine), 6
Waters of Muscle Shoals, The, 2
Waters of the Perkiomen, 2
Waupanseh, 2
Wayawais, 5
Wayside Spring, 1
We Have Met to Remember The Day, 1
Wenona, 2
Wenonah, 2
What Cheer, 2
When I Wanna—You No Wanna, 4
When Our Country Was Born, 6
When the Moon is a Silver Canoe, 6
Where Hudsons Wave, 1
Where the Oregon Rolls, 6
Where the Papoose Swings, 2
While the Tom-Tom Plays, 2
Whippoorwill, 2
Whistling Squaw, The, 2
White Bird, 2
White Dove, 2
White Feather, 2
White Wings, 2
Whoopee, 5, 6
Whoop-Up, 6
Wigwam Courtship, A, 2
Wigwam Dance, 2
Wigwam Melody, 6
Wild Flower, 2
Wild Indian Cherokee War Dance, The, 1
Wild Rose, 2
Wildflower, 2
Winnebago, 2
Winnetou, 5
Winona, 2, 5

WirreisennachWildwest, 4, 5
Wise Old Indian, 4
Witch Queen of New Orleans, 6
Wooing of Sha-Wah-Wah, The, 2
Wyandotte, 2

Y
Yahola, 2
Yaw La Boo La Hoola, 6
Ye Boston Tea Party, 1
Yellow Moccasin, The, 2
Yo-Kum-Kee, 2
You are the One and Only, 2
Youlianna, 2
Young Warriors March, The, 2
Yucatan, 5

Z
Zohima, 5
Zuni Lover's Wooing, 2

ABOUT THE AUTHOR

As a retired university professor of economics with books and numerous articles to his credit, Frank Tinari brings his considerable writing and research abilities to his avocation of sheet music collecting. Originating with his childhood love of music and art, in recent decades he has focused on artistic illustrations and photographs displayed on the covers of printed, popular song sheets in genres of interest to him. Building upon sheet music books of other authors, his aim is to present comprehensive and in-depth coverage of song sheet cover depictions in specific genres. To that end he utilizes his song sheet collection and adds scanned cover images from fellow collectors, museums, and libraries around the world.

www.ingramcontent.com/pod-product-compliance
Lightning Source LLC
Chambersburg PA
CBHW041748290426

44111CB00004B/70